Nature Walks in the Berkshire Hills

An AMC Nature Walks Book

Charles W. G. Smith

APPALACHIAN MOUNTAIN CLUB BOOKS
BOSTON, MASSACHUSETTS

Cover Photograph by the author.
All photographs by the author unless otherwise noted.
Cover Design: Elisabeth Leydon Brady
Book and Map Design: Carol Bast Tyler

Distributed by The Globe Pequot Press, Inc., Old Saybrook, CT.

Library of Congress Cataloging-in-Publication Data

Smith, Charles W. G.
    Nature Walks in the Berkshire Hills / Charles W. G. Smith
        p.   cm.
    "An AMC nature walks book."
    Includes index.
    ISBN 1-878239-57-0 (alk. paper)
    1. Walking—Massachusetts—Berkshire Hills—Guidebooks.
2. Trails—Massachusetts—Berkshire Hills—Guidebooks. 3. Natural history—Massachusetts—Berkshire Hills—Guidebooks. 4. Berkshire Hills (Mass.)—Guidebooks I. Title.
GV199.42.M4B476   1997
917.44'10443—dc21   96-50396
                                                     CIP

The paper used in this publication meets the minimum requirements of the American National Standard for Information Sciences—Permanence of Paper for Printed Library Materials, ANSI Z39.48–1984.∞

**Due to changes in conditions,
use of the information in this book
is at the sole risk of the user.**

Printed on recycled paper using soy-based inks.
Printed in the United States of America.

10 9 8 7 6 5 4 3 2 1   97 98 99 00 01 02

Contents

Northern Region

This book is dedicated to my son, Nathaniel,
who walks with me each time I venture into
the woods whether he is by my side or not.

Walks in the
Southern Berkshire Hills

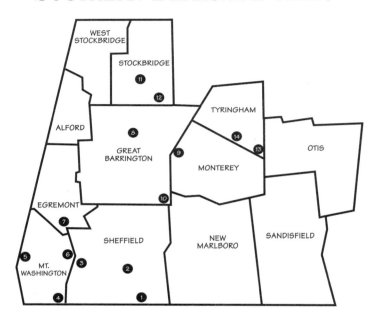

1. Bartholomew's Cobble
2. Sheffield Plain
3. Race Brook Falls
4. Sage's Ravine
5. Bash-Bish Falls
6. Guilder Pond and Mt. Everett
7. Jug End
8. Monument Mountain
9. Benedict Pond
10. Ice Gulch
11. Bowker's Woods
12. Laura's Tower and Ice Glen
13. McLennan
14. Tyringham Cobble

WALKS IN THE
CENTRAL BERKSHIRE HILLS

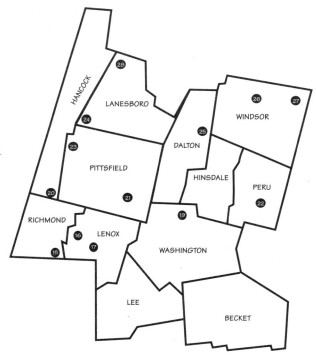

15. Yokun Ridge
16. Pleasant Valley
17. Kennedy Park
18. Finerty Pond
19. Northern Transitional Forest
20. Shaker Mountain and Holy Mount
21. Canoe Meadows

22. Rice Sanctuary
23. Tilden Swamp
24. Balance Rock
25. Wahconah Falls
26. Judges Hill
27. Windsor Jambs
28. Mt. Greylock Visitor Center

Walks in the
Northern Berkshire Hills

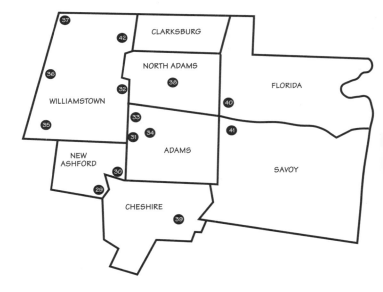

Acknowledgments

A book is a reflection of synergy. A collection of energy and experience gleaned and gathered from many people. This book is no exception. What was given to me I have tried to give back in the chapters that follow.

My thanks to the Appalachian Mountain Club staff, including Dennis Regan, Tim Loveridge, Gordon Hardy, and all the others in the Berkshires and Boston. You guys are the best.

Rick Donovan and his store, Appalachian Mountain Gear, kindly donated a ton of topo maps and Cliff bars so I could have the energy to get lost. He also lets a mountain bum sit in his rocking chair, which I appreciate.

All the people associated with the Trustees of Reservations were very helpful; my special thanks to those at the main office in Stockbridge and to Jean, Shawn, and Andy at Field Farm and Don at Bartholomew's Cobble.

Others who went out of their way to assist me include Tom Tyning and René Laubach of Massachusetts Audubon; Polly Pierce, curator of the historical room at the Stockbridge Library; Tom Donnelly of the Hancock Shaker Museum; George Wislocki and the Berkshire Natural Resource Council; Clebe Scott, John Foster and Bob Hatton of the Massachusetts Department of Environmental Management and Practical Solutions Inc., who kept the computer running.

Also helpful were Bartlett Hendricks, Norm Sills, Dr. Charles Kenny, Peter Arlos, the Berkshire Atheneum, and the Great Barrington Library.

Finally there are those who have helped in ways more personal than words may describe, and I will forever walk with their inspiration. Thank you, Nathaniel, for being who you are and playing Pooh sticks with an old guy. Thank you, Christine, for being the one I climb mountains with and come home to. Thank you to my sister and her entire wonderful family. And thank you to my two mothers, Alta and Bethia, who taught me how to dream.

Introduction

There is an old proverb that says, "Where you walk is where you are. Where you have walked is who you are."

This is a book of forty-two walks through the Berkshire hills. The trails described will lead you to mountaintops with gorgeous views and along windy ridges that pulse with energy. There are paths to waterfalls that are slender veils of lacy mist, and powerful cataracts with drumbeat crescendos. You will walk around ponds where geese and ducks paddle across the water and beaver ferry sticks to their sinuous dams. And tramp to the marshes and swamps where great blue heron, moose, and bear live. There are trails that follow the courses of wide rivers as they wind through the limestone valleys, and paths where wildflowers bend on their slender stems beneath the shade of maidenhair ferns.

Everything along the trail—each stone and flower, every view, cellar hole, field, and tree—has a story to tell. The stone may be a bit of quartzite that began as a sandy beach along an ancient tropical sea, and the flower may be a hawkweed that will tell you of a coming storm hours before it hits. The views may show you valleys carved by glaciers or shorelines at the edges of enormous lakes that existed here at the end of the last Ice Age. And the cellar holes can tell you of the human dramas that were acted out in the wilderness of the Berkshires centuries ago. There are overgrown fields that were once Indian villages and sugar maple trees that were once tapped by the Mahicans.

Homer wrote that the value of a voyage lay not in the destination, but in the journey. This is a book of forty-two journeys that will take the curious and the patient to unforgettable places. I hope you enjoy them as much as I have.

How to Use This Book

Each walk begins with a listing of important facts that includes the *names of the trails*, the *total length* of the walk in miles, the *elevation gain* or change along the hike, an approximate time range needed to complete the walk, and a *rating of the terrain* covered.

Of these criteria the last two are subjective. The time ratings for completing each walk are based on a very relaxed pace that allows for plenty of observation and hanging out. Most people *can* finish the hikes in less time than I have allowed, but I hope they won't want to. The faster the pace, the less is learned and observed.

The ratings for the type of terrain covered include **easy, moderate,** and **difficult.** In general the terrain rating is a reflection of the total length of the walk, the elevation gain, and any unique features, such as scrambles or very steep sections, of that walk. Remember that a faster pace will make any walk more difficult and that it is possible to encounter poor footing on all trails, regardless of rating.

The second section consists of a short summary of that walk as well as a description of how the trails are marked. This introduction is followed by a *Look Forward To* list of that walk's highlights.

The Trail is a guided tour of the entire walk. Landmarks are used as reference points so you can know where you are along the walk at almost any given time. Plants, rock formations, animal burrows, and the like are described in the text in relation to where they appear along the trail, which makes it easier to find these things as you walk along. Unique or special features appear in boldface and are reflected on the accompanying maps. At the end of each trail section is an essay that explores a relevant topic in greater detail.

Getting There gives directions to the trailhead by the most-traveled routes.

What to Bring

Walking or hiking in the Berkshires will take you well away from the conveniences many of us have grown dependent on. We are, to be blunt, a wimpy bunch of folks when compared with the animals of the woods that thrive in storms and snows. It takes many years to become as self-reliant as nature originally intended us to be, so in the meantime it is prudent to bring our technological crutches with us where we walk.

Every time you go for a hike you should have a day pack with you to carry the ten essentials. The ten essentials are the Ten Commandments of hiking and will go a long way to making you more self-reliant in the woods. They are:

1. **Extra clothing.** What you bring depends on the season of the year and where you are going. Some of the staples include rain gear, hats and gloves, fleece or wool sweaters, and socks. Bring clothes made of fibers that retain their insulating value when wet, such as fleece and wool, instead of those that lose it, such as cotton.

2. **Water.** Bring it in a shatterproof water bottle—at least one quart per person.

3. **Extra food.** High-energy food such as cereal bars or gorp (a blend of chocolate, raisins, and nuts) help replace what hiking depletes from your body.

4. **Sunglasses and whistle.** Sunglasses are needed in the winter when the combination of snow and sun can bring on snow blindness. The whistle is used if you get lost and need to communicate with rescuers. The sound carries farther than a yell. *Whistles are used only in emergencies.*

5. **Tools-all.** This wonderful invention combines folding pliers with a knife blade, screwdrivers, awl, and other goodies. The Swiss army knife was its inspiration, but the tools-all is even more versatile.

6. **Fire starter.** Campfires are not a part of the wilderness experience anymore, but they do have a place in an emergency. The simplest fire starter to bring with you is a small candle.

7. **Matches.** It doesn't do much good to have a candle that you can't light.

Christine brings along a walking stick to help her maneuver on the trail.

8. **First-aid kit.** Pick up a hiker's first-aid kit from a good outdoor-recreation store, as they are designed for the woods.
9. **Flashlight.** Sometimes it gets dark a lot faster than you thought it was going to. A flashlight will go a long way to helping you find your way in the dark.
10. **Map and compass.** Never go anywhere without these.

Footwear

You can wear hiking boots to play tennis or wear sneakers to hike the Appalachian Trail, but why? Woodland trails are best negotiated in a pair of hiking boots. They give good footing and protect your ankles from twisting. Today you can get hiking boots that are hybrids between cross-trainers and sturdy leather boots. They are light and versatile and usually meet the challenges of the Berkshires quite well. Inside the boots should be a good pair of hiking socks made of a fabric other than cotton.

Southern Region

The Southern Berkshire Hills

On a river it is difficult to tell exactly where the rapids end and the quiet pools begin. The waters flow from one into the other, displaying their differences but never losing continuity. So the southern Berkshire hills are different from the regions to the north.

The towns and villages of the south are the quiet waters of the Berkshires. Time is measured more with the lengthening shadow than the hour hand. Even the landscape is less hurried; the rolling hills like long waves rippling across a peaceful sea.

The most prominent feature of the southern region are the mountains of the Taconic Range, a long uninterrupted wall of rock that forms the area's western border. Chief among these peaks is Mt. Everett, reaching 2,624 feet. Five different walks in this section explore the rivers, waterfalls, and mountains of this beautiful massif.

Directly east of the Taconics is the wide valley of the Housatonic River, the largest waterway of the southern Berkshires. The river runs along eroded beds of limestone and marble, forming broad wetlands and cobbled fields. Three walks take you through these areas where a wonderfully diverse community of plants and animals thrive.

To the east of the Housatonic valley is the Berkshire plateau where countless isolated mountains feed the rushing streams that carve their dendritic valleys across the landscape. Six walks take you from monuments to glens in some of the most wild lands in all the Berkshires.

Enjoy.

Bartholomew's Cobble
Ashley Falls

- **Ledges Trail, Baily Trail, Spero Trail, Tulip Tree Trail, Hurlbert's Hill Cart Path**
- **3.0-mile loop**
- **364 ft. elevation gain**
- **3.0–4.0 hours**
- **moderate sections**

Astride the narrow intervale between the Housatonic River and Miles Mountain lies the National Natural Landmark called Bartholomew's Cobble. The cobble (the name New Englanders give to rounded hills of rock) sits at the confluence of an astounding number of habitats, providing unequaled opportunities to observe all aspects of nature across its 277 acres.

Bartholomew's Cobble is owned and maintained by the Trustees of Reservations. On the property is a natural history center and a network of well-maintained trails. The most popular path is Ledges Trail, an easy half-mile loop. An interpretive booklet for this trail may be obtained at the center, so a discussion of that trail is not included here. The cobble is open from 9:00 A.M. to 5:00 P.M. every day. There is a small admission fee.

Sections of five trails make up a beautiful three-mile loop that takes you from geese, muskrat, and warblers

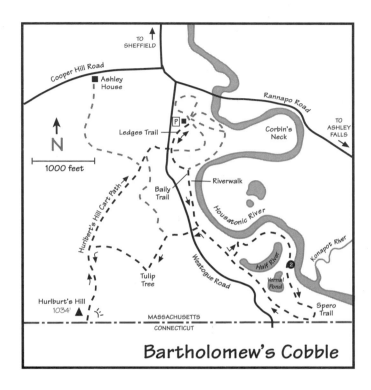

Bartholomew's Cobble

along the riverbank through forests where wildflowers, woodpeckers, and bobcats live, and culminates on a majestic hilltop that holds one of the best views in the Berkshires. All trails on the cobble are clearly marked and each junction accurately signed.

Look Forward To

- a riverside walk
- lots of bird and plant species
- a beautiful view from Hurlbert's Hill

The Trail

From the natural history center take the Ledges Trail to its junction with Baily Trail. From the junction the path leaves the red cedar grove and descends into a **wet woodland** of white pine, elm, and ash. The trail crosses two small streams where the broad leaves of **skunk cabbage** may be seen (and smelled if you're not careful) before turning along the sandy bank of the **Housatonic River.** The Mahican Indians, who once traveled up and down this river in their birch-bark canoes, gave the river its name. *Ho-es-ten-nuck* in Algonquin means "the river that flows beyond the mountains." Many of the same kinds of waterfowl they saw on their travels still live here, as well as some more-recent arrivals. Canada geese and mallard, black and wood ducks nest here, along with hooded mergansers. If you are lucky you may also see **bald eagles** flying low over the water or perched in one of the taller riverside trees.

The path follows the river downstream, crossing several small drainages on wooden bridges. The woods become a blend of cherry, ash, maple, and birch, with tangles of barberry, witch hazel, and red osier dogwood beneath. In the colder months the chickadees, nuthatches, and brown creepers will keep you company as you walk along the path. In March the red-winged blackbirds add their song from the riverbank. By mid-May the

Feeding chickadees at Bartholomew's Cobble

warblers, waterthrush, and other migrant songbirds turn a morning or evening walk into an endless serenade.

Baily Trail now intersects with Spero Trail at the edge of a **hemlock grove.** Take Spero Trail straight ahead (south) through the towering hemlock and white pine. Just to the left the evergreens yield abruptly to marshy stands of maple, cottonwood, and elm. The path comes to a wet area where the trail splits. Turn left here (northeast) onto a **sandy flood plain** of elm, maple, and ash that meanders past beached rafts of flood-borne driftwood and detritus. The woods then yield to a grassy expanse of bottomland framed by the river on the left and the stillwater **oxbow** called Half River on the right. An oxbow is a crescent-shaped pond that forms when a waterway changes course and cuts off a river bend. The quiet waters of the oxbow become home to muskrat and mink as well as a refuge for waterfowl and songbirds. In the spring the pond is the stage from which a chorus of wood frogs and spring peepers sing in the warming air.

The trail then climbs into another wide field, where the path follows the riverbank. You can find many different songbirds through here including one of my favorites, the **song sparrow.** Song sparrows are small birds, brown above with a lighter front strongly streaked with brown, their chest marked with a prominent chestnut spot. As they hop through the underbrush they emit a *cheep, cheep* call but when they hear another song sparrow they will fly to a high branch and sing one of the prettiest songs you'll hear.

The path rises above the river to a bluff where a jumble of boulders overlook the valley in the shade of red oak, cherry, and hickory before opening to a **broad view** of Connecticut's northwest hills. The trail then turns southwest into rocky woods where bobcat often leave their footprints in the winter snow. The footway leads through hemlocks to the edge of a **large vernal pond** at the center of which is a tree where **muskrat** sometimes groom themselves. Muskrat are widely misunderstood creatures. Their hairless tail and rodent genealogy led someone to put "rat" at the end of their name, and their lives haven't been the same since. Muskrat prefer quiet ponds and build beaverlike houses in the shallows or tunnel into banks. Nearby they build feeding platforms where they nibble on aquatic plants or catch an occasional frog. Like many animals, muskrat are most active at dawn and dusk. On bright summer afternoons they like to rest in cool, shady spots, whereas they may be active at all hours on a drizzly day.

The path continues past a weathered boulder where **common polypody fern** and **maidenhair spleenwort** grow and passes the west shore of Half River oxbow, again intersecting with Baily Trail.

Take a left onto Baily Trail (west) which immediately climbs the hemlock-covered hill and crosses Weatogue Road. The path continues uphill through a mixed hardwood forest decorated with boulders and such wildflowers as the delicate **pink-veined spring beauty.** Soon the Boulder Trail leaves right (northwest) and the Tulip Tree Trail continues uphill, west. Take Tulip Tree Trail across some wet woodland to the base of an enormous tulip tree. **Tulip trees** got their name from the showy, tuliplike orange and green flowers they display in late spring. The blossoms are difficult to appreciate, however, because the tree holds them high in its uppermost branches. Tulip trees grow very fast, but it still takes the best part of a century for them to grow to their mature height of a hundred feet.

From the tree the trail turns right through moist woods and fields to the signed junction with the cart path. At the junction follow the grassy path uphill into a huge **dome-shaped meadow** where coyotes hunt for meadow voles in the grass and bobolinks and meadowlarks nest. The trail terminates at the crest of Hurlbert's Hill, where a bench invites you to take in one of the **best views in the Berkshires**. To the left is the undulating profile of the Taconic Range, including Bear Mountain to the extreme left, followed by the gray cliffs of Race Mountain. Mt. Everett and its fire tower are also visible. Straight ahead is East Mountain, with the wide valley of the Sheffield plain in between. On clear days Mt. Greylock is visible through the notch just left of East Mountain. This is a very popular place in spring and fall, for the hill is one of the best places to observe the great hawk migrations. It is not unusual to see thousands of **broad-winged hawks** in one day, and even **golden eagles** have flown overhead. The autumn foliage is eye catching from here but still must take a back seat to the avian splendors.

When it's time to go, follow the grassy path downhill along the edges of fields studded with bluebird boxes. Thanks to the vigorous program of bluebird protection on its lands, the cobble now boasts one of the highest populations of **bluebirds** in the county. Watch carefully and you should see the characteristic sweep of indigo as they fly over the fields.

The path then leads back to the road a short distance from the natural history center.

The Coyote on the Hill

Something remarkable is happening at Bartholomew's Cobble. Its fields have more meadowlarks and bobolinks than the surrounding farmland, and the pastures are home to far more bluebirds than nest elsewhere. There are more wildflowers and ferns and bobcats, yet each year you also will see farmers cutting hay from the fields and cows grazing the pastures. In short, nature is prospering on the same land that people are using.

The natural world and the human world get along so well on the cobble because there it is recognized that the two worlds are really one. People are treated as part of the natural ecology. For example, many farmers in the Berkshires try to get three cuts of hay from their fields each year. To do this they make their first cut in June before ground-nesting birds like meadowlarks and bobolinks have fledged their first brood. Many of the young birds then die beneath the mowers. The farmers who harvest the fields at the cobble get only two cuts a year, but the hay is prime and the ground birds survive.

Haying is a human activity that can be modified to fit within the ecologic web of the cobble. Another way of adapting to the local ecology is for humans to appreciate that they are a transient species and not a residential one. Visitors come to smell the wildflowers, not to pick them. They watch the animals, but do not hunt them. In short, people on the cobble are like the flocks of birds that come and relax in the fields before continuing on their way. They take little from the land but the view, leaving its resources to others.

Working within these ideas, the creatures of the cobble have thrived, yet as the tree swallow does not leave the nest unprotected, neither can people rely on their brethren to do the right thing. Poachers have tried to steal rare plants in the middle of the night, and then there is the coyote on the hill.

On the grassy knoll of Hurlbert's Hill live a group of coyote. In the first light of morning you can see them sometimes attentively stalking the field, searching the grass for the movements of meadow voles. One of these animals is different from the rest: it lost a leg to a steel trap a few years ago. To its credit it has survived and adapted, but it is no credit to us that it has had to.

The experiment at Bartholomew's Cobble shows that human beings as a species can be an intricate part of a prosperous ecology if we are viewed as one of the animals within it. It serves us well, however, to remember the coyote of Hurlbert's Hill, for its jerky gait painfully illustrates what kind of an animal some of us can be.

Getting There

From Sheffield take Route 7 south to the junction with Route 7A. Take a right onto Route 7A and drive to the blinking red light in Ashley Falls. Take a right onto Rannapo Road and drive for 0.9 mile to the junction with Weatogue Road. Take a left onto Weatogue Road. Parking is 0.1 mile down the road.

Sheffield Plain
Sheffield

- **Appalachian Trail**
- **1.8 miles (3.6 miles round-trip)**
- **150 ft. elevation gain**
- **2.5–3.5 hours**
- **easy**

The walk through Sheffield Plain incorporates most of the habitats found in the Housatonic valley. There is swamp, field and forest, all of which are home to an amazing number of plants and animals. In addition we discover a real fairy fort as well as a historic battlefield.

This walk is entirely along the Appalachian Trail (AT), through lands owned and managed by the National Park Service and the Appalachian Trail Conference. The AT in Massachusetts is maintained by the Berkshire Chapter of the Appalachian Mountain Club. The trail is marked throughout its length with white rectangular blazes, and turns are designated by two blazes set atop each other.

Look Forward To

- Shays' Rebellion monument
- fields full of birds
- a fairy fort
- a boardwalk through a swamp

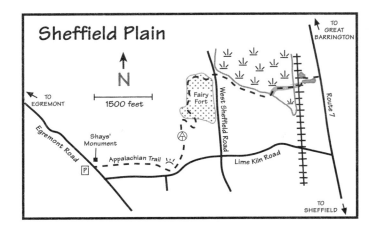

The Trail

From the parking area on Egremont Road, follow blazes southeast 100 feet and cross the road, stopping at the **stone marker** just to the left of the trail. The monument reads:

> *Last Battle*
> *of*
> *Shays'*
> *Rebellion*
> *was here*
> *Feb 27*
> *1787*

The rebellion ended here but the story didn't; see below.

The path follows a tractor road along a **field** whose edge is decorated with the blossoms of milkweed, goldenrod, and Queen Anne's lace each summer, then swings right through a thorny hedgerow of multiflora rose. In June the thorny canes are covered with puffs of single white flowers, and any time of year you can find such birds as sparrows or dark-eyed juncos in the shelter of the branches.

The trail traverses a wet field where in March you can hear the songs of red-winged blackbirds from the wetlands nearby. At the end of the field you pass through an intermittent hedgerow of barberry, with a grove of white oaks to the right. Look among the branches for bluejays and common nuthatches as well as gray squirrels and chipmunks.

The path crosses the field and follows the forest margin gently uphill. This entire area is an example of **edge habitat**, a place where two or more distinct environments overlap. Edges are great places to view wildlife because they contain species from many different areas. Some birds, such as the rufous-sided towhee and the brown thrasher, are edge specialists. Both these birds often feed on the ground, noisily rustling through the dried leaves on the forest floor. Other animals that commonly visit this habitat include white-tailed deer, coyote, red fox, wild turkey, and red-tailed hawks. Edges contain such diversity that regardless of when you visit, you can see and hear many animals and birds.

Near the end of the field is a fine view of the **Taconic range.** The vista extends out over the valley to the mountains. Mt. Bushnell is straight ahead; the prominent shoulder to its right is Jug End. The higher summit to the southwest is Mt. Everett.

The trail now turns left into a **northern hardwood forest** of oaks, hickories, and hop hornbeam. Beneath these trees grow several types of wildflowers including round-lobed hepatica, which throws delicate bouquets of pink, white, and lavender flowers in early spring.

After crossing the mostly level hilltop, the path turns left and descends through a narrow pass, skirting a stone wall as it winds to the base of the hillside and the entrance of a another broad field. As you walk along the field's western edge notice the giant **white oak tree** to the right. White oaks are noted for their high-grade wood and majestic, spreading growth habit. They can survive for hundreds of years, some attaining heights of over 90 feet and a crown spread exceeding 150 feet. In colonial times these great field oaks were sometimes called **fairy forts**, in reference to the little creatures believed to live beneath them.

To many people of Celtic ancestry, fairies are diminutive folk with supernatural powers respectfully included as part of the local flora and fauna. Their preferred habitat is beneath the spreading boughs of giant solitary white oaks. If you rest beneath the tree, don't be disappointed if you fail to see any fairies, as these shy creatures are primarily nocturnal. On bright moonlit nights, however, they throw caution to the wind and dance merrily beneath the leafy branches. If a fairy takes a liking to you it will follow you home, bringing good fortune to wherever you live.

The trail leaves the field at its far northeast edge and crosses West Road before continuing east through the woods. The path soon turns right along the edge of a wooded wetland, then swings left into the **swamp** crossing it on a series of bridges.

Maple, white pine, elm, and **hornbeam** grow in the fragile, mucky soil but are much smaller than their counterparts elsewhere along the trail. Their stunted nature is due in part to the large amount of water present in the swamp's soil, the water limiting both oxygen and nutrient availability, which results in slow growth.

A careful examination of the bridges beneath your feet will show that this is no ordinary boardwalk. In fact most of it is made from grocery store shopping bags. The material, called either plastic wood or Trex, doesn't rot, which means the bridge is installed only once, reducing man-made damage to the swamp. Trex is also very stable and doesn't leach chemicals into the surrounding ecosystem. If the trail is ever relocated, the bridge is simply taken apart and carried away. The material was obtained with the cooperation of the Amoco and Mobil corporations and installed in June 1994 by volunteers from the Appalachian Mountain Club.

After crossing the swamp the trail passes through an area where patches of **princess pine** grow over the ground. This low-growing relative of ferns looks like a miniature evergreen tree and prefers the rich, acidic soils of moist lowland forests.

The path then crosses the railroad tracks (use caution please) before continuing along the shoreline of a narrow alder and red osier dogwood swamp where beaver are sometimes seen. Route 7 is straight ahead.

If you would like a snack or cold drink before heading back, you can proceed along Route 7 North for about a tenth of a mile to a farm store called the Corn Crib. It is the red building on the right. Your return trip follows the AT back to the parking lot on Egremont Road.

Shays' Rebellion

To Daniel Shays there was little difference between Massachusetts before the Revolutionary War and Massachusetts after it. Jobs were still scarce, if anything the currency was worth even less, and the taxes were worse. People who found themselves in debt also found themselves in jail. The Jeffersonian idea of life, liberty, and happiness for all somehow had gotten lost on its way to the Berkshires.

In 1786 Shays and a man named Eli Parsons planned an attack on the arsenal at Springfield, an attack they hoped would spark a revolt against the government. In January 1787, Shays and his followers stormed the arsenal but were quickly routed. In an attempt to regroup, the rebels retreated to the town of Petersham, but government troops followed them and soundly defeated the rebels again. Parsons escaped to New York while Shays found his way to Vermont. Shays would not fight again but the rebellion that bore his name was not quite over.

In the next few weeks Eli Parsons did his best to fire rebellion in the Berkshires from his hideaway in New York. There were minor clashes in Adams and Williamstown, but the largest and bloodiest confrontation was still to come.

On the night of February 27, 1787, a band of about ninety rebels under the leadership of Perez Hamlin crossed into Massachusetts from New York and attacked the town of Stockbridge. They kidnapped some people, ransacked a few homes, and drank all the liquor they could find. With their hostages in tow the mob then marched to Great Barrington, where they unlocked the jail and let everybody go.

The last battle of Shays' Rebellion took place on Sheffield Plain.

About midday on the twenty-eighth, sensing that their welcome was seriously overextended, the little army left town in the hopes of reaching the New York border before somebody tried to stop them.

By this time, however, word of the troubles had reached Colonel Ashley in Sheffield. Ashley, a tough, well-respected commander during the Revolution, soon mustered a militia of eighty men and headed north.

When Hamlin saw Ashley's forces approaching he ordered the rebels to form a line across the road. The hostages were then brought forward in hopes their presence would stop Ashley from opening fire. It didn't. In a split second the report of scores of muskets cracked the winter air as the stunned rebels fell back. Hamlin's troops returned fire, but a quarter of his men were already down, bleeding in the snow. In the time it took the breeze to sweep the clouds of gun smoke from the field, the last battle of Shays' Rebellion was over.

Hamlin and thirty-one of his men were wounded, two fatally, and thirty more were captured. The militia counted one wounded and two killed. The captured and wounded rebels were brought to Great Barrington and locked in the jail they had liberated just hours before. Whatever happened to Daniel Shays? In June of 1788 the government he tried to overthrow granted him a pardon. He died on September 29, 1825, in Sparta, New York.

Getting There

From the southern junction of Routes 23 and 7 in Great Barrington, drive south on Route 7 for 4.5 miles to Lime Kiln Road. Take a right onto Lime Kiln Road and drive 1.2 miles to the intersection with Egremont Road. Take a right onto Egremont Road; the parking area is immediately on the left.

Race Brook Falls
Sheffield

- **Race Brook Falls Trail, Lower Falls Trail**
- **1.0-mile loop**
- **270 ft. elevation gain**
- **1.5 hours**
- **easy**

Race Brook Falls is actually a series of five cataracts that cascade down the steep eastern escarpment between the Taconic peaks of Mt. Race and Mt. Everett. Lower Falls, the last (and highest) in the series and the object of this walk, plunges some 100 feet from the cliff to the rock-filled pool below.

The Massachusetts Department of Environmental Management (DEM) maintains the trails, which are entirely on land owned by the state of Massachusetts. Blue triangles mark the footway and signs appear at critical intersections.

Look Forward To
- a spectacular waterfall
- views from the cliff
- exploring a mountain brook

The Trail
From the kiosk next to the parking area on Route 41, the path leads across a small stream to a sign for the falls

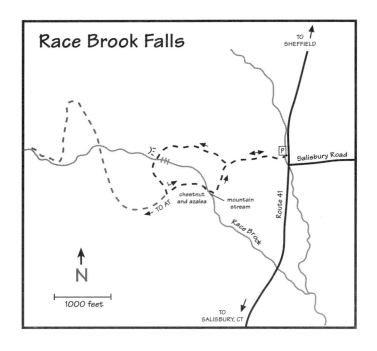

Race Brook Falls

TO
SHEFFIELD

P

Salisbury Road

Route 41

chestnut
and azalea

mountain
stream

TO AT

Race Brook

N

1000 feet

TO
SALISBURY, CT

loop trail. The trail then turns right (west) along the edge
of a small field where clumps of bluestem grass wave in
the breeze. The path enters a moist forest of black and
paper birch mixed with hemlock, the understory a
patchwork of mountain laurel thickets and witch hazel.
After a short walk Race Brook Falls Trail forks left at a
sign marked To AT via Falls. Continue straight ahead on
the Lower Falls Trail, passing a sign marked Side Trail
Dead End to Falls. Don't worry—this really is a loop.

Lower Falls Trail continues northwest, through a **mixed hardwood forest** of red oak, chestnut oak, and ash with increasingly thick tangles of mountain laurel growing beneath, a beautiful walk in June when the mountain laurel is in bloom. Chickadees and nuthatches may be found year-round here, as can bluejays and northern cardinals. In summer red-eyed vireos like to sing from the hardwoods.

The path crosses a small intermittent stream, then follows the bank of Race Brook through a deep hemlock grove that shelters the steep walls of the ravine. The sound of the rushing stream below is melodic compared to the crescendo of the waterfall far off in the distance. The trail then crosses a small tributary stream and winds through a wet, rocky area near the base of the falls before climbing a pile of boulders directly beneath the cascade that offers a dramatic view into the **heart of the waterfall.**

Though this walk is most popular during the warmer months, the harsh cold of winter transforms the waterfall into a spectacular pillar of turquoise ice set against patches of white snow and dark wet rock.

During times of high water it is best to turn around here, as no bridge crosses the stream, but when the water is low you can carefully ford the brook and continue the walk on the opposite bank.

Here the trail turns left and ascends the hill in a wide arc. As the path crests the ridge it reaches a small sign that reads Falls View. Follow the trail straight ahead along the edge of the ravine for about a hundred yards to the **overlook** atop the rocky bluff of Lower Falls.

The view from the overlook peers over the treetops to the distant wetlands of the Sheffield valley to the east.

Lower Falls is the highest and most
spectacular of the Race Brook Cascades.

As you relax among the rocks you can hear the rumble of middle falls higher up the mountain to the west. The few blue and red blazes that still mark some of the nearby trees are remnants of an abandoned trail that once led to upper falls.

To continue the walk, return to the Falls View sign and take a right (south). The path leads through more mountain laurel thickets to a trail junction with a sign on a large hemlock. From here the path to the Appalachian Trail leaves right. Turn left (east) and follow the blue blazes downhill through a mixed hardwood forest of maple, oak, birch, and ash, beneath which grow mountain laurel, witch hazel, and isolated specimens of wild azalea and American chestnut.

About a hundred years ago chestnut made up one-quarter of all the trees in the eastern forests. Then in 1904 an Asian fungus was introduced accidentally into a chestnut grove near Brooklyn, New York. In less than a generation our most important forest tree was gone, as were the thousands of jobs dependent on it. Thin saplings of chestnut survive today because the fungus does not kill the roots, allowing sprouts to grow from old stumps until they, too, are killed. You can find these sprouts by looking for clumps of saplings where the tallest ones are already dead. Look at the base of the dead trees for orange dots of fungus.

The path soon reaches the bank of Race Brook and meanders along the crest of its beautiful steep-sided valley. In this area flocks of golden-crowned kinglets sometimes linger in the hemlocks, sharing the shade with wonderful birds called **brown creepers.** These little birds, brown above and white below, utter a short *theet, theet* call as they look for bugs hiding in the cracks and crannies of tree trunks. Though from a distance they act like nuthatches, you can distinguish between the two because a brown creeper will fly to the base of a tree and climb up, flying off to another tree when it reaches the top. Nuthatches usually start higher up a tree and climb down.

The trail descends the bank, reaching the spot where it again fords the stream. This is the last you will see of

Race Brook so you may want to relax in the cool of the trees or explore the secrets of the mountain stream. The bright orange salamander-like critters you sometimes find in summer near streams like this are **red efts**, the juvenile phase of the red-spotted newt. Beneath some of the flat stones you may see two-lined salamanders or discover the hiding place of an American toad.

After you pick your way across the stream, the trail briefly follows the bank, then turns left away from the brook into a forest of birch and oak, soon reaching the junction with Lower Falls Trail. From here turn right and continue downhill to the parking area.

The Creation of Landscapes

Every waterfall is different. Some are like fragile veils of spindrift while others rage in percussive torrents through the valleys. However different their character, they all have something in common. All the cataracts that sweep down the sides of the Berkshires carry with them bits and pieces of these ancient mountains. Water carries what it can from here to somewhere else. And mountains inexorably fall apart and become the valleys they once towered over.

Over the course of the last 500 million years the peaks of the Berkshires have been raised and then subsequently eroded three separate times. The first episode, named the Taconic Orogeny by geologists, began about 450 million years ago when the ancestral Atlantic Ocean began to close as the continents of the Old and New Worlds started a long, slow drift toward each other. The encroaching landmasses created enormous pressures in the Berkshire bedrock, warping and folding some while thrusting a fifty-mile-long region west in huge landslides. The resulting Taconic mountains were magnificent; they are estimated to have stood 20,000–25,000 feet high.

Over the ensuing millions of years the mountains were worn down by rapid weathering. The wind, rain, and waterfalls eroded literally miles of rock from their slopes, forming huge outwash plains to the west and reducing the majestic mountains to hillocks. Another crustal convergence began the second episode of mountain building, the Acadian Orogeny, about 375 million years ago. Once more, enormous westward pressures folded and compressed the Taconics and Berkshires, rejuvenating their profiles and raising even loftier peaks to the east.

Once more, too, the erosive forces of wind and water began to dismantle this newly elevated landscape as soon as it was created. The higher mountains east of the Berkshires were eroded very quickly, their sediments flowing west, completely covering what remained of the Berkshires. The last event began 250 million years ago; the Appalachians rose, recreating the Berkshires once again. Following this final episode the continents separated, ending the mountain-building cycle (for now) and establishing the Atlantic, an ocean that is still growing wider by about an inch every year.

Today the streams and waterfalls of the Berkshires run through channels cut in rocks called schists, gneiss, marble, and slate. These are all metamorphic rocks that form only deep within the earth. Their presence at the surface testifies to how much material has been washed away by the water, or carried away by the ice of four glacial ages.

Over millions of years the Berkshires have gradually worn away until their hearts have become their summits. Therein lies the beauty. Whatever part of the mountain the waterfall artfully carves, whatever pebble you hold in your hand, it is far older than the Rockies; older than Mt. Rainier or Denali; older even than Mt. Everest and the Himalaya, creating a chronological majesty sheer elevation cannot match.

Getting There

From Sheffield: From Route 7 in Sheffield, take Berkshire School Road (0.1 mile south of the village center) to Route 41. Take a left onto Route 41 south and drive for 1.4 miles to the parking area on the right.

From Salisbury, CT: From the junction of Routes 44 and 41, take Route 41 north to the CT/MA state line. From the state line continue north 2.9 miles; the parking area is on the left immediately north of the intersection with Salisbury Road.

Sage's Ravine
Mt. Washington

- **Undermountain Trail, Paradise Lane Trail, Appalachian Trail**
- **7.8 miles round-trip**
- **1,060 ft. elevation gain**
- **4.0–6.5 hours**
- **moderate with steep sections**

Sage's Ravine is the name for a mile-long valley in the southeast corner of Mt. Washington. Over the centuries Sage's Ravine Brook has artfully carved the folded bedrock into a series of shoots and waterfalls that course through an enchanted hemlock forest. As beautiful as the ravine is, the trip to it is just as delightful, passing through the diverse upland forests in the lee of Bear Mountain.

Because of the long distance traversed, this walk is an excellent choice for an all-day trip. The route also passes two campsites that may tempt some to stretch the walk into a relaxing weekend getaway.

Undermountain and Paradise Lane Trails are marked with blue rectangular blazes, as are the paths around the Paradise Lane and Sage's Ravine campsites. The Appalachian Trail is marked with white rectangular blazes. On all trails turns are noted with two blazes, one atop the other, and well-maintained signs mark all junctions.

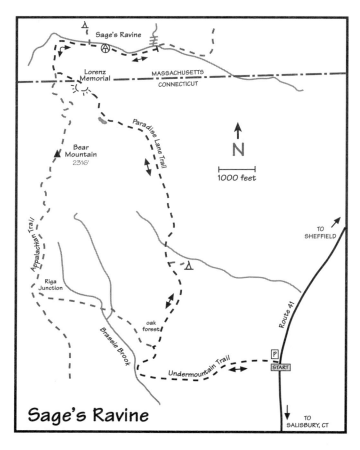

Sage's Ravine
Sage's Ravine
Lorenz Memorial
MASSACHUSETTS
CONNECTICUT
Paradise Lane Trail
Bear Mountain
2316'
N
1000 feet
Appalachian Trail
Riga Junction
Brassie Brook
oak forest
TO SHEFFIELD
Route 41
Undermountain Trail
P
START
TO SALISBURY, CT

The walk passes through lands owned by the states of Connecticut and Massachusetts and by the Appalachian Mountain Club (AMC). The trails are maintained by the Connecticut Chapter of the AMC.

Look Forward To

- waterfalls and deep water pools
- beautiful views
- an ancient oak forest

The Trail

From the parking area on Route 41 in Salisbury, Connecticut, the Undermountain Trail enters the woods near the kiosk, where trail maps are available. A side trail leaves left for the privy. The path heads west into an **open forest** of red and white oak, ash, and hickory. As the trail heads uphill, look for the numerous round leaf nests of gray squirrels high in the branches of oak trees.

As the path climbs higher, chestnut oak and striped maple begin to appear. At about the one-mile mark the trail makes a wide right turn, skirting the bank of Brassie Brook, whose headwaters lie high on the southern face of Bear Mountain. The trail then sweeps gradually left and Paradise Lane Trail enters right at 1.1 miles.

Follow Paradise Lane uphill to a ridge crest in the heart of an **ancient oak forest** where the thin soil and ever-present wind keep even the oldest trees about thirty feet high. These mature oaks, many more than a foot in diameter, don't look any different from the oaks you have been walking past all day, but these are much older. Some were saplings when James Garfield was president in the 1880s.

Many animals live in this mature, or climax forest. White-footed mice and chickadees live in the plentiful hollows that time and pileated woodpeckers have carved in the tree trunks. Ruffed grouse linger near the scattered tangles of mountain laurel while turkeys wander the more open places. Red-tailed hawks often soar overhead, and at night the secretive and mysterious fisher prowl the game trails.

Soon the trail to the Paradise Lane campsite leaves to the right. The main trail passes over undulating terrain thick with June-flowering mountain laurel and rock outcrops, and rich in trailing arbutus, a ground-hugging plant that produces clusters of beautifully fragrant pale-pink flowers in May.

After a long walk the trail passes through a short section of pitch pine, bear oak, and gray birch. Beneath the trees the two-foot-tall fronds of bracken shade patches of wintergreen and lowbush blueberry that grow close to the ground.

The forest now is mostly maple and ash, with a few specimens of shadblow growing in the understory. Shadblow is a small gray-barked tree that throws sprays of delicate white blossoms before the leaves emerge in spring. It got its name because its flowering time coincided with the spring shad run up the coastal rivers. The trail then crosses a stream and soon comes to the shore of a charming little pond on the left.

The path enters a scrubby clearing of bedrock, **blueberries**, and bear oak that offers a **panoramic view** of Bear Mountain that completely fills the southwest horizon. This is a lovely, comfortable place to feel lazy for a while, lie back, and enjoy the sunshine. Do remember that deer also enjoy this spot, however, so watch where you sit.

Just beyond the clearing the trail enters a shady forest of white pine and hemlock, passing the memorial to

Edward H. Lorenz on the right. Lorenz was a charter member of the Connecticut Chapter of the AMC and a dedicated conservationist. In tribute, this grove and the surrounding acreage now bears his name. Look carefully at the trees in this stand and you will notice that some bear the sinuous scars of past **lightning strikes,** testimony to the fact that these woods occupy the highest elevation on this trail. In a few yards Paradise Lane Trail ends at the junction with the Appalachian Trail (AT).

Follow the AT right (north), passing the sign that welcomes you to Sage's Ravine, a beautiful valley named for the family who operated a mill at its eastern end in the 1800s. The trail descends easily through a woodland of birch, maple, and oak, which gradually yields to hemlock by the time Sage's Ravine Brook is reached. The well-trod path then turns right (east) and follows the edge of the stream into the ravine.

The southern wall of the gorge steepens quickly, the slope crowded with boulders and dark ledges of bedrock draped with valances of evergreen wood fern. **Raccoon** tracks often can be found in the soft mud of the stream bank, as can the cloven footprints of passing **deer.** As the forest deepens, the trail to the Sage's Ravine campsites leaves left, crossing the stream on a log bridge. The AT continues along the stream, soon reaching the first in a series of low, melodic waterfalls, each more beautiful than the last. As the north bank steepens, the irrepressible stream collides with a low rampart of bedrock. The resulting cataract sends whitewater tumbling through a ledgy fissure to boil in the deep rock cauldron below. Breathtaking.

One of many waterfalls in Sage's Ravine.

The last waterfall is passed just before the trail crosses the stream on its way to Bear Rock Falls. At the crossing, however, turn back and begin the return journey to the parking lot. But don't rush. The ravine is too beautiful to hurry through. Everytime I visit Sage's I set aside time to linger by some of the deeper pools, searching the waters for the dark, darting streak of a **brook trout** or watching the **water striders** dance on the pool's surface as I cool my toes.

You may return by backtracking the way you came, or, for the adventurous, continue on the AT south past the junction with Paradise Lane Trail for 1.4 miles. The trail will take you over the summit of Bear Mountain and down its south face to Riga junction, where the AT meets the Undermountain Trail. Turn left onto the

Undermountain Trail and follow it 1.9 miles to the parking area on Route 41.

A Delicate Balance

The fisher is one of the largest members of the weasel family, attaining a weight of about twelve pounds and reaching thirty-six inches in length. In temperment it is secretive, but when necessary is unrivaled in perseverance and ferocity. Fishers can climb trees faster than a squirrel and can outrun a snowshoe hare. Its eyes are as black as the night it hunts in, stalking the game trails for its favorite prey.

The porcupine is a creature that exemplifies slow deliberation. With thousands of barbed quills protecting its body, this thirty-pound animal can waddle the woods with impunity, leisurely gnawing the trees to nibble on the soft inner bark, or munching on car tires and tool handles in search of salt. Little troubles it unless it encounters a fisher.

When a fisher meets a porcupine, what follows is a masterful montage of motion. Sensing danger, the porcupine lowers its head and raises its quills, while the fisher approaches carefully. Suddenly the fisher darts around the porcupine, circling it with amazing speed. In response the porcupine thrashes its quill-laden tail at the fisher. The fisher's advantage becomes clear as the two animals joust for position. Porcupines were not built for quick movement, and each time it repositions itself, for a fraction of a second it is off balance. The fisher strikes during one of these fleeting moments, darting in and flipping the porcupine over. There are no quills on a porcupine's belly, and while it is vulnerable the fisher dispatches it with trademark quickness.

The interplay between porcupine and fisher is a paradigm of the delicate balance in nature itself. Every animal is a blend of advantages and vulnerabilities unerringly honed to preserve the species, if not the individual. Every day some will triumph, some will not. Fishers almost always surmount the best efforts of the porcupine, but nature is never a realm of absolutes. Usually the victor walks from the battle, but sometimes it waddles.

Getting There

From Salisbury, CT: Take Route 41 north 3.5 miles to the parking area on the left.

From Sheffield: Take Route 7 to the intersection with Berkshire School Road 0.1 mile south of the village center. Take a right onto Berkshire School Road and follow it to its junction with Route 41. Take a left onto Route 41 south and drive for 5.9 miles to a parking area on the right.

Bash-Bish Falls
Mt. Washington

- **Bash-Bish Falls Trail, Bash-Bish Gorge Trail, South Taconic Trail**
- **2.6-mile loop**
- **900 ft. elevation gain**
- **3.0–4.0 hours**
- **moderate with very steep sections**

Bash-Bish Falls is a uniquely inspiring place. From the rocky aperture at the head of the ravine, Bash-Bish Brook thunders down a narrow gorge of straight-walled cliffs of deformed garnet and mica schist, culminating in a spellbinding, percussive cataract.

The falls are located within Bash-Bish Falls State Park on land owned by the state of Massachusetts and maintained by the Department of Environmental Management. The trail system around the falls also includes acreage in New York's Taconic State Park, the two states working cooperatively to preserve the area. The section of the South Taconic Trail near the falls is maintained by the New York/New Jersey Trail Conference.

Bash-Bish Falls Trail is blazed with blue circles from the lower lot to the viewing area and with blue triangles from the viewing area to the upper lot. Bash-Bish Gorge Trail is blazed with blue triangles and/or circles, and the South Taconic Trail is blazed with small white rectangles.

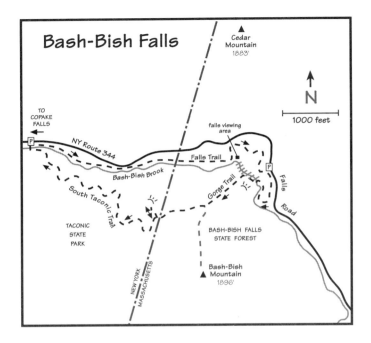

Look Forward To

- a beautiful waterfall
- views into the gorge
- a mountain overlook

The Trail

Caution: The cliffs and falls have proven fatal to many people who chose to disregard the park regulations. The falls and the gorge are restricted areas; swimming is never permitted.

Remember that risky behavior endangers not only yourself but your potential rescuers.

Bash-Bish Falls Trail begins at the east end of the parking area off NY Route 344. The path follows a wide gravel road into woods of hemlock and ash, gradually descending to the stream, then following the brook gently uphill. Christmas and wood ferns line the trail and soon the path passes a large wooden sculpture of a perched bird. To the right across the stream the steep buttress of Bash-Bish Mountain looms above the valley.

The forest changes to a mixture of red oak, sugar maple, ash, and hop hornbeam as the trail passes a sign marking the border of New York and Massachusetts. As the sound of the **waterfall** grows louder the path opens onto a broad viewing area, with a stairway descending to the base of the falls.

This is the picture-postcard view that is used so often as the signature image of the Berkshires. As the brook exits the mouth of the gorge it plummets down the final escarpment in two separate whitewater plumes divided by a massive gray godstone. Beneath it all is a deep viridian pool that is restless and peaceful all at once. It is so beautiful that people often stay for hours just gazing at the falls. It is time well spent.

Falls Trail continues from the west end of the viewing area, entering a **hemlock grove** at the sign for the upper parking area. The path makes a wide turn east as it moderately ascends the bank, passing many boulders that tumbled long ago from higher on the ridge. As the trail proceeds east you may see chipmunks scurry out of your way or watch a red squirrel run up one of the large hemlocks that towers above you. After crossing a

Water roars through Bash-Bish Falls after a summer thunderstorm.

small stream the path winds the last few yards to the upper parking lot on Falls Road, where the trail ends.

Bash-Bish Gorge Trail begins at the gate at the south end of the parking lot and follows a gravel woods road downhill through a **mixed hardwood forest** of ash, black and yellow birch, maple, and chestnut oak. The pale yellow flowers of blue-stemmed golden-rod may be seen in August. The path soon reaches the narrow flood plain of Bash-Bish Brook, and follows the watercourse downstream to the rocky gateway of Bash-Bish gorge. The trail fords the brook just upstream of the restricted area. *Caution: Crossing the stream at high water is dangerous.*

On reaching the far bank the path immediately tackles the very steep scramble up the southwest side of Bash-Bish Ridge, the trail generally following the fence along the precipitous cliff. At the ridge crest is a fantastic overlook that offers a dizzying view into the depths of the ravine. The brook you so recently crossed is just a slender white ribbon far below, noisily rumbling through the jagged canyon.

Leaving the fence, the trail continues uphill through a **storm-damaged forest** of hemlock and red oak with many bare exposures of bedrock. Look for blue circles on the trees as you head southwest. You may hear hairy and pileated woodpeckers in the distance, drumming on some of the many dead trees.

In summer the white stalks of **Indian pipe** appear from the litter of the forest floor. Indian pipe belongs to an interesting group of plants called saprophytes that do not contain chlorophyll and therefore cannot make their own food. Instead they gather nutrients from the decaying leaves and logs of the forest floor. The trail continues up the rugged face of Bash-Bish Mountain to the signed junction with the South Taconic Trail, where you turn right and begin a well-deserved descent.

The South Taconic Trail leads through a **mixed oak forest** accented with rock outcrops and thickets of mountain laurel. This is habitat for the common garter snake as well as the timber rattlesnake, a few of which still live on the mountain (see below), as well as white-tailed deer, coyote, and gray fox. The path passes a rocky area of bear oak and pitch pine and continues downslope to a junction with a blue-blazed trail that leaves right (northwest). Taking a brief detour, follow the blue blazes over bedrock outcrops to an **overlook** that offers the most expansive view of the walk. From the sunny cliff the Harlem Valley opens out to the west, with the little village of Copake Falls visible below. Far to the west is a wonderful view of the eastern Catskills, while Cedar Mountain fills the northern horizon. In March you may see turkey vultures as they return to ride the windy currents that issue from the gorge. Red-tailed hawks also fly over the valley, sometimes with a harassing troop of crows not far behind. In summer the blueberries are a nice nibble, and the view in the fall is superb.

After returning to the South Taconic Trail follow the path downhill through dry patches of pine and mountain laurel, with a few fronds of bracken arching over the rocks. Gradually the forest changes to taller oaks and ash, wandering through moist drainage areas. After turning north into woods of gray birch and hemlock the trail enters the Taconic State Park, skirting a small stream and then following along its bank until the path intersects the wide camping area road near Bash-Bish Brook. Follow the road past some towering Norway spruce, crossing the brook on a stone bridge. The parking lot is a short distance straight ahead.

The Timber Rattlesnake

The Greeks and Romans held them in high regard. They were sacred to Aesculapius and the healing arts, and guardians of the spirit of the temple of Athena. But they weren't perfect, and when the serpent convinced Eve she and Adam should add a little more fruit to their diets, well, that did it. Snakes have had an image problem ever since.

When the Puritans settled in New England the serpent-Satan link already was well woven into common thought; in this new land the timber rattlesnake became its manifestation.

Timber rattlesnakes are large-bodied snakes, historically reaching six feet in length. Today, after generations of slaughter, animals half that size are considered large. They are members of a group of snakes called pit vipers, for the small heat-sensing organ between their nose and eye. During hot spells in the summer rattlers prefer to hunt at night, initiating the belief that the devil gave them the power to see in the dark. But it is the heat-sensing pit, not their eyes, that guides them at night. The organ is so sensitive to thermal energy that a snake can accurately gauge the size, shape, and distance of its prey in total darkness.

Rattlesnakes pass the cold winter months in communal dens usually found in deep, rocky fissures on the ledgy south sides of mountains. Sometimes as many as a hundred snakes will hibernate in the same den. In spring they emerge onto the rocks to warm up in the sun. These congregations, coupled with the fact that they are also venomous, were viewed by the early settlers as more evidence of the snake's allegiance to the devil.

As settlement pushed west timber rattlesnakes were pushed out, killed for being what they were and what they were believed to be. Their range still covers more area than that of any other rattlesnake, extending over most of the eastern United States. Within that range, however, they are rare, surviving in small populations atop isolated mountains.

There are a few places in the Berkshires where rattlers still return in the fall and gather in the spring. These dens may have been in continual use since long before the New World was discovered by the Old. Today you may find the dark-bodied snakes at Jug End in Egremont, on Bash-Bish Mountain in Mt. Washington, on East Mountain in Great Barrington, and on Dry Hill in New Marlborough. If you are fortunate enough to observe one, be also gracious enough to leave it in peace.

Getting There

From Hillsdale, NY: Take Route 22 south 4.1 miles to Route 344. Take a left onto Route 344 and proceed 1.3 miles to the parking area in Taconic State Park on the right.

From Egremont, MA: From the junction of Routes 23 and 41, take Route 41. Drive 0.2 mile and take a right onto Mt. Washington Road. Continue for 7.7 miles to the intersection with Cross Road. Take a right onto Cross Road and drive 4.2 miles (follow signs for Bash-Bish Falls) to the lower parking lot in Taconic State Park on the left.

Guilder Pond and Mt. Everett

Mt. Washington

Guilder Pond Trail
- **1.0-mile loop**
- **30 ft. elevation gain**
- **1.0 hour**
- **easy**

Appalachian Trail to Mt. Everett summit
- **0.7 mile (1.4 miles round-trip)**
- **572 ft. elevation gain**
- **2.0–2.5 hours**
- **moderate**

Mt. Everett is the preeminent landmark of the southern Berkshires, its rounded summit dominating the horizon from nearly every ridge crest and overlook for miles. This walk takes you to the peak of this windblown mountain, where the views are supreme. In a study of contrasts you can also explore the sylvan shoreline of Guilder Pond, the shimmering mountain tarn that lies on the shoulder of Mt. Everett.

Mt. Everett and Guilder Pond are entirely within the state-owned and -operated Mt. Everett State Reservation, maintained by the Massachusetts Department of Environmental Management. Guilder Pond Trail is blazed with blue triangles, while the Appalachian Trail is marked with white rectangular blazes.

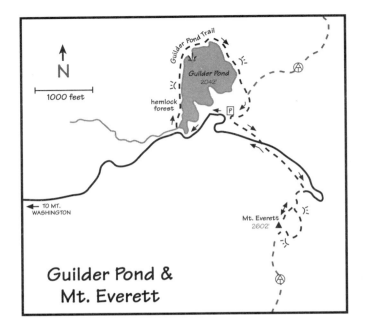

Guilder Pond Trail

Guilder Pond
2042'

hemlock
forest

P

← TO MT.
WASHINGTON

Mt. Everett
2602'

N

1000 feet

Guilder Pond &
Mt. Everett

Look Forward To

- •beautiful summit views
- •a host of interesting plants
- •exploring a mountain lake

The Trail

The Mt. Everett access road runs from East Street in Mt. Washington up the northwest flank of the mountain. At about the one-mile mark the road reaches the picnic area parking lot on the eastern shore of the pond. Both walks begin here. During the more inclement times of year the access road is closed and parking is restricted to the lot at East Street, adding about two miles (round-trip) and 370 feet elevation gain to the walk.

From the picnic area walk the short distance down-hill along the access road to the southern end of the pond, where a sign marks the trailhead of Guilder Pond Trail. The path immediately crosses the pond's outlet on a log bridge and enters a **centuries-old hemlock forest** where the gnarled trees and perpetual shade create a fantastic, Arthurian atmosphere. The path rises on ancient metamorphic bedrock until the path is some thirty feet over the water, offering splendid views across the pond from various **overlooks.** From these vantage points the rounded shoreline typical of glacially molded lakes is obvious. Residents of the woods include chickadees and golden-crowned kinglets. Deer mice nest in the deeper carvings left by pileated woodpeckers in tree trunks, and coyotes wander the deer trails in the oak forest higher up the ridge.

The trail now makes a steep descent to the water's edge and crosses a boggy inlet where sphagnum moss grows in abundance. It is the light green plant that carpets the ground. Sphagnum is remarkable for many reasons, including its ability to hold twenty-five times its weight in water. It also produces an antibiotic that has been shown to promote healing of wounds. No wonder Native Americans used it to dress injuries.

The living sponge created by the mats of sphagnum gives rise to an acid environment used by a few unique plants. **Leatherleaf** is a small evergreen shrub with bronze, leathery leaves and topped with a one-sided tassel of white, bell-shaped flowers which blossoms in late spring and early summer. Less prominent is the **cranberry**, a creeping shrub with small, waxy evergreen leaves; it is most noticeable when the familiar red fruit ripens in the fall. The fortunate will spy the small, misty red rosette of the **sundew**, a carnivore whose leaves glisten with tiny droplets of a sticky exudate that traps and digests small insects (see below).

The path continues across a small peninsula where a picnic table awaits, then wanders along the shore through thick stands of mountain laurel. As the trail reaches the north end of the pond, the hemlock thins and red oak and maple mix in. Some oaks bear the toothy scars of beaver, marks made so long ago that the trees have begun already to cover the wounds with new bark.

As the trail follows the pond's eastern edge it passes through some wet areas where clumps of leatherleaf and sheep laurel grow. Sheep laurel, a small relative of mountain laurel, has small, dark pink flowers beneath the last growth of leaves, its blossoms opening in June. Soon the path comes to a spot where wide sheets of bedrock dive into the water, creating an **open, rocky shoreline** with unrestricted views of the entire pond as well as the summit cone of Mt. Everett. This is a lovely place in fall when the autumn forests scatter leafy sailboats over the pond, or in summer when the gray tree frog's birdlike chorus floats across the water. In late spring, however, the **mountain laurel** blossoms, turning the sedate shoreline into a Monet landscape of antique white and watercolor pink that you will remember long after the flowers fade.

From the rocks the trail passes through a **mixed forest** of yellow birch, beech, and red oak, leaving the shore and heading southeast where the Guilder Pond Trail joins the Appalachian Trail. Both trails then continue through the woods a short distance to the picnic area, where Guilder Pond Trail ends.

From the picnic area the Appalachian Trail heads southeast toward the summit of Mt. Everett. The trail crosses the access road and reenters the woods on the right, proceeding at a moderate uphill grade through woods of black birch, oak, and maple. After a short but strenuous climb the path emerges from the woods where the access road ends and continues uphill a short distance to a clearing just above an old stone shelter. This broad **overlook** offers the best views to the north and east, with the wide sweep of the Housatonic valley framing the mountains all the way to distant Mt. Greylock.

As the trail climbs still higher, bear oak and pitch pine dominate with a few examples of **wild azalea** offering their pale pink blossoms to the late-May breeze. The path then reaches the summit just south of the old fire tower. The crest of Mt. Everett is cloaked in a sea of **bear oak thickets**, with islands of bedrock offering distinctive views to the south and west. Race Mountain is due south, Bear Mountain to the south-southwest. Mts. Frissell and Ashley are southwest, and the Catskills of New York form the bulk of the western horizon. I have spent many happy hours hopping from one outcrop to another taking in the ever-changing view. Bird lovers come here throughout the year but especially in September during the **annual hawk migrations**. Many different species may be seen, but the most spectacular show

Mt. Everett rises above the calm waters of Guilder Pond.

often is put on by the **broad-winged hawks** that fly over the Berkshires in huge autumnal flocks sometimes numbering in the thousands.

As beautiful as the panoramic vistas are, there are other summit sights you shouldn't miss, such as the blueberries that crowd the cracks in the bedrock or the dainty white flowers of three-toothed cinquefoil. This plant, whose flower resembles a strawberry's, blossoms in July. It is more common in the cold of Canada but some live on the higher ridges and mountaintops of the Berkshires, botanic reminders of much icier times.

The Sundew Solution

The shallow boggy places in the marshy corners of some Berkshire ponds are not friendly places in which to grow.

Sphagnum moss engulfs the ground in fluffy wet mats that chill the ground and help make the soil acidic. The nearly stagnant exchange of air and water depletes oxygen and slows the natural process of decay that returns nutrients to the soil. Plants that live in such places must, of necessity, be different from those in fertile fields and forests. Some become more adept at using what little the environment offers, while others have evolved a beastly side, gleaning sustenance from those who happen to wander by.

There are many predators in the plant world, from fungi that snare tiny worms called nematodes to bladderworts that trap water fleas. Venus' flytraps cage prey in toothed traps and pitcher plants create deadly swimming pools. But perhaps the most fascinating is the sundew.

Sundews are small plants, their spatulate leaves forming a basal rosette two to four inches across. Each leaf is graced with hundreds of tiny red spurs capped with a drop of sticky, sweetish liquid. In the sunlight the leaves and drops combine to create what looks like a vague vermilion mist sparkling with tiny earthbound stars.

The beauty of the sundew is also the key to understanding its ingenuity. The sweet liquid attracts small insects, which become mired in the sticky stuff as soon as they touch it. As the insects struggle to escape the leaf slowly curls inward, wrapping itself around its prey. At this point the liquid around the insects begins to change from a sweet lure to an acidic bath of digestive enzymes. As the bugs dissolve in the fluid, their nutrients are absorbed by thin-walled cells that line the pad of the leaf. When the process is complete the leaf unrolls, the tiny red hairs again adorned with inviting luminescent dewdrops.

Sundews don't fit very well into the simple food chain diagram chalked onto classroom blackboards. Nature so simplified couldn't have solved the problem facing the sundew, or for that matter, created human beings. If plants are not capable of solving problems, then they are certainly intimate parts of a system that is, a system that creates the sundew solution as well as our curiosity to comprehend it.

Getting There

From the junction of Routes 23 and 41 in South Egremont, take Route 41 south 0.2 mile. Turn right onto Mt. Washington Road and drive for 7.4 miles. Turn left at the sign for Mt. Everett Reservation and follow the access road to a picnic area. Parking is available near a large sign for Appalachian Trail.

Jug End
Egremont

- **Appalachian Trail**
- **1.1 miles (2.2 miles round-trip)**
- **968 ft. elevation gain**
- **2.5–3.5 hours**
- **moderate with steep sections**

Jug End is the name given to the prominent northwest shoulder of Mt. Bushnell, a peak in the Taconic Range of the southern Berkshires. The steep profile of Jug End allows those atop its summit to enjoy what some call the best view in the Berkshires, a panorama reaching all the way to Mt. Greylock. The view makes this short but strenuous walk very popular and rewarding.

The walk to the crest of Jug End and the summit of Mt. Bushnell is entirely along the Appalachian Trail (AT). The path is marked with white rectangular blazes, with turns noted by two blazes set one atop the other.

Look Forward To
- a witches'-broom
- boulders
- commanding views

The Trail
The parking area is a small pull-off at the side of Jug End Road. From the trailhead the path enters the woods and

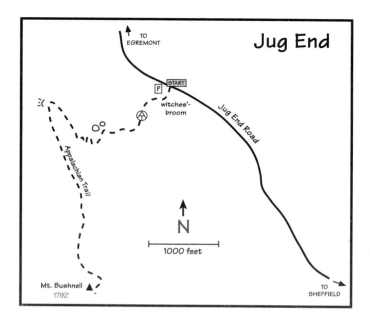

immediately begins to ascend the forested hillside. Large specimens of **white pine** are scattered through a woodland made up of ash, maple, and cherry. When the path passes through a small level spot, proceed to the next blaze and stop. Within a few feet of this blaze are two tall white pine. If you look up toward the top of the closer one you will see a large, dense growth of branches that at first glance look like a huge bird nest. This compact structure is called a **witches'-broom.** In some species of plants brooms result from a pathogenic infection, but on white pine these extremely rare forms are due to a spontaneous genetic mutation. This alteration promotes the dwarf, multibranched growth that is so different from the rest of the tree. As you have no doubt guessed, many of the dwarf pine cultivars you find in garden centers owe their origins to witches'-brooms.

The trail continues to make a gradual ascent along the edge of the rocky ridge that appears on the right. The path then turns into the ridge and wanders through a level section where **oaks** predominate. Mountain laurel grows beneath them interspersed with clumps of witch hazel. **Witch hazel** flowers are small, with long, twisted yellow petals. When they bloom in September the flowers look like delicate golden spiders clinging to the ends of the twigs.

The buttress of Mt. Bushnell now becomes visible straight ahead. At the base of the ridge are **two large boulders.** Hidden about the larger one are small cavities in the rock that hide troves of little quartz crystals. These crystals formed when the rock was thousands of feet underground. Intense geologic compression melted the rock, allowing the quartz to recrystallize as it cooled. If you like antiques you will love these rocks: they formed even before the dinosaurs evolved.

The trail now tackles the steep ridge, using switchbacks to keep the grade moderate. At the top of the highest switchback the path turns north, traversing the slope. This is a lovely section of the trail, as boulders litter the forest and the plentiful rock ledges teem with clumps of **common polypody fern.** You can recognize this plant easily by the throngs of small, six- to ten-inch fronds that grow in compact clusters atop the rocks. To many there is a hopefulness that issues from places favored by these plants. Henry David Thoreau called it "the cheerful community of the polypody." Jug End's rocky slopes are also home to the common garter snake and the timber rattlesnake.

As you progress north you are rewarded with tantalizing glimpses of the view to the east that momentarily appears through the trees. The trail then turns left and climbs the last few feet to the base of a large, blazed **pitch pine** pocked with holes chiseled into the trunk by hungry **pileated woodpeckers.** From the pine take the side trail (right) through the scrub to the north. This short trail was once part of the AT and still has some white blazes on it. It leads in a few yards to a rugged rock outcrop at the edge of the precipice. This is Jug End overlook and the view is extraordinary. The sheer drop of Jug End is before you, with a wide plain extending north. The first prominent mountain ahead is Tom Ball Mountain in Great Barrington. Monument Mountain is just to its right. The mountain visible between these two peaks is Mt. Greylock, some forty miles north in Adams.

The path heads south from here over the level plateau. Notice that the forest is now dominated by two species of trees that were absent from the areas below, the pitch pine and a small tree called the **bear oak.** Both species do well in the thin, rocky soil of windblown mountaintops. The bear oak got its name because its acorns are so bitter that it was believed bears were the only animals that would eat them. Some of the **animals** that frequent the slopes and ledges of Jug End are the white-tailed deer, eastern coyote, and bobcat.

The trail continues south, climbing over large stretches of exposed bedrock often rimmed with **wild**

blueberries. It descends briefly through an open woodland where the pink-blossomed **wild azalea** grows, then climbs again over some bedrock outcrops, finally scrambling up to an open area marked by a small cairn that designates the summit of Mt. Bushnell, with extensive views to the north and west. The Fenton valley to the west separates Mt. Bushnell from Mt. Darby, recognizable by the radio towers atop its summit. The view to the north again extends all the way to Mt. Greylock. This area is a wonderful place to linger and enjoy an afternoon exploring. The return trip is made by following the AT back to the pull-off on Jug End Road. Use caution on descending the buttress, as the footway can be slippery.

Bear Oak

There are about three hundred different species of oak that grow around the world, thirty-four of which are indigenous to the eastern United States. Historically these trees have been one of the most important sources of high-grade lumber. The bark has been used for tanning and cork and the acorns are a significant source of food for wildlife. In European tradition the tree was venerated by the Druids and used to build English warships, and served as the hiding place for Robin Hood's treasures. In New England the Charter of Connecticut was hidden within a great oak when royal agents demanded its surrender in 1687.

All of this nobility and purpose, however, have managed to elude the little bear oak. While some oaks can reach 100 feet in height, the bear oak is stretching things if it gets 20 feet tall. It is too small for lumber, and

Bear oak grows in profusion on many ridges of the Taconics.

its nuts are so full of bitter tannin that almost no animal will eat them. Yet the nobility in nature, if not always obvious, is always present. Bear oaks are celebrated because they can survive where no other oak can.

This little tree thrives in the nutrient-starved soils that often drape the highest Berkshire summits, helping to stabilize these fragile areas. Its small size makes it less prone to wind damage, and the hardy twigs can survive frigid winter winds that would kill other trees. In addition, bear oaks tend to grow in dense thickets which serve as hiding places for wildlife such as birds and chipmunks. Bear oak is recognized easily by its small, sometimes holly-shaped leaves that are dark green above and gray beneath. In autumn the leaves turn a muted red.

Getting There

From Great Barrington take Route 23 west to Route 41 in Egremont. Take a left onto Route 41 and then make an immediate right onto Mt. Washington Road. Proceed about 0.8 mile to Avenue Road. Take a left onto Avenue Road and continue for about 0.9 mile to a small pull-off on the right.

Monument Mountain
Great Barrington

- **Hickey Trail, Indian Monument Trail**
- **2.5-mile loop**
- **800 ft. elevation gain**
- **2.5–3.0 hours**
- **moderate**

Monument Mountain is, quite simply, a magnificent place replete with history and natural beauty. While the bedrock of the surrounding hills is made primarily of schists and gneiss, the distinctive white cliffs of Monument Mountain are composed of pure quartzite hundreds of millions of years old. Over the centuries water and ice have cleaved the stone into sheer rock walls that loom over the valley like ghostly ramparts, a pale Devonian fortress visible for miles. The long, narrow ridge called Squaw Peak at the mountain's summit is known for its inspiring views, and the needle-shaped spire of rock called Devil's Pulpit attracts rock climbers from across the region.

The 500-acre Monument Mountain Reservation is owned and maintained by the Trustees of Reservations. No fee is charged but there is a donation box at the northwest end of the picnic area. The two trails that encircle the mountain are marked with blue circular blazes. Turns are noted by two blazes set one atop the other or by arrows.

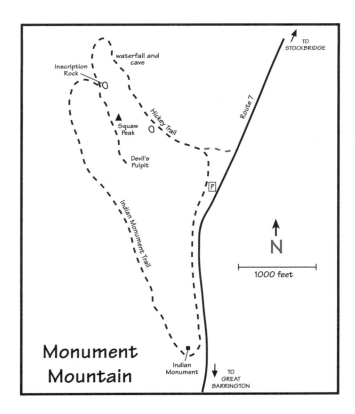

Monument
Mountain

Look Forward To

- a waterfall over a shallow cave
- boulders to explore
- fantastic views from the summit ridge
- Indian Monument

The Trail

The most popular route follows the Hickey Trail, which enters the woods amidst **sassafras** and red pine at the north end of the parking lot. Sassafras is the bushy tree with one or two deep-cut lobes in the leaves that give the foliage a mitten shape. The Indians used sassafras in healing ceremonies, and in colonial times tons of it were exported back to England for medicinal use.

After a gentle walk that passes some large white pine and oak there is a wet area with an abandoned stone-lined well close by. Soon a side trail enters from the right and shortly thereafter a false trail leaves left. The path, still heading north, then begins a steady climb, passing a huge boulder that is home to a large colony of the dainty common polypody fern and also serves as a good rest stop. **Mountain laurel,** which grows well in rocky woodland soils, forms gnarled thickets throughout this area of the mountain. In June the bushes are peppered with blush-red buds and creamy blossoms. A little farther on you come to a brook that flows through a small but beautiful ravine. The trail follows the brook a short way, then crosses it on a small bridge. Soon a **waterfall and cave** appear on the left. The falls are small and are most impressive during spring runoff or in winter when they are transformed into a still life of ice. The cave is shallow but large enough for most folks to sit in. The rocks can be a little damp, but they encircle you with a wonderful silence that enhances the song of the falling water beside you. Please note that if the summer has been dry the little waterfall may be also. The trail continues up a dry ravine to the ridge crest, crosses the stream again on another bridge, then reaches the junction of the Indian Monument Trail, which enters on the right.

Inscription Rock is here; carved on its face is the tale of how the original property was donated to the people of Berkshire by Helen Butler in 1899. Take a moment to look at the large holes chiseled into the oak near the rock. They are the calling card of the pileated woodpecker, a crow-sized bird plumed in black and white with a pronounced red crest on its head. These birds have a large home range, so you are much more likely to see their handiwork than the birds themselves.

Hickey Trail continues past the rock and soon tackles a short scramble to the summit. The top of the mountain is a jumble of weather-worn quartzite boulders with lots of hideaways to relax in and enjoy the view. In summer you can enjoy a trailside nibble of the tart blueberries that grow in abundance on the summit. The winds that often rake the ridge discourage most trees from growing here but the hardier pitch pine and bear oak do well enough amidst the rocks. They do, however, pay a price for the view: the prevailing breezes kill many of the windward buds and twigs, while those on the leeward side continue to grow, resulting in trees that always look as if they are blowing in the wind. These sculpted trees are called flag trees.

A short walk along the ridge brings you to the precipitous cliffs of **Squaw Peak,** immortalized in William Cullen Bryant's poem "Monument Mountain." **Devil's Pulpit** is the spire of rock that hangs teasingly out over the valley. You will often see rock climbers here negotiating the vertical pitches. Take a moment to watch the turkey vultures flying out over the valley. The warmth of

The Devil's Pulpit rises dramatically from the shoulder of Squaw Peak on Monument Mountain.

the sun produces thermals, rising currents of air that such gliding birds as vultures and hawks use to soar through the sky. Sometimes there are more than twenty of them sailing the thermals at once. If you watch long enough you will see them beat their wings, but turkey vultures are master gliders; they don't have to flap their wings very often. Sometimes if you're quiet and lucky, they will soar up from below and pass over the ridge just a few feet overhead. It's quite a sight.

In addition to the natural wonders of this spot, it also has an artistic story as well. On August 5, 1850, Nathaniel Hawthorne, Herman Melville, Oliver Wendell Holmes, and other friends came up the mountain on an outing. Hawthorne's friendship with Melville began that summer day. On the top of this white mountain the two spoke about a great white whale. To a large degree it was Hawthorne's influence and continued support that helped turn *Moby Dick* from a great sea story into a masterpiece of mankind's lonely journey in the borderland between good and evil. Melville dedicated the book to Hawthorne.

When the time is right, backtrack to Inscription Rock and bear left down Indian Monument Trail. This is a gentle downslope walk through tall hardwoods and thickets of mountain laurel interspersed with hemlock groves, the omnipresent cliffs always nearby. Deer, who seek out the easiest passage from one place to another, like to use this section of trail when they cross over the mountain. In the spring look for **lady-slippers** and other wildflowers. Almost anytime there are flocks of chickadees, titmice, and nuthatches, as well as golden-crowned kinglets, flitting among the hemlocks. These birds are tiny things, smaller than chickadees and almost as friendly. The cliffs grow smaller the farther south you walk. When they disappear look for a stone wall that comes out of the woods on the left. This wall is only a few yards long and leads to the old stone mound called the **Indian Monument.** Follow the wall back to the trail; the path swings to the north and ends soon at the south end of the parking area.

The Mystery of the Monument

Many people who have hiked Monument Mountain for years have never seen the rough pile of stones that gave the place its name. It sits just off the trail at the south end of the ridge at a spot where the quartzite bedrock dives beneath the ground and an ancient stone wall wanders between the trees.

When you first see this rocky cairn it honestly does not look like much, just a heap of stones in the woods. Why would anyone name an entire mountain after a pile of rocks? Perhaps because that pile of rocks was here in the woods even before the Pilgrims landed at Plymouth Rock.

The Mahicans who lived nearest the mountain had many traditions regarding the origin and purpose of the mound. Some believed that the cairn was built over the burial site of the first Mahican sachem. Others claimed it honored a great military victory over another tribe, and still others that it marked the grave of a heartbroken Indian maiden who threw herself in despair from the cliffs. The last version was immortalized in William Cullen Bryant's poem, "Monument Mountain."

In 1735 the sachem of the Stockbridge Mahicans told the English that the stone monument also served as a boundary marker. Under a treaty with the Mohawk the Mahicans were entitled to all the land within one day's walk from the mound.

In 1824 William Cullen Bryant last visited the monument he helped make famous. Shortly afterward some misguided people destroyed it. They scattered the stones and dug into the earth in search of the monument's secrets, but they found nothing. No deceased maiden who died for love, no sachem of a proud nation, nothing. For sixty years Monument Mountain had no monument. Then in 1884 a group of citizens from Great Barrington, guided by the directions of an old man who had visited the mound with Bryant years before, rebuilt it.

Why or even when the cairn was built may never be known for certain, but one tradition concerning the monument is well known. Whenever the Mahicans walked the trail over the mountain they would stop at the stone mound. As they gave thanks to the Great Spirit, they would add one more stone to the pile. It is a custom that continues today. Before they end their walk many people stop at the monument, give thanks for their blessings, and add one more stone to the pile. It is a tradition that makes a hike on Monument Mountain different from any other you will take.

Getting There

From the south: At the northern junction of Routes 23 and 7 continue north on Route 7 for 3.0 miles. The parking area entrance is on the left.

From the north: From the Red Lion Inn at the junction of Routes 102 and 7, continue south on Route 7 for 3.0 miles. The parking entrance is on the right.

Benedict Pond

Great Barrington and Monterey

- **Pond Loop Trail**
- **1.5 miles**
- **30 ft. elevation gain**
- **1.0–2.0 hours**
- **easy**

Benedict Pond is the largest of the dozens of small ponds scattered through the expansive woodlands of Beartown State Forest. Pond Loop Trail wraps itself around the often-shallow shore, offering many views across the water as well as opportunities to watch the activities of the pond's diverse wildlife.

Blue triangle blazes mark Pond Loop Trail throughout its length. At the pond's south end you will also find the white rectangular blazes of the Appalachian Trail (AT). Beartown State Forest is owned by the state of Massachusetts and maintained by the Department of Environmental Management.

Look Forward To

- wild azalea and mountain laurel
- a beaver lodge
- salamanders and turtles

The Trail

Pond Loop Trail begins near the shore next to the boat ramp, heading east into a forest of red maple, yellow

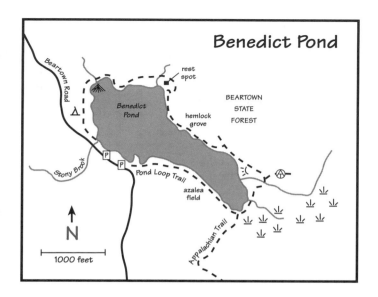

Benedict Pond

rest spot

BEARTOWN STATE FOREST

hemlock grove

Benedict Pond

Beartown Road

Stony Brook

Pond Loop Trail

azalea field

Appalachian Trail

N

1000 feet

birch, red oak, and white pine with a tangled understory of hemlock, mountain laurel, and azalea. The trail slowly swings southeast as examples of beech and gray birch add to the already varied forest, and wild azalea becomes very common. There are many species of azalea, both native and cultivated escapees, that live in the Berkshires but you are most likely to bump into the pinxter and mountain azalea. Both species have flamboyant pale-pink-to-white tubular flowers in showy clusters blossoming in May, just as the new leaves are unfolding. This section of shoreline is unusually endowed with these beautiful plants.

The path now makes its way through patches of trailing arbutus and wintergreen before joining the

Appalachian Trail at the marshy south end of the pond. In conjunction with the AT the path wanders northeast by a small grove of white cedar, passing small mats of evergreen partridgeberry and a plant called shining club moss, a relative of the more common ground cedar and princess pine. The trail crosses a small drainage on a wooden bridge and a larger stream on a picturesque stone bridge, after which the AT immediately leaves right.

Pond Loop Trail continues along a wide, graded woods road to an **overlook** on the left where bracken fern grow beside shrubby hawthorn trees. This rocky crest offers a nice view across the narrow southeast neck of the pond and is especially pleasing in May and June when the blooms of azalea and mountain laurel cover the far shore.

From the overlook the trail soon turns left (west), leaving the woods road and descending along the shore into a **hemlock grove** filled with mossy rock outcrops, the largest of which hosts communities of polypody fern and hemlock growing from deep fissures in the rock.

As the path turns north red maple, yellow birch, ash, and red oak replace the hemlock, with patches of princess pine and wintergreen along the ground. At the northeast corner of the pond the trail passes a sturdy bench that begs to be sat upon. From its sturdy wooden comfort you can view a cattail marsh to the right where tiny tree frogs called **spring peepers** sing in April.

From the bench the path switchbacks east and wanders through a marshy forest in a wide northeast arc, encountering the shore again at a boggy inlet where red-spotted newts swim in the shallows. These are the adult stage of the bright orange-colored red efts you see so often along the trail after a summer rain. Also look for colorful painted turtles in the marsh to the left.

The trail continues along the north shore, passing another bench, this one set beneath a spray of white pine where more trailing arbutus hides among the rocks. In a wet area just beyond, sensitive fern grow beside the yellow August blooms of goldenrod. The path crosses a stream on a wooden bridge and soon comes near a **beaver lodge,** where the chewed stumps of maple, oak, and hop hornbeam litter the shore. Beaver don't always build their domed lodges in the middle of ponds; some, like these, construct shelters very close to the bank. Sometimes, if the beaver live along a stream, their home isn't a lodge at all but a burrow dug into the bank.

Beavers build their lodges along the shore of Benedict Pond.

The path now turns south through a camping area before emerging just north of the spillway along the dam. Cross the spillway bridge and proceed through the swimming area to the parking lot a few yards beyond.

"Eye of Newt and Toe of Frog"

There it is, in act four, scene one of *Macbeth*: that newt thing. Whenever nasty old witches brew up some noxious poison they always add the eye of some poor newt. Is there some reason for this salamander slander or did Shakespeare just have a thing against newts? It turns out that Shakespeare had his reasons, but more on that later.

Newts are small amphibians closely related to salamanders. There are about twenty or so species around the world, from Europe to Africa, Asia, and the Americas, yet the red-spotted newt is the only one indigenous to the Berkshires. The life cycle of the red-spotted newt is a complex series of metamorphic changes that begins when small larvae hatch from eggs in ponds in early spring. A larva, complete with gills, stays in the pond until summer, when its body undergoes a metamorphosis, exchanging gills for lungs and acquiring the blaze orange color characteristic of the newt's juvenile phase, or eft stage. Red efts then leave the water and begin a long, long walk through the woods, which is where we usually find them.

Red efts eventually change into the olive green adults you see swimming in the pond in spring, unless of course they are found by wandering witches and brought back to a boiling cauldron. Which brings us back to *Macbeth* and Shakespeare. Newts and efts have glands in their skin that exude a toxic substance when

A red eft atop white puffball mushrooms near Benedict Pond.

they are injured. These compounds render them very distasteful to potential predators. That is why red efts can walk the woods so cavalierly and why they are a favorite ingredient in any witches' brew.

Getting There

From Stockbridge: Take Route 7 south to Monument Valley Road, the first left south of Monument Mountain

High School. Follow Monument Valley Road to Stony Brook Road. Take a left onto Stony Brook Road and drive for 2.8 miles. Take a left onto Benedict Pond Road and drive for 0.4 mile to the parking area.

From Great Barrington: Take Route 7 north to the intersection with Monument Valley Road just south of Monument Mountain High School. Follow the directions above to the parking area.

Ice Gulch
Great Barrington

- **Appalachian Trail**
- **1.1 miles (2.2 miles round-trip)**
- **525 ft. elevation gain**
- **2.0–2.5 hours**
- **easy**

Ice Gulch is one of those rare places that doesn't seem to belong in modern times. There is a prehistoric quality about the chasm and the shadowy forest that surrounds it. Of course, there are no saber-toothed tigers lurking on the mossy ledges, but your imagination may tell you differently.

Just beyond the gulch is the Tom Leonard Shelter, where tired hikers may spend a restful evening. The shelter is also a great rest stop for day hikers, and the nearby overlook provides a beautiful place to have a quiet lunch.

The walk to Ice Gulch is entirely along the Appalachian Trail (AT) and passes through state-owned East Mountain State Forest. The Massachusetts Department of Environmental Management oversees the forest and maintains the trail cooperatively with the Berkshire Chapter of the Appalachian Mountain Club. The AT is marked throughout its length with white rectangular blazes; turns in the trail are noted with two blazes set one atop the other.

Look Forward To

- an Ice Age ravine
- Tom Leonard Shelter
- beautiful views from the overlook

The Trail

The Appalachian Trail intersects Lake Buel Road about fifty feet southeast of the trailhead parking area, entering the woods on some wooden steps beside a large white pine. The path leads uphill into a mixed **second-growth**

forest of white pine, paper and black birch, sugar maple, ash, cherry, and hemlock. Beneath them grow many ferns including the familiar, glossy green Christmas fern and the burgundy-stemmed ebony spleenwort.

The trail passes a low **stone wall,** a quiet reminder of a time when farmers cleared Berkshire of its forest and pastures, building stone rows for boundary markers. When people abandoned the farms in hard times a succession of shrubs and trees swallowed the walls.

The path continues gently uphill through groves of white pine, striped maple, and hemlock. As the path levels out, listen for the songs of chickadees, a clear *fee-bee,* or the familiar *chick-a-dee-dee-dee.* Male woodpeckers often can be heard drumming on trees in the spring as part of their annual courtship ritual. When you cross a vernal stream the bulk of East Mountain is visible straight ahead through the trees. At the base of the escarpment the path crosses an intermittent stream, then veers left along a cliff. The trail steepens, crossing the streambed at a place favored by Canada violet and spring beauty, two wildflowers that bloom in May. A sharp left turn takes you into a primeval hemlock forest.

Hemlocks prefer to grow in the cool, moist shelter of stream-cut ravines, where they form pure, slow-growing stands. This maze of mossy rock outcrops and dark, thickly needled boughs represents such a grove, an evergreen sanctuary where some of the trees are well over a hundred years old. While still in the hemlock woods the trail skirts the first shallow scarp of Ice Gulch, retreats through a wet sag, then emerges at the rocky scar of **Ice Gulch lookout.**

As you stand on the promontory at the head of the gorge, notice the web of deep vertical fissures on the cliffs. As these faults enlarge by erosion and alternate freezing and thawing of ice, they calve huge boulders that tumble into the ravine. Over time these boulders have filled the valley, burying the stream that runs through it and creating countless caverns and **boulder caves** on the valley floor. On quiet, windless days you can hear the watery whispers of the brook as it flows through the stony hollows far below. Local legend says that ice remains in the deeper catacombs well into summer.

The rugged habitat of Ice Gulch is home to many deer, though they prefer to stay in the deep woods on the other side of the gulf where people rarely go. **Eastern coyote** live in the ravine, as do red squirrels, chipmunks, and raccoon.

The trail continues to the right, descending onto a shelf bounded on the right by rocky cliffs and on the left by a sheer drop into the gulch. When it looks like there is nowhere to go, look for a sharp right turn that threads through the rock on a stone stairway. Follow the path downhill. The **Tom Leonard Shelter** is just across the stream.

As you enter the shelter you will notice that this is not just some lean-to in the woods but a beautiful, cozy hideaway. A plaque on the wall relates the history of this showpiece shelter.

Welcome
To the Tom Leonard Shelter
This shelter is dedicated to the memory of a young man who spent his few years of adulthood in service to the Appalachian Trail as a Ridge Runner. In 1985 his life

Tom Leonard Shelter in Ice Gulch.

*was cut short by an unexplained, brief neurologic ill-
ness.*

*This shelter was designed and built by volunteers from
the Appalachian Trail Committee of the Appalachian
Mountain Club during the summer of 1988. The material was airlifted to the site using a Sikorski Skycrane
helicopter of the Air National Guard.*

*Materials were purchased with funding from the AMC
and an anonymous donor. The Massachusetts Department of Environmental Management donated the land
and the outhouse.*

The trails around the shelter are marked with blue
rectangular blazes. Paths to the tent platform/overlook
as well as to the outhouse and camper's water supply

are marked with white circles. No permit is required to stay at the shelter overnight or camp at the platform, and no fee is charged. To reach the overlook climb the steps in front of the shelter and follow the bedrock outcrop a few yards to the cliff.

The **overlook** (which was also the landing site for the helicopter that brought the building supplies in 1988) offers the most expansive view of the trip. The vista opens south, overlooking a beautiful valley. To your right is the southern shoulder of East Mountain. The first prominent hill straight ahead is Sisson Hill in New Marlborough, and those pale blue hills against the horizon are the Litchfield Hills of Connecticut.

As you enjoy lunch or just relax, notice that the forest around you is different from either the second-growth forest or the hemlock grove near the gulch. This is an **upland hardwood forest** characterized by red oak and beech, with clumps of June-blooming mountain laurel and wild azalea scattered beneath. The heart-shaped flowers of Dutchman's-breeches bloom at the edge of the cliff in May.

After exploring the lookout area, return to the AT and follow it back to the parking area on Lake Buel Road. (From Lake Buel Road, if you proceed for about a mile northbound on the AT, you will be in the heart of the forest destroyed by the tornado that tore through this section of the Berkshires on Memorial Day, 1995. This area suffered almost complete devastation from winds estimated to have approached 300 miles per hour. The storm was so powerful most of us never will witness sights like this again in our lifetime, or feel the disturbing emotions a walk through here creates. Following the policies of the National Park Service enough downed material was removed to reduce the fire hazard, with the remainder of the mangled forest left to recover through nature's own processes.)

The Evolution of the Eastern Coyote

According to local legend the last timber wolf in New England was killed in 1918 in the Berkshire town of New Marlborough. With the passing of that animal a gaping hole was created in the ecology of the Northeast. A hole that would be filled through nature's never-ending ingenuity in less than a hundred years.

Historically the range of the coyote was generally limited to the vast expanse of territory west of the Mississippi River. Yet in the early years of this century, for some unknown reason, a population of western coyote then living in northeast Iowa began a slow infiltration of the lands to the east. Through DNA analysis scientists have discovered the animals migrated into areas around the Great Lakes and into Ontario, where they met and interbred with their cousin, the timber wolf.

By the time the first coyotes were seen in New England in the late 1950s and early 1960s, they were remarkably different from their western cousins. Their muzzles were shorter, with much stronger jaw muscles. Their bodies were stouter and larger, some reports insisting twice as large as their thirty-pound western kin.

A debate ensued as to what these animals were. Were they coyotes or were they wolves? Again DNA studies provided the answer. The animals that now live in the Berkshire hills are coyotes that have wolf DNA.

Eastern coyotes are beautiful animals, very intelligent and usually quite secretive. They move about mostly at night or near dawn and dusk in small family groups of three or four. Their calls range from the happy yips and yaps they exchange while walking the trail to the mournful howls they sing to stay in touch with their kin. Yet their most amazing trait is their seemingly endless reservoir of adaptability—a trait that has allowed them to thrive in the Berkshires. The wolves are gone and yet, in a very real sense, they have returned.

Getting There

From the north junction of Routes 7 and 23 in Great Barrington, take Route 23 east toward Butternut Basin Ski Area. Drive for 2.3 miles and take a right onto Lake Buel Road. Proceed on Lake Buel Road for 1.3 miles to a small parking area on the left.

Bowker's Woods
Stockbridge

- **Bowker's Woods Lower Trail**
- **1.0-mile loop**
- **50 ft. elevation change**
- **0.5 hour**
- **easy**

In the early decades of the twentieth century Richard Rogers Bowker was one of the most influential editors in America, polishing the prose in such publications as *Publishers Weekly* and *Library Journal* among others. He helped found the American Library Association and was president of the town library in his adopted home of Stockbridge. One of his favorite places was where the Housatonic River wrapped itself around a forest of tall pines and marble boulders. It was magical to him, and when he died in 1933 he gave the magic to us.

Bowker's Woods is owned and maintained by the Laurel Hill Association. The trail is marked with yellow blazes throughout its length.

Look Forward To

- a stroll along the Housatonic River
- marble boulders and rare ferns
- tall pines and forgotten trolleys

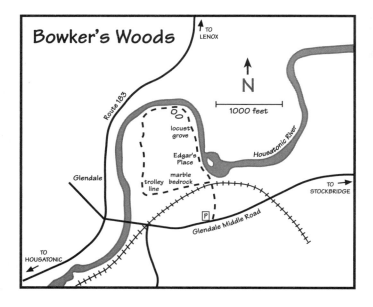

The Trail

From the trailhead on Glendale Middle Road the path enters a **second-growth forest** of ash and pine, with a rough understory of burning bush and cherry. The trail heads downhill and soon crosses the railroad tracks. Near the riverbank the path splits, with one branch leaving left (west). Continue straight ahead along a high bluff directly over the river. Tall pines and hemlock shade the sky above you as mallards and black ducks swim in the river below. A short walk brings you to a bench that overlooks a small island in the river. A plaque on the bench reads: "Edgar B. Taft, 1916–1993, who loved this spot." Don't hurry on, because Edgar was right. This spot is the first magic place. When I come here I like to watch the ducks paddle by like little riverboats or imagine my footprints on the sand of the island's shore. Stay too long and the spirit of Huck Finn will have you dreaming of building a raft for a long float downriver.

From the bench the path follows the riverbank to a place where the towering pines suddenly yield to a grove of **black locust trees.** Hundreds of years ago these tall, hauntingly contorted trees grew only in the central Appalachians far to the south, where the hard, heavy wood was used for house timbers and fence posts. Each spring the leafy twigs harbor clusters of fragrant white flowers. The early settlers planted it far from its original home, until now the locust is naturalized throughout

A view of the Housatonic River from Edgar's spot.

New England and even parts of Europe. In the Berkshires the trees blossom in June and are so richly perfumed that the breeze may carry their undiluted fragrance for hundreds of yards.

From the locust grove the trail quickly encounters a mossy green wonderland of **weathered boulders** to the left. These massive stones are made of calcium-rich marble and limestone, which has a high pH. Raindrops often form in association with low-pH particles, creating precipitation that is weakly acidic. When the rain contacts the stone a chemical reaction takes place and a tiny bit of rock dissolves in the water. Over the centuries this process creates the cavities and potholes that pock the rock's surface. This gentle erosion also provides a home for a select group of plants, including common polypody fern that grows atop the boulders and the rare **walking fern** that may be found on the east side of the largest stone. Walking fern is so named because, when the tip of its slender frond stays in contact with its mossy neighbors, a little fern plant grows from the frond, enlarging the colony. Each plant lives only for a few years, but some believe that the colony itself has occupied the same patch of rock for hundreds, even thousands of years. Please be careful not to disturb it.

Beyond the boulders the path comes to a stone wall where the trail turns away from the river as it makes a wide oxbow turn to the south. The path follows the wall lined with even greater pines that rise some one hundred feet above the Christmas and wood ferns below. The trail then turns left (east) along a wide, level road where bushes of honeysuckle blossom in June. This section of the trail follows the **old trolley line** that once ran from town to town throughout the Berkshires in the early 1900s. Invented in 1880 by Stephen Dudley Field of Stockbridge, the electric trolley seemed a good solution to public transportation at the time. The trolley, however, was prone to accidents, the most infamous coming in 1902 when a trolley car ran over the carriage carrying Theodore Roosevelt, killing a Secret Service agent and injuring the president. In spite of the accident the bruised Roosevelt continued his itinerary, giving a speech later that day in Stockbridge.

A short way down the path the trail passes through an exposure of grayish rock. This outcrop is called **Stockbridge marble** by geologists. It was formed when soft limestone was compressed as the continents of Africa and America drifted together. The intense pressures metamorphosed the limestone into marble. These stones are more than 400 million years old.

From here the path recrosses the railroad tracks and wanders back to the road.

"Pure Leaves"

Generations ago ferns were considered very mysterious things. They produced no fruit, no flowers, and no seeds, yet the forests were full of their graceful fronds. No matter how carefully the problem was investigated, no one could determine how they spread across the shady forest floor. The longer the problem remained unresolved, the more magical ferns became. In Shakespeare's *Henry IV,* fern dust even made Gadshill invisible.

Gradually the secrets of ferns have been pieced together. Ferns produce extremely small spores that contain only a few cells apiece. A spore is released from the frond and floats away on the breeze. If it lands in a favorable place the spore begins to grow into a flat disc called a prothallium. The prothallium is larger than a spore but is still very small, usually about a quarter of an inch across. As the disc matures male and female organs appear, and if enough moisture is present the sperm cells swim across to what will become the egg cell. This union results in a young fern plant called a sporophyte, which grows on the prothallium. As the sporophyte matures it develops roots and fronds, growing into the plant we recognize as a fern. These ferns then produce more spores and the cycle begins again.

Regardless of how much we understand about them, however, ferns never lose their mystery. A fragile tuft of maidenhair spleenwort will always seem too delicate to touch. And by lying down in a thicket of cinnamon fern we can be as invisible as Gadshill. It is, at last, the mystery of ferns that inspired Thoreau to write, "Nature made ferns for pure leaves."

Getting There

From Stockbridge: Take Route 102 west to Glendale Middle Road near the bell tower. Go 1.0 mile on Glendale Middle Road to the trailhead. Pull off the road as far as possible.

From Lenox: Take Route 183 south to Glendale and the junction with Glendale Middle Road. Take a left onto Glendale Middle Road and drive for 0.3 mile to the trailhead. Pull off the road as far as possible.

Laura's Tower
and Ice Glen
Stockbridge

- **Laura's Tower Trail, Ice Glen Trail (including sections of Ice Glen Road, Route 7, and Park Street)**
- **3.3-mile loop**
- **640 ft. elevation gain**
- **2.5–3.5 hours**
- **moderate**

The walk to Laura's Tower, atop the hill named Laura's Rest, and the walk through Ice Glen are along trails maintained by the Laurel Hill Association, a village conservation and improvement society. The Laurel Hill Association, founded in 1853, has the distinction of being the oldest organization of its kind in the United States.

These trails offer panoramic views from Laura's Tower, sky-scraping conifers, and the mysterious world of Ice Glen, all within a few minutes' walk of the Stockbridge village center. The beauty of this area, coupled with its easy accessibility, has made this hike a favorite of visitors and residents alike for well over a century.

Look Forward To
- cathedral pines and hemlocks
- the view from Laura's Tower
- Ice Glen

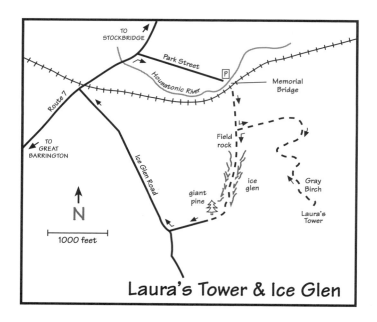

TO
STOCKBRIDGE

Park Street

Housatonic River

P

Memorial
Bridge

Route 7

TO
GREAT
BARRINGTON

Field
rock

Ice Glen Road

giant
pine

ice
glen

Gray
Birch

Laura's
Tower

N

1000 feet

Laura's Tower & Ice Glen

The Trail

The trails for both Laura's Tower and Ice Glen begin at the parking area at the end of Park Street in Stockbridge. There you will find a trail map and other information posted on a prominent sign just north of the bridge. Over the years various colors have been used to mark these trails; *both* trails, however, are now marked with yellow rectangular blazes for their entire length.

The trail begins by crossing the Housatonic River on the **memorial bridge,** a secure but bouncy structure that gives good views up and down the waterway. Look for black ducks feeding in the shallows along the riverbank.

They especially enjoy the area just upstream from the bridge.

The path crosses the railroad tracks, beside which goldenrod, blackberries, and sensitive fern grow, then enters a forest of maple, ash, and beech. These hardwood trees share the woods with towering white pines. The trail proceeds gradually uphill to a large three-trunk pine where the Ice Glen Trail leaves right (southwest)

Memorial Bridge crosses the Housatonic River at Ice Glen trailhead.

and Laura's Tower Trail turns left (east). Follow Laura's Tower Trail through a level, storm-damaged landscape where majestic pine and hemlock share the woods with windfalls. Weather-worn boulders accent an understory of **striped maple** and **hobblebush.** Striped maple is a small tree of the northern temperate forests. It gets its name from the pattern of green and white lines along its trunk. Hobblebush is a shrub best known for its showy clusters of white flowers in May. This area is habitat for red squirrels, friendly creatures you will bump into often. They are notorious for scolding anyone who has the gall to walk in their woods. Deer and coyote are also frequent visitors.

Soon the trail swings right, crosses a small stream, and turns uphill, passing a springhouse on the right. The cathedral pines yield to an upland forest of **red oak** with **hemlock** lining the moist drainage areas. The path meanders up the sometimes steep slope, using wide switchbacks to moderate the grade, and enters a disturbed area where **gray birch** are common. You can distinguish gray birch from paper birch by its sooty white bark. Paper birch is known by the clean appearance and prominent peeling of its bark. Gray birch is a pioneer species, a tree that naturally reclaims abandoned pasture or areas damaged by logging or fire. As the forest matures, the gray birch eventually yields to other species.

The top of Laura's Rest is maintained to preserve the view, and the trail now enters this managed area characterized by a uniform growth of saplings that form a dense thicket of striped maple and birch. Soon the path opens onto the brushy summit, where the **gray metal tower** reaches skyward.

The stairway of the tower is steep and a bit intimidating, but the view from the top is magnificent. From the lookout you can see clearly to the east, north, and west. The first hill due north is Rattlesnake Hill, with West Stockbridge Mountain to its left. On clear days the view extends to Mt. Greylock in the north and to the Catskills to the west-southwest.

While you enjoy the view from Laura's Tower atop Laura's Rest you just might want to know who Laura was. Laura was Laura Belden, daughter-in-law of the well-known David Dudley Field (we will bump into him again later in the walk). Field was extremely fond of Laura, but this affection could not alter the tragedies that awaited her. Her husband and children died untimely deaths. This hilltop became her refuge and over time a memorial. The original wooden observatory was replaced in the 1920s with this metal tower; "Laura's Tower."

From the tower the trail continues on to Beartown State Forest in Lee, but we are going to backtrack down the hill to the junction with Ice Glen Trail. On the way listen for the coarse drone of **cicadas** "singing" in the treetops in summer. According to folklore these large red-eyed insects are harbingers of frost, the first icy morning coming six weeks after they are first heard.

From the three-trunk pine, Ice Glen Trail heads left (southwest) into a deep, mossy forest of hemlock and black birch. Hemlock is also the understory here, turning the path into an enchanting emerald tunnel. Soon the steep slopes of Little Mountain appear and a very short side trail right leads to an **enclave of sheer rock.** On the sharpest wall is carved an ancient message, the neat block letters enveloped beneath a palette of rich green moss. The inscription reads: Ice Glen, the gift to Stockbridge of David Dudley Field, 1891. The Field family is one of the area's most accomplished, their members responsible for reforming laws, laying the trans-Atlantic cable, and even (by Darby Field in 1642) the first known European ascent of New Hampshire's Mt. Washington.

As you return to the trail the prominent V-shaped entrance of Ice Glen is before you, guarded on either side by steep ridges clothed in statuesque pine and hemlock. Boulders are everywhere, creating an ethereal beauty reminiscent of a Maxfield Parrish landscape. The path snakes its way through the ravine, dipping under windfalls and around boulder caves capped with the ubiquitous **polypody fern.** The rough-hewn beauty of Ice Glen is accented by its omnipresent chill. The deep shade of the trees and the steep-sided mountain, coupled with the jumbled matrix of boulders, create an environment that allows the ice of winter to linger in the ravine's deepest recesses sometimes well into summer.

The path wanders from bank to bank, carefully negotiating the steeper crevices on a series of wooden bridges. After passing some deep boulder caves, the trail exits the rocks where a monstrous **white pine** guards the entrance to this side of the glen.

Today this giant tree is exceptional, yet in colonial times it would have blended anonymously into the massive tracts of pine forest that covered precolonial New England. White pine is the fastest growing and largest of all northeastern conifers, reaching 100 feet today and historically 150 feet. There are no words to describe the beauty a forest of such trees would impart, but gazing at this one tree stirs the mind to imagine such magnificence.

This area of ancient timber is also home to the **barred owl.** During the day this large gray or brown bird roosts in a sheltered grove of trees waiting for nightfall, when it most often hunts for food. The barred owl is one of the few owls that has dark eyes, their deep, penetrating stare a fitting complement to the shadowy depths of the glen.

The yellow-blazed trail stops at the gravel road just ahead. Follow the road downhill a short way to its junction with Ice Glen Road. Take a right on Ice Glen Road, along which are beautiful houses as well as a pastoral view to the west encompassing the broad wetland surrounding Konkapot Brook and the signature white cliffs of Monument Mountain to the southwest. At the end of Ice Glen Road take a right onto Route 7, then another right onto Park Street and the parking area.

Yellow Eyes and Silent Wings

We are attracted to our opposites but live with the familiar. One holds mystery, the other comfort. One is the owl, the other is not.

In our culture the owl's habitat is the unknown, the darkness. It haunts our Halloweens and teases our insecurities with its ghostly nocturnal confidence. But rather than stir the suspicious within us the owl should be the subject of admiration.

Owls have evolved beautifully for their habitat. They are predators of the night, a time prey find safer because most creatures don't see very well in the dark. Owls have overcome this hurdle in many ways. An owl can see perfectly well in daylight but can still see well with just 1 percent of the light we would need to register an image. In addition an owl's eyes are set so that it has the greatest range of binocular vision of all birds. Binocular vision allows for more accurate depth perception and thus locating of prey. To aid an owl even further in locating its target precisely, its ear openings are large and asymmetrical, creating an ability for the bird to locate prey by audile triangulation.

Once the prey has been located the attack begins. An owl's wings soar and create high lift, perfect for flying through forests. The feathers on the wings' leading edge have an abraded texture that eliminates wind noise—an owl can fly right over your head and you won't hear a thing. And the owl's strong raptorial talons decisively hold captured prey.

Owls are fascinating creatures, but still, when you come eye to eye with one, it is not uncommon for fascination to yield to a more visceral emotion. It is the eyes, of course, the unblinking golden eyes. As cryptic as they are hypnotic, they represent that part of nature that has not surrendered its mysteries.

Getting There

From the Red Lion Inn on Route 7 in Stockbridge, follow Route 7 south for 0.2 mile and take a left onto Park Street. Continue down Park Street to its end, where there is a parking area.

McLennan
Tyringham

- **Round Mountain Loop Trail**
- **2.0 miles (2.8 miles includes walk to reservation entrance on Fenn Road)**
- **443 ft. elevation gain**
- **2.0–3.0 hours**
- **moderate**

McLennan is a reservation of beautifully wild land that includes all of Round Mountain, wonderful waterfalls, and a fascinating upland beaver swamp. Black bear, coyote, fisher, and bobcat still freely stride the woodlands. Yet if this isn't enough, the forests of McLennan hold even more. Running through the woods are miles of stone walls that still frame forgotten roads and ring the cellar holes of long-abandoned farms. It is a ghost town in the wild.

McLennan's 491 acres are owned and managed by the Trustees of Reservations, who maintain the two-mile-long Round Mountain Loop Trail that encircles the mountain. The trail is marked with white circular blazes, with turns designated by two blazes set one atop the other. The section of trail on the upper part of Fenn Road is not blazed but the treadway is easy to follow.

Look Forward To
- a mountain stream and waterfalls
- a beaver swamp
- ghostly ruins

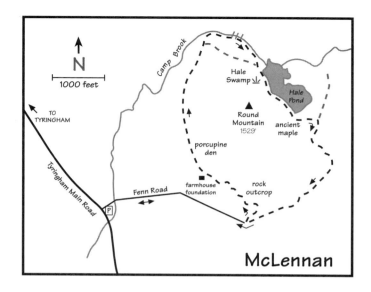

McLennan

The Trail

People park along Tyringham Main Road, then walk 0.4 mile up unimproved Fenn Road to the entrance of McLennan. (Please do not block Fenn Road or park on the lawn near the road.) Regulations and information are posted at the trailhead. The Trustees ask people who enjoy their properties to please donate or become a member.

From the trailhead on Fenn Road (which continues straight ahead) take the footpath into a **hardwood forest** of sugar maple, black birch, and red oak. The trail ascends a brief, steep pitch along a stone wall, then turns left (north-northwest), passing large outcrops of rock on the right. The convolutions you see in the layers of stone were created when Africa slowly crushed against America millions of years ago. The unimaginable force of that collision deformed the bedrock's flat stratifications into the motionless waves before you.

With the talus slope of Round Mountain always on the right, the path joins a stone wall that leads to a large stone foundation built into the hillside on the left. Ruins are **islands of diversity** in the deep woods. The neatly placed stones that once supported the farmhouse are now home to chipmunks and garter snakes, deer mice and toads. Redbelly snakes hunt earthworms beneath the large flat stones of unused walkways. Each autumn the **deer** browse apples fallen from a vestigial orchard and coyotes stand watch atop the stone walls.

The trail continues along the stone wall into a thick forest of hemlock that meanders gradually uphill. The stone wall then leaves left. To the right is a large tree where **porcupines** sometimes den. You can recognize it by the large pile of scat at its base. Porcupines eat twigs and bark from a variety of trees, which makes their scat look like pellets of sawdust. They den in hollows beneath trees, like this one, or in rocky crevices on hillsides.

The path continues uphill, making a wide swing to the southwest before coming to a junction where the trail splits. The right fork goes directly to Hale Pond while the left gets to the pond via the **waterfalls.** The path left proceeds a short way to the bank of Camp Brook, where the sound of the rushing water seems as cool as the evergreen forest around it (this stream is called Camp Brook because each spring the Mahican Indians built their sugar camp along its banks, but more on that a bit later).

Camp Brook cascades over worn stones at McLennan.

The path follows the stream along a series of low cascades that cut through the rocky ledges along the bank. There is no one beautiful spot through here, but a collection of wonderful places, each a little different than the last. It is one of the most tranquil places you will find.

A brief walk brings you to the open horizon of **Hale Pond.** Hale Pond isn't always a pond, so what you see here depends on what the **beaver** have done lately. Beaver eat aspen and alder, and when these trees grow along the shore the beaver come and repair the dam at the pond's north end. The waters then flood the meadow, turning the clearing into a broad, shallow pond. Cattails and bur reed grow in the shallows where red-spotted newts swim and wood frogs quack in the spring.

Black ducks, mallards, and wood ducks swim in the water and kingfishers and hawks perch in the driftwood-gray skeletons of dead trees along the shore. When the food runs out the beaver leave. In a little while the dam gives way and the pond once more becomes a marshy meadow where deer, black bear, coyote, fisher, and the occasional moose wander the grassy field.

The path follows along the edge of the pond until the trail turns left (east) at a huge old **sugar maple tree.** This tree is about four hundred years old, which brings us back to the Mahicans.

Once their camp was set up along the brook, usually in early March, the Indians would venture into the sugar woods. On each maple they would cut a gash into the trunk that ran to a wooden spout. The sap would run along the wound and drip from the spout into a birch bark bucket. The full buckets then were emptied into a large container. Hot stones were dropped into the sap to boil it down until the sugar crystallized. The Indians stayed at the sugar camp until they had made enough maple sugar for the year, then they would store the equipment and return to their village. This tree is one of the only maples still alive that was probably tapped by the Mahicans hundreds of years ago. Just to the west of the tree are the remains of another farmhouse whose occupants probably tapped the same tree centuries later. What stories the tree could tell.

From the maple tree the path joins the rutted remains of Fenn Road, turning right and heading downhill through an area frequented by ruffed grouse and deer. In April the beautiful flowers of spring beauty dot the woods beneath the boughs of black birch, oak, and maple. The trail passes a collapsed springhouse and then one last forgotten foundation to the right before returning to the trailhead.

Sweet Waters

To the Indians, maple sugar was one of the greatest gifts of the forest. They used it to season their food, much as we use salt or pepper, or added it to flour or meat to make more substantial meals. How they learned to make it is lost in the antiquity of the art, but an art it certainly is.

Sugar maples are unique things and each tree in a sugar woods may give sap of different quality and quantity. Trees that grow along wet meadows or in moist drainages will give the most sap but yield the least sugar. The best-quality sugar comes from trees in open, upland woods. Usually the sap of these trees contains about 3 percent sugar, but trees producing up to 6 percent are not uncommon. Taps set on the east and south sides of the tree will run earlier than those on the west or north side. Some folks believe they can even forecast the weather by watching their sugar taps in spring. A strong flow of sap foretells a northwest wind, sunny skies, and cold nights, while a weak flow means a southwest wind, warm nights, and stormy weather.

Maple sugar is like no other sweet thing in the world. It is pleasingly different in character from honey and a million times superior to that stuff in the sugar bowl. The art of maple sugar making represents one of those rare times when humanity mingles with nature and neither is compromised. It may also be the oldest continuous tradition in New England, reaching back from the present to a time long centuries ago when an anonymous person discovered the gift from the tree of sweet water.

Getting There

From the junction of Routes 102 and 20 in Lee, take Route 102 west and immediately take a left onto Tyringham Road. Take Tyringham Road to Tyringham village. From the village proceed on Tyringham Road 1.9 miles to Fenn Road on the left. A reminder: Fenn Road is a public way but the areas around it are private property, including the grassy area near Tyringham Road; please respect the rights of the owners.

Tyringham Cobble
Tyringham

- **Tyringham Cobble Trail**
- **1.9-mile loop**
- **423 ft. elevation gain**
- **2.0–3.0 hours**
- **moderate**

Tyringham Cobble is the name of the steep, bouldered hill that rises abruptly above picturesque Tyringham village. Though its highest reaches are forested, most of the cobble is still pastureland and brushy fields that harbor a vast array of birds, mammals, and plants. As an added bonus there are superb overlooks along the ridge crests. The unforgettable views are especially striking in autumn.

The geologic definition of a cobble is a rock larger than a stone but smaller than a boulder. In New England, however, the word also means any large, rounded outcrop of rock.

Tyringham Cobble Reservation is owned and maintained by the Trustees of Reservations, a Massachusetts conservation organization that owns and protects more than 18,000 acres across the state. The loop trail that winds through the cobble's 206 acres is marked with either blue or white circular blazes; turns are noted with signs, painted arrows, or two blazes set one atop the other.

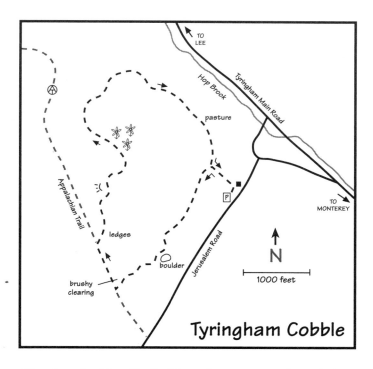

The Appalachian Trail skirts the eastern edge of the reservation and the Cobble Trail coincides with it for a short distance. The junctions are well signed.

Look Forward To

- beautiful views
- many different birds, mammals, and plants
- a mysterious marble boulder

The Trail

From the parking area on Jerusalem Road follow the short trail to the kiosk beside the red barn, where there is information about the cobble, a posting of regulations, and a donation box.

From the kiosk the trail heads northwest along the pasture fence where nest boxes used by eastern blue-birds hang from some of the fence posts. In August look for the pink thistlelike flowers of burdock blooming among the yellow plumes of goldenrod. Just past the gate take a left and ascend the hill, entering a **young forest** of white pine, elm, and ash bounded by an old windrow of sugar maple. In spring you can often hear the thumping wing beats of male ruffed grouse as they try to impress the females. Large colonies of Christmas fern blanket the ground here, providing cover for the mouselike voles and hairy-tailed moles that live here.

The path descends to where a **monolithic boulder** rises some ten feet out of the ground. This huge stone is made of marble, the metamorphosed successor to lime-stone. Marble is composed of calcium-rich compounds that dissolve slowly when in contact with such acidic substances as rainwater or fog. Over thousands of years this process has gently sculpted the stone into a natural work of art. The rock's south face is also pocked with small holes called solution potholes, which form in a similar way. In the evening red fox sometimes sit at the base of the stone.

The trail continues uphill, the woods melting into a bushy highland clearing of red cedar, common juniper, apple, and barberry. Dewberry runs its thorny vines along the ground and bittersweet drapes the trees. Birds

A hairy-taled mole

love it up here, and most any time you can see or hear many different kinds. Turkey vultures, crows, and hawks often soar overhead. Robins are here, and as chickadees lightly land on pliant strands of steeplebush, rufous-sided towhees rustle among the fallen leaves. Red fox, eastern coyote, and deer frequently use the trail, though mostly at night. In the fields visible below you might spot wild turkey and Canada geese.

The path briefly joins the Appalachian Trail, then veers right to a **ledgy outcrop** of rock that offers a beautiful view to the southeast. The Tyringham valley is straight ahead, its narrow intervale eventually swallowed by the mountains in the distance. Round Mountain is the smaller hill nestled against the grander escarpment of Long Mountain (1,950 ft.) on the northeast side of the valley.

The trail scrambles up a rocky slope to the height of land (1,358 ft.) in a young woodland of hemlock, white and gray birch, ash, and red oak. Partridgeberry creeps along the ground and a few clumps of common juniper and barberry line the path that leads to a spectacular **rocky overlook.** From the open ledge the view sweeps down to the little village below. This is a wonderful place in the fall, when migrating birds soar by and the patchwork fields of the town resemble a Grandma Moses painting. This is also a great place to ponder the geologic history of the cobble. The rocks you are sitting on are older than the ones at the base of the hill, a situation opposite from the way things should be. Sometime in the past the huge mass of rock that makes up the cobble was part of the mountainous escarpment to the west. An unimaginably powerful geologic event (such as an earthquake) flipped it over, landing it in the valley. A bit mind-boggling, isn't it?

The path continues through shady woods of hemlock and hop hornbeam; a particularly old gnarly one is on the right as you descend the hill. The trail then crosses a sag and climbs onto an open shoulder of the cobble where field-grown birch oversee a grassy **oasis of wildflowers.** Black-eyed Susan, goldenrod, thimbleweed, and shrubby cinquefoil all grow here, as does wild thyme, a creeping plant with lavender flowers and spicy-smelling foliage. This is a wonderful sunny place to spend lazy hours smelling the flowers and looking at the view.

From the hilltop the trail descends through the woods beneath a canopy of cherry, ash, and oak, joining a woods road for a while before turning right and entering a large pasture filled with barberry and juniper.

Barberry is a low-growing thorny shrub with small, pendulous clusters of pale yellow flowers in June. It is beautiful in fall when scarlet berries cling to stems aglow with wine-colored leaves. Common juniper is a stiff-needled, shrubby evergreen that often forms impenetrable stands in the sunny clearings it prefers. Its berries provide food for such birds as ruffed grouse, while the thick foliage shelters songbirds and rabbits. As you walk along the path look for the tall stalks of thistle, their soft pink flowers opening from spiny buds in summer. Thistle attracts many butterflies including tiger swallowtails, and their seeds are a favorite food of the bright yellow goldfinch. Also growing here are oxeye daisy and wild thyme.

The path traverses the field, turning right along a windrow of sugar maples. Listen for the sharp call of killdeer through here. Killdeer are the Berkshires' shorebird; their sharp call is similar to that of their plover relatives who scurry along the beaches of Cape Cod. The trail then turns through the gate and returns to the parking area.

The Blue Bird of Happiness

In 1908, three years before he was awarded the Nobel Prize for literature, Maurice Maeterlinck wrote a play called *The Blue Bird*. The story chronicles the journey of two children in search of an ethereal blue bird believed to be the source of all happiness. Their travels take them through timeless lands farther and farther from hope and home. Eventually, however, they return to the place their journey started, a place where they unexpectedly find the secret of the blue bird.

In the early part of the twentieth century, when Maeterlinck's play was written, people in the Berkshires did not have to journey far to find their own bluebirds. Every hayfield had its birds of azure and orange that flew over the timothy grass, and pastures were host to gathering sapphire flocks in late summer. But then things began to change. English sparrows and starlings, European birds naturalized in the United States, used the same nesting sites as bluebirds did, yet were more aggressive at claiming them. Pesticides were increasingly used in the fields where bluebirds flew, while the open spaces themselves were abandoned to forest as farmers left their unprofitable rocky fields and moved away.

Every year fewer and fewer bluebirds returned, until by about 1950 they had almost completely disappeared. It was about this time that we realized what we had done and tried to fix it. Bluebird mortality was decreased by banning the worst of the pesticides. The nesting site problem was solved in a most ingenious way with the creation of the bluebird box.

Bluebird boxes are now familiar sights in fields and backyards all over the Berkshires. If you look at how they are made you will see that the entrance hole is always 1.5 inches in diameter. This is large enough for the bluebird to use but too small for a starling. English sparrows are small enough to fit through the entrance hole, so their competition had to be approached in a different way: notice that most bluebird boxes are placed in pairs, the two boxes sometimes back to back or a few feet apart. When a bluebird builds a nest in one box, a competing species often uses the neighboring one. Many of these competitors are stronger defenders of territory than are bluebirds; as they defend their own nests they inadvertently protect the bluebird's as well.

It has taken the better part of fifty years but it is now common for people to find this beautiful bird singing in their own backyards once again, which, by the way, is where the children in Maeterlinck's play find theirs. When they helped someone less fortunate than themselves, the blue bird came to them. They did not have to seek it after all, only earn it. A few bluebird boxes in your backyard is a small gesture of assistance to another living thing, a gesture that in turn may bring the blue bird of happiness to you.

Getting There

From Lee: Take Route 20 to the junction with Route 102 near the Massachusetts Turnpike interchange. Take Route 102, then turn immediately left onto Tyringham Road. Take Tyringham Road 4.2 miles to Tyringham village and the junction with Jerusalem Road. Take a right onto Jerusalem Road and proceed 0.2 mile to a parking area on right.

Central Region

The Central Berkshire Hills

It isn't easy being the middle child, sandwiched between siblings who are like you but different, too. So the central Berkshires lie between the mountains and broad valleys of the south, and the shadow of Greylock to the north.

The massive Taconic Range, the defining feature of the southern region, continues north forming the western border of the central Berkshires as well. These majestic hills offer breathtaking views and long walks on windy ridges. Four different walks explore the central Taconics from the ridge crest named for a Mahican to the holy mountains of the Shakers.

As the Taconics form a barrier to the west, so the Berkshire Plateau rises to the east. This ancient mountain range has been leveled by millions of years of erosion, its undulating highlands home to northern forests, waterfalls, and wildlife. Five walks explore this isolated woodland, where bears still forage for blueberries in the swamps and balsam fir fills the air with its cool, invigorating fragrance.

In between the mountains and the plateau lie the headwaters of the Housatonic River. Here are forested valleys, waterfalls, and bottomlands where beaver swim and songbirds sing. Four walks explore this diverse area from the waterfall with a legend to the most pleasant valley in all the hills.

At the northern edge of the central region is the looming presence of Greylock. As a taste of things to come, one walk wanders the southern shoulder of this unique massif as it pokes into the central hills. Enjoy.

Yokun Ridge
Richmond and West Stockbridge

- **Walsh Trail, Ridge Trail**
- **1.1 miles round-trip**
- **262 ft. elevation gain**
- **1.0–1.5 hours**
- **easy**

In the early years of the eighteenth century Yokun, son of the chief of the Hudson River Mohicans, came to live in the Indian town at Stockbridge. By about 1740 Jehoiakim Yokun owned much of the land between Stockbridge and Pittsfield, but unsuspectingly sold it a decade later to another Indian working for English land speculators. Today Yokun is remembered in the names Yokun's Seat, the highest point on Lenox Mountain, and Yokun Ridge, the beautiful northern shoulder of West Stockbridge Mountain.

The walk along Yokun Ridge is a mountaintop stroll easy enough for almost anyone. There are pastoral views all year long from the rocky ledges, and in summer the blueberries and soaring hawks may coax you to linger longer.

Walsh and Ridge Trails are in the Yokun Ridge Forest Reservation, a preserve owned by the Berkshire County Land Trust and Conservation Fund. The area is managed by the Berkshire Natural Resource Council and maintained by volunteers. Walsh Trail is marked with red blazes, the Ridge Trail with blue, and signs are logically placed at overlooks and trail junctions.

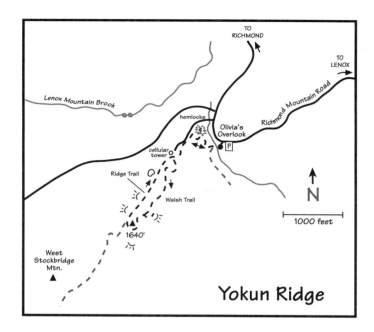

Yokun Ridge

Look Forward To

- many different views from the ridge
- spring wildflowers and autumn foliage
- hawks and vultures

The Trail

The parking area is also the site of **Olivia's Overlook,** a
rolling promontory with a beautiful view of Stockbridge
Bowl far below. On bright sunny days the blue sky adds
shades of sapphire to the water, enhancing an already

captivating scene. Beyond the lake is Rattlesnake Hill, a wooded ridge that hasn't seen a rattlesnake in many, many years. Olivia's Lookout was named in honor of Olivia Stokes Hatch, whose family donated the lands to the Berkshire County Land Trust and Conservation Fund. The overlook itself was provided by the Tennessee Gas Pipeline Company.

Walsh Trail begins at an engraved stone at the west end of the parking area, passing through a clearing where mats of crown vetch cover the ground. Vetch is a fast-growing legume planted in areas prone to erosion. In summer small spikes of pea-like purple flowers poke through the dark green foliage. At the far end of the clearing the path crosses an intermittent stream on a wooden bridge at the edge of the woods. An unmarked trail leaves left, downhill, and the red-blazed Walsh Trail continues right heading uphill into a **northern hardwood forest.** Black birch and white and red oak rise high overhead, while shrubby witch hazel bend over dark boulders. Here and there a few hemlock grow among the rocks, some of which have been here since the Civil War. In the morning or at dusk the early-summer air is filled with the songs of veeries and hermit thrushes, and autumn brings the honking of Canada geese as they fly toward Stockbridge Bowl.

The path weaves through the picturesque forest to the junction of the Ridge Trail just south of a cellular telephone tower. From this junction Walsh Trail continues southwest into woods of red oak, maple, and **hawthorn,** a small, shrubby tree with long, woody thorns along its branches. The barbs help protect the tree and are useful to a bird called the northern shrike. The shrike captures

The Walsh Trail begins at a prominent stone marker.

rodents and impales them on the strong thorns until it is ready to eat them—a little gruesome but practical.

The path gradually gains elevation and passes through patches of **woodland savannah** where oaks and hickories oversee a forest floor of wavy grass and rock. A short side trail then leaves left to a rocky ledge. In winter there is a nice view of Stockbridge Bowl to the southeast. When spring comes a number of **wildflowers** bloom here, including pale corydalis, which offers its uniquely shaped red and yellow blossoms to passersby in June.

From the ridge the path makes a short climb to another side trail right that leads to an **overlook** on the Ridge Trail. Walsh Trail continues straight ahead, ending at a clearing where a bench awaits the weary. From this restful spot the white cliffs of Monument Mountain dominate the distant southern horizon with the misty form of East Mountain rising even farther in the distance. Chokeberry is the low-growing woody plant that forms dense thickets among the rocks. In June vast bouquets of small white blossoms appear, perfuming the air with their sweet fragrance. Near here the bright pink flowers of gaywings also can be found as well as wild azalea, both of which bloom in early June.

Ridge Trail leaves from the west edge of the clearing and immediately turns right (northeast). The blue blazes quickly lead to a rocky ledge with a wide view northwest. Cone Hill in Richmond provides the horizon's undulating profile, while Cone Swamp winds through the valley below. Hawks and turkey vultures often glide on the air currents that sweep along the ridge. Mountain ash is the small tree with powder-puff blossoms in early summer. In fall both the leaves and berries turn bright red, lending color to the shortening days. You can also find tart blueberries and aromatic sassafras here.

From the overlook the trail follows the edge of the ridge through **hemlock** groves and stands of oak, passing a few limited views to the west. Chokeberry and blueberry line the path with an occasional sprig of columbine lending color to the gray rocks. The path then winds around a large boulder where polypody fern grows. As you continue downhill the shady hemlocks yield to maples whose leaves shelter patches of bunch-berry and bluebead lily. Ridge Trail then ends at its junction with Walsh Trail near the cellular tower. From here follow the red blazes of Walsh Trail back to the parking area at Olivia's Overlook.

Wilson's Thrush

Each spring when May is passing and the ephemeral wildflowers are fading, Wilson's thrush returns to the dappled shadows of the Berkshire woods. It is a quietly reclusive bird, its fawn-colored plumage blending with last year's leaves as it hops along the forest floor looking for insects. It is easy to overlook until it flies into the trees and begins to sing.

It is a song that beckons you to stop and listen. It begins with a series of harmonic chords, simultaneous tones that energetically chase each other in melodious circles. And it ends with an echo that gently passes through this world into another, leaving the memory of its beauty even as its substance vanishes into silence.

Wilson's thrush is a migrant songbird that nests in broad-leaf forests from New England to Oregon and winters far to the south. Many migrant songbirds spend the colder months in Central America or on islands in the Caribbean. Wilson's thrush, like broad-winged hawks and barn swallows, flies all the way to South America, where it lives in the tropical evergreen lowland forest of Amazonia.

The name Wilson's thrush was given in tribute to Alexander Wilson, America's first ornithologist. Born in Scotland in 1766, Wilson came to Philadelphia in 1794. Nine years later he began to teach himself about the birds of the United States. In the next few years Wilson wandered across the country observing, painting, and writing about every bird he found. In 1808 the first volume of this compilation was published under the title *American Ornithology*. In the pages of this and the following installments were the first descriptions and engravings of more than 40 birds, including the goshawk, pine siskin, and song sparrow. By the time the ninth and final volume was published in 1813, Wilson had painted and described more than 300 species.

Alexander Wilson died of exhaustion and dysentery in 1813 at the age of forty-eight. For a brief time his book was the bench mark of avian art. Then, twenty-five years after Wilson's death, John J. Audubon produced his masterwork, *Birds of America*. It was an amazing achievement, with 435 life-size color plates of unequaled beauty. As Audubon's star rose Wilson's set.

Today the name of Audubon still shines down from its artistic heights, unchallenged and untarnished after all these years. Wilson's, on the other hand, clings to the wings of the migrants when they fly, Wilson's warbler to Mexico and Wilson's thrush to Amazonia. Yet even this legacy is fading, for the thrush no longer carries his name. Today Wilson's thrush is called the veery, a name that sounds like the song it sings.

When he traveled through the forests of America, Alexander Wilson carried a flute with him. Alone in the woods he would play the somber melodies of Scottish ballads, the melancholy notes nourishing the memory of things long left behind. The next time you hear the hauntingly beautiful song of the veery, stop and listen carefully. As the melody trails off into tremolo tones there is a flutelike sound that seems to usher in the silence that follows. It is a coincidental tribute, but for that moment the veery is once again Wilson's thrush.

Getting There

From the junction of Routes 7 and 102 in the center of Stockbridge, take Route 102 west to the junction of Route 183. Take a right onto Route 183 north and drive for 4.1 miles to the junction with Richmond Mountain Road (immediately past the entrance to the Kripalu Center). Turn left onto Richmond Mountain Road and drive 1.4 miles to the parking area on the left.

From the junction of Routes 7A and 183 in the center of Lenox take Route 183 south 1.6 miles to the junction with Richmond Mountain Road. Take a right onto Richmond Mountain Road and drive 1.4 miles to the parking area on the left.

Pleasant Valley
Lenox

- **Bluebird Trail, Alexander Trail, Yokun Trail, Old Wood Road, Saint Francis Spring Trail, Great Hemlock Trail, Laurel Trail, Ravine Trail, Trail of the Ledges, Pike's Pond Trail**
- **2.1-mile loop**
- **315 ft. elevation gain**
- **2.0–2.5 hours**
- **moderate**

If every place named Pleasant Valley really was, the country would be a much happier place. This Pleasant Valley, however, lives up to its name. There are marshes and beaver ponds all along the meandering course of Yokun Brook, as well as hillside trails that scale nearby Lenox Mountain. You can spend a delightful few hours walking the paths, or find a secluded bench by an enchanted pond and while away the hours.

The 1,450 acres that comprise the Pleasant Valley Sanctuary are owned and maintained by the Massachusetts Audubon Society (MAS). The sanctuary is open every day except Mondays, with an admission fee for adults of $3 and $2 for children. Fees do not apply to MAS members.

The trail system is well maintained with signs at all junctions. Blue blazes mark all outbound paths while inbound ones have yellow blazes. Trail maps are available at the office.

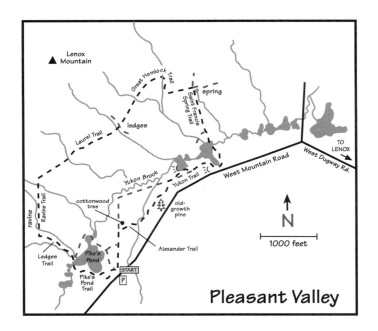

Look Forward To

- marshes and beaver ponds
- boardwalks and benches
- a mountainside spring

The Trail

From the parking area on West Mountain Road proceed to the office, where all visitors are asked to register. From the office follow the lawn north past a red barn on the left where wild honeybees have built a hive between the barn boards. Continuing north the path leads past a kiosk to the sanctuary museum, where interactive exhibits of raptors, songbirds, and ferns line the cozy walls.

Just west of the museum is a field where goldenrod, milkweed, and cinquefoil grow. In spring and summer bluebirds and swallows fly in graceful arcs over the flowering field searching for tasty bugs.

The path continues north along the edge of the field, soon coming to a large **cottonwood tree** where the Alexander Trail leaves right (northeast). The trail then skirts the south edge of a narrow field before entering a **mixed hardwood forest** of ash, black birch, maple, and red oak. Evergreen Christmas fern mingles with starflower as you descend to a small brook where yellow-bellied sapsuckers dine on the wintergreen juices of black birch. A little farther on, large specimens of white pine and ash loom over their diminutive neighbors. Some of these trees are more than three feet in diameter and probably began growing here about the time George Washington retired from the presidency.

At the base of the slope turn right (east) onto Yokun Trail. In a few feet turn left along a short side trail that leads to a secluded bench on the **shores of a beaver pond.** Tangles of willow, alder, and red maple ring the waterline as red-winged blackbirds and goldfinches fly over the sedges and cattails in the shallows. Peepers and wood frogs are here in spring; summer belongs to green frogs.

From the pond return to Yokun Trail and turn left (east). The treadway is straight and level with peekaboo views of the cattail marsh on the left. After the woods have teased you long enough they fall away to reveal a **wide view** of a beautiful beaver pond. Shrubby growths of willow and alder frame the linear wisps of cattails and sedges that bend in the breeze. Monet's waterlilies float in random rafts on their dark, fluid canvas while water birds push rippled wakes across the pond. There is another bench here, thoughtfully perched on a low rise that overlooks the peaceful scene.

The path briefly continues east, then turns left (north) onto the Old Woods Road, which crosses some interesting shallows on a wooden bridge. The lance-shaped foliage of broad-leaved cattail points skyward like so many emerald Excaliburs, and bunches of bulrush shade shiners that flash in the sunlight as they swim nearby.

The Old Woods Road then guides you away from the pond to the Saint Francis Spring Trail that leaves right (north). The route to the spring passes through a forest of black birch, cherry, and maple, their trunks and canopies draped in the twisted stranglehold of wood vines. The soil is moist and rocky here, conditions that cause a few trees a year to crash down in windy storms.

Saint Francis Spring is just off the right side of the path a few feet before the next junction. The water is clear and inviting, but one of the rules of the woods is to drink only water that has been purified.

Saint Francis Spring Trail turns left (west) passing beneath robins' nests in spring and summer. The path climbs into drier uplands where ash and maple creak in the wind and Christmas fern covers the ground.

Great Hemlock Trail then turns right (north) at a great red oak on the bank of a rocky stream. The path ascends the hillside, keeping the brook just to the left, then crosses it near a low bedrock overhang. From here you begin to traverse a slope where large ash and white pine seem lost amidst the thick forest of **second-growth hardwoods.** Deer and coyote use the trail in their wanderings, and chipmunks hide in the half-buried boulders. After passing a large tombstone-shaped outcrop the footway descends around stark gray ledges to the next junction.

From this intersection continue west across the brook, following the rocky course of Laurel Trail as it climbs the steep slope. Near the crest of the hill turn left (southwest) onto Ravine Trail. The yellow blazes lead you over a low, stony cobble to the edge of a **shallow ravine** where hemlock and yellow and black birch shade an undergrowth of witch hazel and mountain laurel. The path descends a slippery rock pitch then crosses the stream near a leaning birch.

Ravine Trail then ends at Ledges Trail, which guides you down a moderate slope along a tumbling stream to Pike's Pond Trail. Turn right (southwest) and proceed to a wooden bridge that spans a **narrow cove.** Common yellowthroat nest in the marsh grass; their sharp *chip, chip* can be heard as they gather insects for their brood in summer. Along the shore blueberries, azalea, and beaked hazelnut grow beneath a vanguard of white pine, while the wetter spots are home to forget-me-nots and joe-pye weed.

The path briefly leaves the water, passing patches of spring flowering red trillium and false Solomon's seal, and goes to a large sugar maple that shades a restful view of Pike's Pond. Some years a pair of Canada geese

White pine and blooming laurel surround the walkway at Pike's Pond.

raise their family here, the downy goslings dutifully following their parents as they cruise the water.

The trail then swings south, skirting a small field before coming to a boardwalk that weaves through a wooded swamp of tamarack, red maple, ash, and quaking aspen. The wet soil is home to skunk cabbage, horsetail, and a beautiful iris called yellow flag that blooms in June and July (see below).

Pike's Pond Trail then ends a few yards from the parking area.

The Flower of the Rainbow

In 507 A.D., Clovis led his army of Franks against the Visigoths. At first the Franks had the upper hand, but in a vicious counterattack the Visigoths succeeded in trapping Clovis's troops against the banks of the Rhine. For much of its length the river was too deep to ford, and for a moment all hope seemed lost. Then, as the Visigoths regrouped for another assault, Clovis noticed the golden blooms of yellow flag growing in the middle of the river. Knowing that yellow flag grew only in shallow water, the king of the Franks quickly led his army across the Rhine at the place where the wild iris grew. The Visigoths did not follow and the Franks escaped.

Yellow flag displays its sulfur-colored flowers in June and July, adding a unique brightness to the marshes and wetlands where it grows. It is a member of the iris family, a group of plants named for Iris, the messenger of the gods in Greek mythology. She would travel between the heavens and earth as a rainbow, thereby connecting the two realms. The flower honors Iris because its complex petals are often marked with multi-colored patterns that reminded ancient botanists of rainbows.

If you look at an iris flower you will see not only rainbows but an example of ingenious natural engineering. Iris are pollinated by bees that land on the wide lower petals of the flower. To get to the blossom's nectar the bee must climb under the small overhanging petal where the female stigma and male pollen are. The insect first brushes the receptive side of the stigma, the sticky surface of which gathers any pollen from other iris clinging to the bee's body. As it drinks the nectar pollen from the anthers collects on the insect's body again. When the bee leaves the flower it doesn't lose any of its new pollen because it brushes the nonsticky face of the stigma. The bee then flies off to the next flower. This process ensures genetic diversity by inhibiting self-pollination.

After his narrow escape, Clovis changed the emblem on his coat of arms to a yellow flag iris. The next year the Visigoth empire fell to the Franks, creating the framework for what would one day become the country of France.

Getting There

From the south: At the junction of Routes 7 and 20 in Lenox drive 2.9 miles north to West Dugway Road. Turn left onto West Dugway and drive 0.8 mile to West Mountain Road. Turn left onto West Mountain Road and continue for 0.8 mile to the parking area.

From the north: At the junction of Routes 7 and 20 in Pittsfield drive south 4.6 miles to West Dugway Road. Turn right and drive 0.8 mile to West Mountain Road. Turn left and drive another 0.8 mile to the parking area.

Kennedy Park
Lenox

- **Main Trail, Red Neck Trail, Lookout Trail, Balance Rock Trail, Pondside Trail, Kirchner Trail, Summit Trail**
- **3.4-mile loop**
- **305 ft. elevation gain**
- **3.0–4.0 hours**
- **easy with some moderate sections**

The Aspinwall Hotel opened its doors in 1902 and immediately became the queen of Lenox resorts. It had 400 rooms (each with its own fireplace), an orchestra in residence, and even telephones. From its perch high above the town, the Aspinwall was the preferred place to stay for nearly three decades. Then, in 1931, it burned to the ground.

In the 1950s the town turned the abandoned land into a huge reserve of cross-country ski trails and hiking paths. Today Kennedy Park occupies about 500 acres of forests, ponds, and hillsides in the heart of Lenox. It is a rare treat to have miles of trails within walking distance of the center of a town.

Kennedy Park is owned by the town of Lenox and maintained by volunteers. There are signs at all junctions (and there are many of them), for the trails constantly crisscross each other. Do not count on seeing any blazes, but the paths are all well-worn and easy to follow. Trail maps are available at the kiosk near the entrance to the park and posted at major junctions throughout the park.

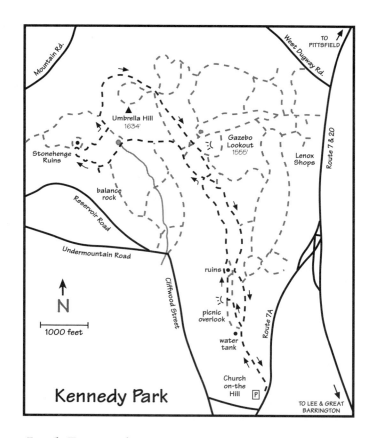

Look Forward To

- another Balance Rock
- a ridge-crest gazebo with wide views
- a restful forest pond

The Trail

From the parking area at the Church-on-the-Hill walk north along Route 7A about ten yards to the park entrance on the left. A short walk along the paved entrance road brings you to a kiosk where a large map of the park is posted. Trail maps are also usually available here.

From the kiosk continue uphill along the road to a large green water tank, where Main Trail begins at a chain-link fence. The trail is paved here, as it follows the old hotel driveway, and immediately forks. Take the left fork past the rotting remains of an ancient **grape arbor** now dwarfed beneath the lanky branches of fifty-foot ash and maple trees.

Arbors are built in open, sunny places, which this was eighty years ago when the hotel was still here. When the land was abandoned by people it was reclaimed by nature, which, in turn, created the **second-growth hardwood forest** you now walk through.

Follow the graded driveway to the crest of the knoll, where a short side trail leads to the **picnic overlook** with fine views to the west. When the hotel was operating it was fashionable to come to the lawn of the Aspinwall and socialize amidst the panoramic view.

Far below to the west is a wide wetland called the marsh, with the buttress of Lenox Mountain looming beyond it. Just south of Lenox Mountain is the long, serrated ridge of West Stockbridge Mountain. To the south the undulating profile of Monument Mountain rises from the distant valley while East Mountain, its slopes home to the Butternut Basin ski area, forms the southern horizon.

At the north end of the picnic area a short trail leads through hemlock woods to the brick foundations of once-elegant buildings. The path weaves around the crumbling Ozymandian ruins and joins the Red Neck Trail just north of the Main Trail junction.

Red Neck Trail then crosses a utility clearcut that offers a limited view left (west) of Lenox Mountain and then continues through rolling hills shaded by black birch, maple, and red oak to Main Trail.

Bear left (northwest) onto Main Trail. In summer the trees shade the red and yellow blossoms of columbine that hang from their slender stems like tiny floral flames. Columbine likes to grow in the places other plants forsake. It springs from clefts in fractured boulders and in the sandy soil of roadsides. It doesn't compete well with other plants, so it finds the lonelier spots more to its liking.

Cutoff Trail then leaves right, followed quickly by Overview Trail. At Overview junction bear left (northwest) and continue on Main Trail. There are **two enormous oaks** here, each more than a hundred years old. The first is a white oak. Sheathed in pale bark, white oaks produce acorns sweet enough to eat as they fall from the tree in autumn. The second is a red oak. Cloaked in bark of battleship gray, red oaks produce large, bitter acorns laced with tannic acid. There is a reason for the difference. White oak acorns can germinate as soon as they fall from the tree, and if they do they don't get eaten. Red oak acorns must be chilled through the winter before the seed will sprout. The bitter tannins help protect the seed from being eaten.

Aspinwall Trail now leaves right, followed by Undermountain Trail to the left. The wide walkway leads through a deep hardwood forest of tall oaks, ash, and beech to the banks of a **quiet woodland pond.** Turn left onto Pond Trail, where a bench sits near the noisy outlet.

Most forest ponds are shallow, weedy things but this one is an exception. The boughs of beech trees reach out over the dark, still water that reflects the forest. It is a magical place where you could half-expect the Lady of the Lake to rise from the depths and give you Excalibur.

From the pond the trail rises to a T-junction with Balance Rock Trail. Bear right, following the path uphill to the top of the ridge where there is a limited but picturesque view of the marsh to the southwest. Far in the distance the rounded dome of Mt. Everett is visible on clear days.

A short side trail left leads to **Balance Rock,** a marble boulder that rests comfortably on a triad of stones. Geologists believe this formation was created thousands of years ago during the last great Ice Age, deposited here as the massive glaciers retreated northward. Others believe such balanced sculptures were constructed by Native Americans as sites for religious ceremonies.

From Balance Rock the trail climbs into a **woodland savannah** of hop hornbeam, oak, and maple where the rough contours of rock outcrops are softened by waves of bending grass. After descending to a sag the Kirchner Trail enters right just below a bluff studded with the concrete footings of vanished towers, fancifully known as Stonehenge. Turn right (northeast) onto Kirchner Trail, which leads downhill to a junction with Main Trail. Bear left (northwest) onto Main Trail and then right (north) onto Summit Trail.

The Balance Rock of Kennedy Park.

The path now climbs at an easy grade up a breezy, forested ridge. This is a lovely place to walk in autumn, when the woods are cloaked in the russet tones of a hardwood forest at season's end. After swinging to the southwest the trail comes to another multiple junction. Umbrella Trail loop leaves right and ascends the short way to the wooded height of land at 1,634 ft. Umbrella loop is a nice add-on walk in the winter when the leafless trees allow a view southwest.

From the multiple junction, Summit Trail heads downhill, following the course of an underground telephone line. Chipmunks live among the rocks you pass. When disturbed they scurry out of the way, leaving their piercing alarm call to rattle in your ears. Their panic seems a bit exaggerated until you realize that chipmunks are the preferred snack food of just about every predator in the woods.

Overview Trail then crosses at the base of a short, steep pitch that leads to Lookout Trail, where a sturdy **gazebo** is thoughtfully perched on a 1,555-foot-high ridge. Inside are benches and helpful signs pointing out the distant landmarks. Lenox Mountain and its fire tower are to the northwest. The best view, however, is to the northeast, where the Mt. Greylock massif rises in front of a horizon dominated by Vermont's Green Mountains.

From the gazebo take Lookout Trail south to Main Trail. Turn left (southeast) on Main Trail through a beautiful forest of tall oak and hemlock. Stokes and Upper Trails leave left before Main Trail crosses the utility clearcut, where views extend out to the east and west. The path then descends to a multiple junction where Main Trail forks left and right. Either path will return you to the main gate, though the left branch is an easier walk. From the gate by the water tank it is a short stroll to the parking area at the Church-on-the-Hill.

The Tree of the Universe

In Norse mythology its straight, columnar trunk supported the weight of the earth, holding the world securely between the depths of hell and the heights of heaven. From its base three massive roots grew down to the underworld, where they wrapped themselves around the realms of death, of the giants, and of the gods. The crown of the tree was an enormous canopy, its topmost branches reaching beyond heaven itself while the lower ones shaded the earth. Within the tree perched the eagle of storms and the squirrel of strife.

For generations this mystical tree grew in the fertile mythology of the land of the midnight sun. It was the symbol of wisdom and knowledge, forever joining heaven, hell, and earth in a trinity of existence.

Pretty heavy stuff, but what kind of tree was it? What noble species did the ancient Scandinavians hold in such high esteem? The tree of the universe was not the oak or the spruce, but the ash.

Species of ash grow across Europe, Asia, and North America. All are deciduous hardwoods with bipinnately compound leaves— leaves with many blades, each blade separately attached to the main leaf stem. To those new to the woods the ash is one of those trees that gets lost in the green matrix of the forest. It just isn't flashy. It *is* extremely adaptable and amazingly useful.

There are three species of ash indigenous to the Berkshires; white ash, green ash, and black ash. (Mountain ash is not an ash—it's actually part of the rose family—but carries the name because its leaves are ash-like.)

White ash is the most common of the three. It grows in upland and well-drained bottomland soils in the company of oak, maple, and beech. White ash is also the tallest native ash, reaching a mature height of 80–100 feet. The hard wood is excellent for almost everything from baseball bats to furniture.

Green ash prefers the shorelines of ponds and the banks of streams. It is much more common west of the Appalachians and is used to stabilize land that has been disturbed.

Black ash is the smallest of the three, reaching a height of about 50 feet. It is a tree of the cold swamps in northern transitional forests where its neighbors are balsam fir, red spruce, and white cedar. Black ash is also called basket ash because it was the species used by the Indians to make baskets.

The easiest time to tell one tree from another is in the autumn, for each species has a distinctive fall color. The leaves of the white ash turn a beautiful, earthy maroon-purple. Green ash fades from green to yellow, though the color is not as clear and brilliant as in tamarack or aspen. The black ash seems content to have its leaves just turn brown and fall off.

Whatever species you see on your walks, the ash is a tree of subtle beauty and nearly unmatched utility. And, of course, it holds up the world.

Getting There

From the south: At the junction of Routes 183 and 7A in Lenox center take Route 7A north for 0.5 mile. The parking area is on the left behind the Church-on-the-Hill.

From the north: At the junction of Routes 7 and 7A just south of the Lenox Country Shops bear right onto Route 7A. Drive for 0.6 mile to the parking area on the right, behind the Church-on-the-Hill. From the north the parking lot entrance is on a blind curve, so use caution.

Finerty Pond
Washington

- **Appalachian Trail**
- **3.2 miles round-trip**
- **187 ft. elevation gain**
- **4.0–5.0 hours**
- **easy with some moderate sections**

Finerty Pond is an unspoiled sheet of water nestled in the hemlock and beech forests of southern Washington. It is what the mind conjures up when imagining what a wilderness pond should look like. In addition, the walk to the lake passes by beautiful marshes and vestigial beaver ponds that are home to a wonderful array of wildlife.

The path to Finerty Pond is entirely along the Appalachian Trail (AT), a National Scenic Trail extending from Maine to Georgia. The AT is managed by the Appalachian Trail Conference and maintained in Massachusetts by the Department of Environmental Management (DEM) and the Berkshire Chapter of the Appalachian Mountain Club (AMC). The trail is well marked with white blazes, and turns are noted by two marks placed one atop the other.

Finerty Pond is located in the southeast region of October Mountain State Forest, which has more than 14,000 acres of woodlands and reservoirs to explore.

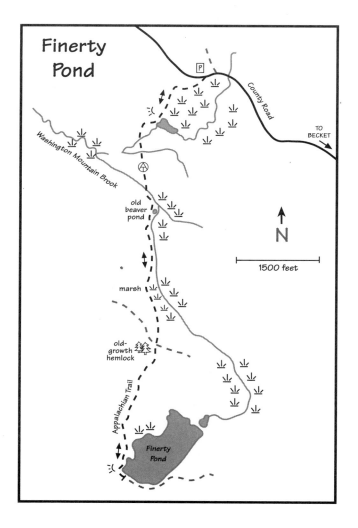

Finerty Pond

Washington Mountain Brook

County Road

TO BECKET

N

1500 feet

P

old beaver pond

marsh

old-growth hemlock

Appalachian Trail

Finerty Pond

Look Forward To

- a pristine forest lake
- marshes and beaver ponds
- birds and animals

The Trail

From the small pull-off on County Road the trail heads southwest into a **transitional forest** of ash, maple, red spruce, and balsam fir. Between the fractured, moss-covered boulders grow beds of bluebead lily and evergreen princess pine.

As you walk downhill watch for **porcupines** in July, when these dark-colored animals are most active. Many times you will see them quietly munching fresh green twigs and leaves just off the trail. Porkies are very gentle, patient creatures and it takes a lot to tick them off. Once angered, however, they will raise the quills on their back and swing their tail at whatever threatens them. If this doesn't work they run away.

The trail meanders along the wooded shore of a wide, grassy marsh, passing through thick emerald stands of balsam. Of the many birds you may find here one of the friendliest is the common yellowthroat, which builds its nest in the marsh grass at the edge of the woods. The yellowthroat is a small, brownish bird with a yellow throat and a black, "Lone Ranger" eye mask. It winters in the tropics but visits the Berkshires from spring through late summer.

At the end of the marsh the path opens to a **beautiful view** of a small pond. A short side trail leads to an open area where the fragile flowers of blue flag (a wild

A porcupine lumbers along the Appalachian Trail at Finerty Pond.

iris with purple blue flowers) blossom in summer. The trail then leaves the pond and marsh behind, crossing two small brooks amidst the shamrocks of wood sorrel and the dogwood blossoms of bunchberry. In the moist lowlands hemlock, maple, and yellow birch rise above a path lined with trillium and starflower that leads to yet another stream.

This one is larger than the others and crossing it at high water may be a problem. When the brook is shallow, however, the steppingstones keep your feet dry. The trail then turns upstream, following the bank to a **vestigial beaver pond.**

The beaver left this spot many years ago and the few gnawed stumps that remain are mossy with age.

Dendritic rivulets drain the mucky bed of the pond, and the trunks of long-dead maple and spruce stand like the pillars of some driftwood parthenon. At the center of it all the remains of the beaver lodge rise above the marsh grass and provide a summer home to great blue heron. Swallows sweep across the sky like little fighter planes while the herons methodically stalk the shallows for frogs and fish.

From the banks of the old pond the trail follows its feeder brook uphill through a **northern hardwood forest** of maple, ash, and beech. Chipmunks race out of the way with their patented squeak, and thrushes fill the warmer months with song.

The meandering path leads to a third marsh, this one resonant with the sounds of green frogs and American toads. In the colder months it can be strangely silent here, the woods left to the deer and coyote until spring.

A short walk south leads to a junction with a motorcycle trail. Here the second-growth hardwoods are dwarfed by a few enormous **old-growth hemlock** probably about two hundred years old. As you pass these magnificent trees look for the dead one a few yards south of the intersection. If you examine its trunk you will find the thin scar that lightning etched into the tree. It survived for centuries only to die in an anonymous flash a few years ago.

The path then climbs a moderately steep hillside peppered with stones before descending the rocky path to the northwest corner of **Finerty Pond.** As you leave the woods the fresh air of the lake is sweet and invigorating. Boulders line the shoreline and clusters of mountain laurel light the water's edge in late June. Yellow pond lilies float in the shallows, providing a pastoral foreground for the rounded hummock of Walling Mountain that rises to the southeast. Canada geese and many different ducks visit the marshy northern shore, and sometimes you can see deer emerge from the forest to drink.

After loitering for as long as you like follow the AT back to the road.

Great Blue Herons

It moves across the muddy shallows with unhurried deliberateness, long legs and neck in slow-motion synchrony. The controlled ballet continues until the bird suddenly stops in midstride, the dance suspended in time. For a moment it is as still as the driftwood stumps of the swamp. An instant later, quick as lightning, the bird's long beak pierces the water like a saber. As it pulls its head from the water the bird's bill securely holds a dripping fish—nature's compensation for the water dancer.

Of all the birds you might encounter in the Berkshires, one of the largest and most fascinating is the great blue heron. It can stand four feet tall, with wings that span more than six feet. A male heron's back and wings are covered with muted steel blue feathers accented with black and white. The female has less blue and more mottled brown in her coloration.

Great blue herons are short-distance migrants, each fall flying off to winter in the southern states (a few stay much farther north). Though the birds have become common throughout the Berkshires, they breed in only a few locations, a number of pairs building their stick nests in one selected marsh.

As impressive as this bird looks on the ground, it is in the air that the true beauty of the great blue heron reveals itself. It usually flies just over the treetops at a pace so slow you wonder why it doesn't just drop out of the sky. The experience of having one suddenly soar overhead has been likened to standing at the edge of a runway watching gliders land.

At one time, not so very long ago, herons and their egret cousins were routinely killed for the few graceful plumes that adorned the breeding birds. These fragile feathers were sold to the fashion industry, where they adorned hats and garments instead of herons and egrets. Today we have laws that protect these animals from the myopic and selfish among us. In response the heron is free to fly over our heads and refresh our spirits with an experience of unique beauty.

Getting There

From the center of Becket take Route 8 south about 1.7 miles to Cripple Creek store. Turn right onto Tyne Road. Drive on Tyne Road and then County Road a total of about 5.0 miles, following signs to October Mountain State Forest. The pavement ends shortly before the AT crosses the road. There is a small sign that marks the crossing, but it and the parking area pull-off are easily missed.

Northern
Transitional Forest
Washington

- **Appalachian Trail**
- **2.0 miles round-trip**
- **80 ft. elevation gain**
- **1.0–2.0 hours**
- **easy**

The Berkshire Plateau is a vast level highland that serves as the meeting ground of two very different environments. Here the hardy northern forest intermingles with the more southern broadleaf hardwoods. Red spruce touches American beech, and balsam fir grow with hemlock. The resulting montage is called the northern transitional forest. Replete with wildlife from the north and the south, it is one of the richest habitats in the Berkshires.

This walk is along the Appalachian Trail (AT) on land owned by the National Park Service. The AT is managed by the Appalachian Trail Conference and maintained in Massachusetts by the Berkshire Chapter of the Appalachian Mountain Club (AMC) and the Department of Environmental Management (DEM). The trail is marked with white rectangular blazes throughout its length, with turns noted by two blazes set one atop the other.

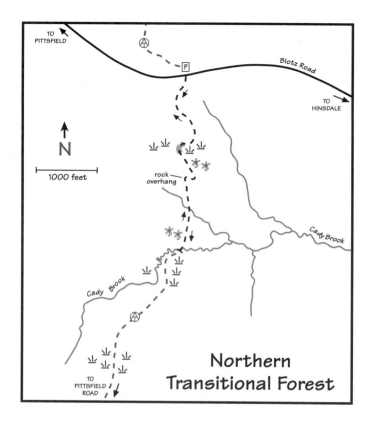

Look Forward To

- birds and wildflowers
- a rocky overhang
- sandy Cady Brook

The Trail

From the parking area on Blotz Road head south along a log walkway into a **transitional forest** of yellow birch, aspen, and ash with an understory of red spruce and cherry. Wood thrushes return from the south at the same time the red trillium are in bloom in late April or early May. In winter the chickadees keep you company in the cold.

The trail wanders through alternating wet and dry patches before climbing a modest hill where thick colonies of princess pine and wood fern grow. White pine and red maple intermingle with yellow birch and red spruce to form an overhead mosaic of different shades of green. A stand of slender beech dominates the top of another low knoll before the path gently descends to a small wetland traversed by a **long wooden bridge.**

The Berkshire Plateau is the vestige of an ancient mountain range, its relief slowly stolen by millions of years of erosion. The resulting landscape is an undulating quilt of boggy recesses and drier hillocks. In spring the forest is dotted with vernal pools where salamanders, wood frogs, and peepers gather. This wetland is choked with massive growths of a plant called shining club moss or running pine, an evergreen herb with long, spreading roots. Woodpeckers have carved deep holes in the trunks of the dead trees around the swamp, creating homes for both chickadees and flying squirrels. Hermit thrushes often dip their tails as they perch in nearby trees. In winter look for brown creepers in the hemlocks.

From the wetland the trail climbs into a **mixed hardwood stand** of yellow birch, red maple, and beech, with hobblebush and striped maple growing beneath. Bluebead lily and painted trillium blossom along the path in

May. Painted trillium is a beautiful flower with blush-white petals accented by a hypnotizing central magenta eye. Yellow-bellied sapsuckers are large woodpeckers whose sharp call is often heard from nearby treetops.

The trail then briefly follows the edge of a ridge before descending past a **ledge of overhanging rock** that would afford some protection in a sudden storm. Some

The Appalachian Trail skirts this ledgy overhang in Washington.

of the boulders near the ledge are topped with clusters of polypody fern at home in the shade of the yellow birch and red spruce.

From the ledge the path crosses a small brook before beginning a long walk through beautiful examples of a transitional forest. The scattered stands of red and black spruce prefer the cool, rocky spots while red maple and yellow birch do well in the moist soils. Look for slate gray juncos in the lower branches of the undergrowth and thrushes in the saplings near wet places. Deer, coyote, and black bear wander through from time to time, as do fox, porcupine, and fisher. There are a few white pine here, too, the most notable being a towering giant just off the trail. Even though white pine is very fast growing, this tree must be more than a hundred years old.

Just after passing the large pine you'll reach the **bridge to Cady Brook.** This is a wonderful place to have lunch and explore. The stream bottom is soft and sandy, and in May its banks are dotted with the yellow flowers of trout lily, wild oats, and scores of delicate spring beauty. Spring beauty is a small flower with pinkish petals and an enchantingly light fragrance. The water of the brook is always cool and a delight to sink your toes in.

To return to the parking area simply retrace your steps.

Shadow Tails

One of the most common animals in the Berkshire forests is the flying squirrel, but you may never see one. In daylight these diminutive creatures are asleep in their nests, their bodies rolled up into tight furry balls. It is the dusky twilight that stirs them to open their large dark eyes. As the evening deepens they climb onto the lip of their nest high above the forest floor and, after a moment of stillness, leap into the night.

Flying squirrels don't fly but rather glide from one place to another. Once a squirrel launches itself into the air it spreads its legs, opening a fold of skin that acts as an airfoil. As the squirrel sails through the air its flattened tail acts as a rudder, steering its descent. When the squirrel approaches its target, usually another tree trunk, it raises its front legs, lightly landing on all fours. Lightly, however, is a relative term. Every summer at least one flying squirrel uses the screens on our windows as a landing strip. Its arrival is announced by a loud *whack*. The squirrel hangs on for the few seconds it takes the screen to stop vibrating and then scurries off across the logs of the cabin into the darkness.

There are two species of flying squirrels that call the Berkshires home. The northern flying squirrel, the region's most common flying squirrel, weighs about two ounces, with soft earth brown fur covering its tiny body. The smaller southern flying squirrel exists in a few isolated populations, including Bartholomew's Cobble in Ashley Falls (see chapter one). Both species are active all year long but more so in the warmer months.

The word squirrel is not lyrical in its sound and the animal it describes is common. But the word is actually beautifully poetic, for it comes from two Greek words meaning *shadow tail*. And there is nothing common in the ability to leave the earth behind in favor of the sky. Night in the forest intimidates many people, the cloak of darkness keeping them from exploring beyond the friendly light of day. There are things that go bump in the night, but there is infinite beauty as well: huge green luna moths, night-flying warblers, and shadow tails that fly in the light of the moon.

Getting There

From the junction of Routes 7 and 20 and Holmes Road in northern Lenox, take Holmes Road to the traffic light at the intersection with Williams Street. Take a right onto Williams Street and proceed to the Pittsfield/Dalton town line, where the Burgner Farm is straight ahead. Take a right at the Burgner Farm, then bear left onto Kirschner Road. Follow Kirschner Road to the reservoir on the right. From the reservoir continue 1.0 mile to a parking area on the left.

Shaker Mountain and Holy Mount
Hancock

- **Shaker Trail**
- **3.5 miles**
- **787 ft. elevation gain**
- **3.5–4.5 hours**
- **moderate**

More than a century ago a religious society called the Shakers lived and worshipped in the hills of southern Hancock in the central Berkshires. They are gone now, yet as you walk the woodlands along the Shaker Trail their influence is as close as your shadow. Stone dams and mill foundations, cart paths, stone walls, and holy mountains blend with the waves of wildflowers that bloom along the brook and the rare chestnuts atop Shaker Mountain. The sacred ground atop Holy Mount is a particularly striking combination of the spiritual and natural worlds.

Shaker Trail passes through both the Pittsfield State Forest, a 9,000-acre woodland owned by the state of Massachusetts and maintained by the Department of Environmental Management (DEM), and land of the Hancock Shaker Village Museum. The trail is maintained by DEM and the Boy Scouts of America and is blazed with large green triangles with a white circle in the center.

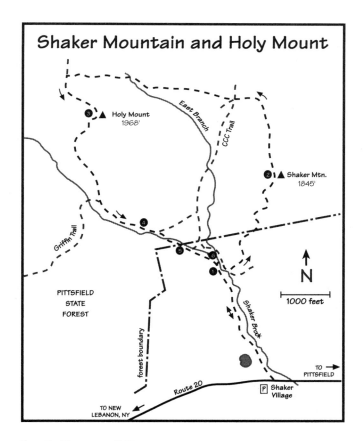

Shaker Mountain and Holy Mount

▲ Holy Mount
1968'

East Branch

CCC Trail

❸

❷ ▲ Shaker Mtn.
1845'

Griffin Trail

❹

❺

❻

❶

N

1000 feet

PITTSFIELD
STATE
FOREST

forest boundary

Shaker Brook

TO →
PITTSFIELD

Route 20

Ⓟ Shaker
Village

TO NEW
LEBANON, NY

Look Forward To

- mountains held sacred by the Shakers
- streams and hardwood forests
- dams, stone walls, and a marble quarry

The Trail

From the parking area at Hancock Shaker Village walk to the visitor center and register to hike the trail. They will give you a white Hiker sticker that allows you to walk across the grounds to the trailhead. There is no charge for the sticker.

From the visitor center proceed east along the shoulder of Route 20 to the crosswalk opposite the large brick meeting house. Cross the road and pass through a gate to a grassy cart path that runs northwest through the well-tended grounds. As you pass between the large earthen dam of the village reservoir on the left and Shaker Brook on the right there are good views of Shaker Mountain to the north. Continue across the fields to the first blaze at the edge of the woods. Turn right along a woods road whose shoulder is dusted with the dainty white flowers of bloodroot each April. Along the stream maple, ash, cherry, and yellow birch grow in the moist soil. Yellow birch is the tree with curls of exfoliating bark clinging to the trunk.

The trail soon comes to the gray rocky rampart of the **lower dam** constructed by the Shakers over a century ago. It still supplies water (via the iron aqueduct) to the village reservoir, while the waterfall created as the brook tumbles over the spillway conjures nostalgic visions of Emersonian New England.

Just north of the lower dam turn right and cross the stream on a wooden bridge. Follow the woods road right (south) past the cellar holes of old mills. Soon the path turns left and begins the ascent of Shaker Mountain. Gray birch and white pine grow in the well-drained upland soils, with hop hornbeam and saplings of maple contributing to the thick understory. The pale leaves of trailing arbutus contrast with the deep emerald of wintergreen as they intertwine along the forest floor. In midspring the tiny white flowers of Canada mayflower appear, lending their rich lily-of-the-valley fragrance to any passing breeze.

Using switchbacks the trail enters a northern hardwood forest of red oak and beech amidst scattered stands of hemlock and soon crests the hill at a sign that marks the boundary of the mountain's **holy ground.** The Shakers left their horses and wagons here as the worshippers, following ancient Old Testament tradition, bowed seven times before entering the sanctuary, or feast ground.

Today this holy place is a dense thicket of young birch, beech, and American chestnut. Some of the chestnut trees are almost six inches in diameter and scatter a layer of spiny burs on the ground each autumn; a rare treat since the chestnut blight nearly wiped out the species early in this century (see below).

The path enters the feast ground from the south, passing a depression in the soil just to the left of the trail that marks the place of the fountain, the center of activity of each outdoor service. A few feet north of the fountain was a four-foot marble slab called the **fountain stone,** placed here in 1843. On its face was carved a sacred dedication that sanctified this spot. After the Shakers ceased their hilltop ceremonies a decade later it disappeared. Its location today is a mystery but some experts believe the Shakers buried it somewhere on the mountain 150 years ago. About thirty feet north of the fountain you will find the remains of the circular **stone altar,** and beyond that the outline of a small building of unknown use called the **shelter.**

The trail leaves the sanctuary and follows the level ridge of Shaker Mountain's north shoulder. A wooden bench affords a place to rest, offering a winter view of Holy Mount through the trees to the west. The walk through the woods along the ridge is lovely any time of year. There is usually a breeze that combs the upper canopy and the fortunate will see deer or porcupine cross their path.

The trail then turns west, descending through shady hemlocks to an old clearcut. Tree stumps dot the sapling woods and carpets of princess pine and wintergreen grow amidst the wood fern. At an intersection of woods roads the path turns left, then immediately right along a stone wall, passing through the col between Doll Mountain and Holy Mount. After crossing the east branch of Shaker Brook the trail continues uphill on the woods road through tall white pine and cherry to an **abandoned orchard.** The road now leaves right and Shaker Trail turns left.

In spring small tree frogs called peepers sing from the nearby vernal pools and wood thrushes flit among the tangle of young apple trees that grow beneath the pines. The path now begins to climb the southeastern side of Holy Mount, the sacred mountain of the Shaker society of New Lebanon, New York. The trail now follows the route they once used to the crest of the hill, where an opening in the stone wall marks the entrance to the **feast ground of Holy Mount.**

Holy Mount is only about a mile from Shaker Mountain and the two societies held their outdoor services in concert so spiritual gifts could be exchanged across the mountaintops. The New Lebanon Shakers constructed their feast ground to the same plan as that

The stone wall built by the Shakers around Holy Mount still stands.

of the Hancock Shakers, but on a far grander scale. This feast ground is huge. Follow the path southeast along a beautiful stone wall to the drywall foundation of the shelter building on the left. To the right is the stone circle of the altar, which in turn is a few feet from the fountain. Holy Mount also had a marble fountain stone, which has never been found. A short side trail left leads to a section of wall that exemplifies the simple but lasting craftsmanship of the Shakers. This wall was constructed more than 150 years ago, yet generations of icy winters have not dislodged a single stone.

The path turns right (west) through a grove of Scotch pine to another stone wall. This wall completely encircles the sacred summit of Holy Mount, wrapping the mountain with a stony necklace more than one mile long. The trail follows the wall downhill through a northern hardwood forest of beech and red oak to a magical place where a spring seeps through the rocks of the perimeter wall. Nearby the yellow flowers of trout lily enchant the springtime, and in autumn the russet leaves of gray-barked beech bathe a restful afternoon in amber.

From the spring you pass through drifts of snow white paper birch before joining the Griffin Trail on a woods road perched above the west branch of Shaker Brook. The Griffin and Shaker Trails continue together along the bank of the stream past **ancient specimens of oak and ash,** some more than 200 years old. In May the nodding flowers of trillium blend with sharp-lobed hepatica, blue cohosh, and yellow violets to create a pastel painting of lavender, wine, and gold. In summer the brook invites bare toes to walk the smooth streambed, while red-eyed vireos sing from the trees.

Soon the Griffin Trail leaves left and the Shaker Trail crosses, then skirts, the brook. The path follows the stream to a small sign (right) marking the site of the old Shaker **marble quarry.** For nearly a century this hillside supplied the village with marble for everything from doorsteps to foundations. The fountain stone for Shaker Mountain may even have come from here. Shortly after the Civil War, with the village in decline, the quarry was abandoned. What mankind worked for a century, nature has reclaimed for the same length of time. Today the once-sharp contours of cut stone are muted beneath the tangled roots of yellow birch and the gossamer fronds of maidenhair fern. Maidenhair fern is one of the most delicate plants in the Berkshires, its finely dissected leaves growing from soil buffered by the slow dissolution of marble or limestone beneath its roots.

The woods road continues along the stream to **high dam.** This huge construction was built about 1810 of massive stone blocks. Behind the dam a long, narrow pond filled the valley while downstream a sawmill straddled the brook. Over the years a thick mantle of silt settled in the pond. In 1976, long after the sawmill was gone, a violent storm sent flood waters down the valley, collapsing a section of the dam and scouring a deep trough through the black sediment.

From high dam the path follows the woods road back to the village.

Ruins of high dam built by the Shakers about 1810.

American Chestnut

In the early years of the twentieth century a ship docked at the port of New York. In its hold, along with its cargo of goods from the Far East, was a fungus called *Endothia parasitica*, better known as chestnut blight. As the ship was unloaded the freshening breeze blew the tiny fungal spores inland, and the country has not been the same since.

A hundred years ago 40 percent of all the trees growing in the forests of the eastern United States were American chestnut. Its light, strong wood was used for almost everything you could think of and its nuts filled the woods each fall with plentiful food for wildlife. It was the most valuable timber tree in the country and an integral part of the economy of hundreds of cities and towns. If something were suddenly to steal away the chestnut, it would be devastating.

In 1904 a caretaker at the Bronx Zoo noticed a collection of orange dots at the base of a dying chestnut tree. Beneath the lifeless bark was a canker, a large wound of dead wood interlaced with moist fungal fibers. The fungus continued to grow until the entire trunk was girdled and the tree was dead. It was only the beginning.

With amazing speed the blight spread from New York to infect forests all over the Northeast. Within ten years Pennsylvania was spending hundreds of thousands of dollars trying to stop the destruction of its woodlands, as did other states in turn. But at the time no amount of money could buy a solution and the trees kept dying. By the end of the 1930s all the chestnuts, millions of trees, were gone.

But the blight only killed the tops of the trees and in a few years slender stump sprouts grew from the still-living roots. These trees grew to be about ten years old before they, too, fell prey to the fungus. This cycle of death and rebirth has continued in the forests ever since.

In 1976 a grove of chestnut was found on a Michigan golf course that was infected with the blight but was still alive. Samples of the fungus were taken from those trees and sent to the New Haven Agricultural experiment station in Connecticut, a headquarters of chestnut research. The Michigan fungus turned out to be a weakened strain of the original blight and gives new hope that a remedy will be found. The research at the Connecticut experiment station continues.

The chestnut trees atop Shaker Mountain are not immune to the disease that has almost destroyed their species. The fungus is killing them as it did their ancestors. Yet they are special because some of them have lived long enough to generate seed. Seed that may produce saplings just different enough from their parents to survive what other chestnuts could not. Control of the chestnut blight may come one day from far away laboratories, or perhaps it will grow in the grove on the holy ground atop the mountain.

Getting There

From the intersection of Routes 7 and 20 just south of the rotary in Pittsfield, take Route 20 west (West Housatonic Street) for 4.2 miles to the Hancock Shaker Village. Park in the Shaker Village parking lot and register to hike the trail in the nearby visitor center.

Canoe Meadows
Pittsfield

- **Sacred Way Trail**
- **1.2 miles**
- **no elevation gain**
- **0.5–1.0 hour**
- **easy**

It is not surprising that the old fields and wetlands of Canoe Meadows are home to coyote and red fox, beaver and mink. Or that deer often drink at the pond where muskrats swim. What is surprising is that all this happens within a few minutes' drive of the center of Pittsfield.

Canoe Meadows is a 262-acre mosaic of swamps, ponds, fields, and woodland bordered by the Housatonic River and quiet residential neighborhoods. It offers not only relaxing, easy walks through diverse ecosystems, but access to inventive educational programs as well.

Canoe Meadows is owned and administered by the Massachusetts Audubon Society (MAS) and is open from 7:00 A.M. to dusk Tuesday through Sunday. Admission is $2 for adults; $1 for senior citizens and children (MAS members and children under six free). The trails are lightly blazed and it is best to rely on a map and the well-defined treadway.

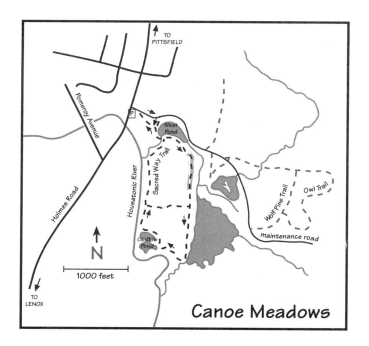

To Pittsfield

West Pond

Pomeroy Avenue

Housatonic River

Sacred Way Trail

Holmes Road

Wolf Pine Trail

Owl Trail

maintenance road

N

1000 feet

Ox-Bow Pond

To Lenox

Canoe Meadows

Look Forward To

- a long boardwalk through a swamp
- ponds with geese, ducks, and muskrats
- birds and wildflowers

The Trail

From the kiosk at the east end of the parking area, follow
the maintenance path to the grassy junction of the Sacred
Way Trail near the west shore of the pond. The path

turns right (south) and follows the shoreline to a concrete bridge that spans the pond's shallow outlet brook.

From the bridge the wide, level wetlands and meadows extend out to the east, where the land rises to form the soft contours of October Mountain. The bridge also offers a relaxing view of **West Pond,** where tall white pine shade the eastern bank, and honeysuckle, alder, and red osier dogwood grow in patchwork thickets along the rest of the shore. Playful muskrats live near the bridge and can often be seen floating in the shallows nibbling on aquatic grasses. These furry little creatures are much smaller than beaver, and the muskrat's tail is long and vertically flattened while a beaver's is short and flattened horizontally.

Red-winged blackbirds and kingfishers like to perch on the high branches overlooking the water, while Canada geese and mallard ducks cruise the surface.

From the bridge one branch of the trail follows the brook south while the other continues east along the shore of the pond. Proceed east into dense stands of willow that mark the boundary of a vast **woodland swamp.** The swamp is traversed by a boardwalk that weaves through a constantly changing tapestry of alder and dogwood, spirea and honeysuckle. Through here a seemingly endless array of birds flit among the twiggy tangles. Cardinals, catbirds, goldfinches, sparrows, and yellow warblers are just a few of the many you may see.

At the end of the boardwalk a shortcut that connects with the western branch of the Sacred Way loop leaves right (northwest). The trail now turns left (southeast) into an overgrown field that rises above the wetland to the left. Spirea and scrubby cherry struggle to grow in the nutrient-poor alluvial soil of the field, while taller aspen and birch colonize the more fertile slopes near the swamp.

In summer watch for blue jays as you walk along. They are pretty birds but are also arboreal nest predators, animals that steal eggs from tree-nesting birds. When a blue jay discovers the nest of another bird it swoops down and lands on a branch near the eggs. The pair of nesting birds then tries to drive off the jay. Larger songbirds such as cardinals accomplish this fairly regularly, but it is a much tougher task for smaller birds like warblers. If the jay is not driven away, it spears an egg from the nest and flies off to consume its meal elsewhere.

Beaver are active in the wetland to the left. Until 1987 there were no beaver here at all, but in that year they returned and built their first pond. Since then they have completely colonized the area, becoming the chief architect of environmental change in the sanctuary.

At the bank of a narrow brook the trail turns right (west) and enters a **bottomland forest** of hornbeam, gray birch, beech, and maple. The land rises gently to the shore of **Ox-bow Pond** where wooded bluffs overlook the dark, still water. Gardens of yellow and pink waterlilies bloom in early summer and great blue herons stalk the shallows for fish. On warm days painted turtles like to bask on the half-submerged logs that poke out from the shore, and occasionally a water snake slips silently between the lily pads.

Oxbow ponds form in an interesting way. As water flows around a bend in the river the currents deposit sand on one side of the channel and remove it from the other. Over time this inequity creates a loop in the

Waterlilies.

riverbed called a meander. Gradually this same process narrows the neck of the meander until one day it is breached and the loop is cut off from the main riverbed. The isolated body of water is an oxbow pond.

The path follows the shoreline of the oxbow, passing through groves of paper birch wrapped in bark the color of clouds. At the north end of the pond, where the waterlilies are shaded by sugar maples, the trail turns right (north).

From here the footway leaves the pond behind, briefly skirting the **Housatonic River** on the left and passing through an old field overgrown with spirea and honeysuckle. The daisylike flowers of fleabane blossom in June and the white umbel of yarrow points skyward in midsummer. At the edge of a wide, **wet meadow** the link trail enters right as the Sacred Way continues straight.

The name Sacred Way refers to the Mahican Indians, who would come every summer to the meadow and grow corn, squash, and beans. The Sacred Way was the spiritual path people would follow on their journey upon the earth. Those who followed it would learn wisdom and understanding.

In summer the meadow is a sea of waving grasses with islands of alder and willow. Look for the colorful caterpillars of monarch butterflies as they crawl along the stems of milkweed and the sudsy, white homes of spittlebugs hidden in the grass. A spittlebug is the immature form of an insect called a froghopper, so called because it looks like a little frog. If you carefully look inside the foamy spittle you will uncover the bright green spittlebug. The suds protect the bug while it feeds on the plant, as well as keeping its body moist.

The path through the meadow brings you again to the south bank of West Pond, which in turn is a short walk from the parking area.

Disappearing Honeybees

There is a morning in late winter when a southwest wind scents the air and chickadees greet the dawn with tentative but cheerful songs. From that time on, the Berkshires slowly waken to spring. Each year it comes in the same way until the meadows are once again in flower and the birds have again returned to fill the woods with song. But one time, the spring of 1996, was different, for that was the year the honeybees disappeared.

Honeybees were one of the first creatures we domesticated, and for more than four thousand years we have gone through time as partners. The bee pollinates the vegetables and fruits we grow and produces the thick golden liquid that was the sweetener of every Old World civilization. In turn we protect the bees from predators and provide the hive with nourishment in the cold winter months. It is a relationship that is almost as old as civilization itself.

The honeybee is a creature of the Old World and came to America with the first European colonists. The insect thrived in New England, and within decades of its introduction it had escaped the Puritan towns and become naturalized in the wild.

For almost four hundred years we have taken its presence for granted; most of us never realizing that the wild honeybee is the primary pollinator of backyard vegetables and fruit trees.

Then, in the early 1990s, beekeepers began to notice large numbers of dead bees outside their hives. Scientists who investigated the kills discovered that the bees had been parasitized by a species of tiny mite. The only known control was a single chemical which did slow the carnage, but the wild bees had no such overseers and the stage was set for disaster.

The winter of 1995–96 lingered long into spring. The cool weather weakened the bees, which made them more prone to infection by the mites. In one season some beekeepers lost 40 percent of their hives. But in the hollow trees that sheltered the hives of the wild bees the toll was far worse. Just how many bees died that winter and spring no one can know, but estimates range from 50 percent to 90 percent. In some places of the Berkshires, however, the honeybee has simply disappeared, and the prospects for its future remain unknown.

The Romans believed that Jupiter, their most powerful god, was nourished by honeybees. It seems that for a while at least, even the gods will go hungry.

Getting There

From the south: At the junction of Routes 7 and 20 and Holmes Road in north Lenox take a right onto Holmes Road. Continue on Holmes Road for 2.7 miles to the entrance on the right.

From the north: At Park Square in Pittsfield follow East Street three blocks to the junction with Pomeroy Avenue. Take a right onto Pomeroy Avenue and follow it to its end at Holmes Road. Turn left onto Holmes Road. The entrance is at the first right beyond the Housatonic River bridge.

Rice Sanctuary
Peru

- **Pink Trail, Red Trail**
- **1.5 miles**
- **150 ft. elevation gain**
- **1.0–2.0 hours**
- **easy with moderate sections**

The Rice Sanctuary is nestled in the heart of the moist highlands that make up the Berkshire Plateau. The trails that wander over the preserve's 273 acres will take you from Massachusetts to Maine in less than a mile. The forest of red spruce and mountain maple is still visited by black bear, and the wet meadows are home to nomadic flocks of cedar waxwings. In addition the sanctuary is just far enough off the beaten path to offer its visitors a rare treat: solitude.

The Rice Sanctuary is managed and maintained by the New England Forestry Foundation and is open from 8:00 A.M. to 7:00 P.M. daily. The trails are uniquely blazed with colored blocks of wood and are marked in only one direction.

Look Forward To

- a woodland lawn of birds and bumble bees
- an old beaver pond
- winter views

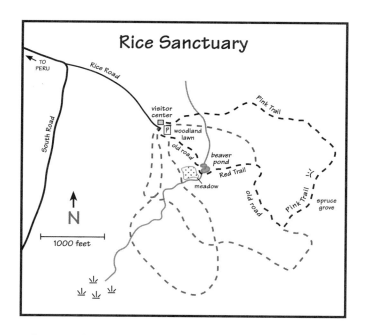

The Trail

Near the parking area is a large map of the sanctuary, a signpost that serves as the trailhead for all the paths, and a small visitor center. Surrounding this is a **woodland lawn** of mown grass generously planted with a variety of shrubs and trees. In purpose this area imitates an overgrown field, providing habitat and food for a vast array of birds and animals. In practice it is also a delightful distraction, for many of the plants offer colorful, fragrant flowers in the warmer months. As you wander about you can find locust trees and lilac bushes that bloom in May and June, sweet-scented balsam fir, and mock orange, the early summer flowers of which look and smell like orange blossoms. Apple trees grow by blueberries and Russian olive keeps company with red spruce and white pine.

This eclectic collection attracts everything from hummingbird moths and rabbits to cedar waxwings and deer. For those not up to a walk in the woods, this little spot is a nice place to enjoy the day.

At the signpost turn right (southwest) and follow the grassy path into the woods, where the white trail exits and returns on the right. The Pink Trail swings left (southeast) into a second-growth sugarbush of thirty-year-old maple and gradually descends through a forested **stone wall corridor.**

When New Englanders built a road through the wilderness they methodically stacked stones on both sides to mark its course. The result was miles of parallel tracks of stone walls that snaked across the countryside. This rocky avenue is all that remains of the eastern portion of Rice Road.

Red maple, beech, and apple now dominate a woodland where white-throated sparrows, thrushes, blue jays, and robins live. The path turns right and crosses the stone wall into a **wet meadow** with an old beaver pond at its southeast corner. Wide colonies of sensitive fern mingle with majestic blue flag, a wild iris whose blooms look like sky blue butterflies in flight. As you approach the pond the bright yellow flowers of mouse-ear hawkweed and Indian paintbrush greet you in summer, while bushes of blueberries ripen in the August sun.

There are many places near the water to stop and watch the life of the pond. Dragonflies and their smaller relatives, damselflies, streak over the sedges and spirea in search of bugs to dine on, while whirligig beetles spin

Blue flag blooms in a meadow near the beaver pond.

in chaotic circles over the surface of the pond. The shallows are home to spotted newts whose greenish skin blends nicely with the waterweeds.

The path follows the bank of the pond and crosses its outlet on a wooden bridge before swinging along the southern shore. Thick glens of alder and aspen hide misty white foamflower, which yields to patches of bluebead lily as the trail climbs higher. After reentering the stone corridor of the old road the Red Trail leaves left, while the Pink Trail continues uphill straight ahead (south). Red maple, spruce, and ash shade a dense understory of mountain ash and mountain maple. Black bear and deer pass through here, and thrushes, chickadees, and blue jays often flit about the brushy thickets.

The trail then leaves the vestigial road, turning left (northeast) into a wet area where yellow birch and maple oversee raspberry, Indian cucumber, and wood fern. A short walk brings you to a **northern transitional forest** where beech and red spruce grow above trillium, Canada mayflower, and bunchberry. Storms have uprooted many of these century-old spruce from the sodden soil, creating a maze of windfalls to wander through.

The path now tackles a moderate scramble past weathered boulders and rocky outcrops to a limited view at the top of the hill. Pileated woodpeckers have carved their concave sculptures into many nearby trees, and the wing beats of ruffed grouse can often be heard in the forests below. In winter the leafless trees share **an expansive view** that rolls over the rounded hills toward October Mountain in the southwest.

After following the edge of the ridge crest past bushes of blueberry and azalea the trail swings left, descending through tall ash, maple, and cherry to the bank of a small stream. From the brook the path climbs into an attractive woodland of thick red spruce, beech, and white pine, with saplings of balsam fir brushing your shoulders as you pass. A short walk brings you back to the woodland lawn by the parking area.

The Great Bear

Each winter evening, as the sun retreats behind the western horizon, the gossamer lights of the stars begin to illuminate the sky. As the darkness deepens, the images of the constellations grow stronger until the heavens become a sparkling quilt of ancient tales.

There is Orion, a great cluster of stars that the Egyptians believed was the home of the dead kings and the Greeks named the hunter. On his shoulder is Betelgeuse, a red giant star swollen with age, while at his heel is the brilliant dog star, Sirius. In between are the three stars of

Orion's belt, their orientation perfectly duplicated on earth by the three great pyramids at Giza.

Nearly opposite Orion is the Big Dipper or great bear, the most familiar constellation in the northern sky. The seven stars of the great bear form a huge trapezoid accented with a sweeping tail. Close by the great bear is the little bear that carries the North Star, Polaris, on its tail.

The bears in the sky were hunted by many different peoples, each weaving words and stars into a tapestry of tradition. Of all these, perhaps the most eloquent one comes from the Mahicans of the Berkshires.

Once, a very long time ago, the seven bravest hunters of the Mahicans were transformed into stars and sent to live forever in the heavens. The seven hunters then began to search the sky for the great bear and in the spring found its tracks. All summer long the hunters followed the bear, but the wise old animal eluded them. Then, as the nights grew longer, one of the hunters wounded the bear, its blood becoming the crimson and scarlet of the autumn leaves. In winter the fat of the bear fell upon the earth as snow. When spring came again the fat melted into the earth, where it nourished the soil and became the sap that rose into the trees. As the world awakened, the seven hunters once again found the tracks of the great bear in the sky, and the story began again.

Getting There

From the junction of Routes 8 and 143 in Hinsdale, take Route 143 east 4.4 miles to the intersection with South Road in the center of Peru. Turn right onto South Road and travel 1.0 mile. Rice Road is the dirt road straight ahead as South Road turns sharply right. Follow Rice Road 0.3 mile to a small parking area next to the visitor center.

Tilden Swamp
Hancock

- **Hawthorne Brook Trail, Pine Mountain Trail, Parker Brook Trail**
- **3.5-mile loop**
- **1050 ft. elevation gain**
- **4.0–5.5 hr**
- **moderate with steep sections**

"Whenever I looked out on the pond it impressed me like a tarn high up on the side of a mountain." Thoreau wrote those words shortly after moving to the shores of Walden, yet they come to mind each time I sit by the waters of Tilden Swamp. It is a magnet to wildlife and its ambiance soothes the soul. This walk climbs over the rounded summit of Pine Mountain, explores the shores of Tilden Swamp, and returns along the plentiful cascades of Parker Brook.

The trails are in Pittsfield State Forest, a 9,000-acre reserve of mountains, ponds, and hardwood forest managed by the Massachusetts Department of Environmental Management (DEM). The trails are marked with blue blazes and some junctions are signed. In winter the forest is a popular destination for cross-country skiers. A small fee is collected per car as you enter the reserve.

Look Forward To
- a climb up Pine Mountain
- a walk around mountain pond
- waterfalls and wildflowers

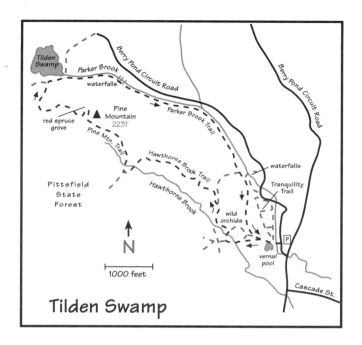

Tilden Swamp

Map labels:
- Tilden Swamp
- Parker Brook
- Berry Pond Circuit Road
- waterfalls
- Pine Mountain 2231'
- red spruce grove
- Parker Brook Trail
- Pine Mtn. Trail
- Hawthorne Brook Trail
- Hawthorne Brook
- Pittsfield State Forest
- waterfalls
- Tranquility Trail
- wild orchids
- vernal pool
- Berry Pond Circuit Road
- P
- Cascade St.
- N
- 1000 feet

The Trail

From the kiosk opposite the parking area and ski lodge head west across the wooden bridge. The paved walkway of Tranquility Trail, a path designed for the physically challenged, immediately leaves right. Continue straight past a large vernal pond on the left where spring peepers and wood frogs herald spring. A red-blazed ski trail soon leaves right through a **hardwood forest** of red oak, black birch, maple, and ash. The approach to Hawthorne Trail passes many side paths. In an effort to make the trailhead easier to find, To H has been painted in blue on selected trees along the way. The path continues northwest through sprays of spicebush and clusters of trout lily and red-flowered trillium, which blossom in May.

After crossing a small brook the blazes of Woodland Ramble Trail continue straight and Hawthorne Trail swings right, recrossing the stream. The path immediately comes to a signed junction where Hawthorne Trail turns left and heads uphill beside the brook. As you climb look for clumps of wintergreen, May-flowering trailing arbutus, bluets, and the exotic **rattlesnake orchid.**

There are some 20,000 species of orchids in the world, the most of any family of flowering plants, yet relatively few call New England home. Rattlesnake orchid, also called rattlesnake plantain, is easily recognized by its deep green rosette of richly variegated leaves. In summer a slender flower spike supports its cluster of small but complex ivory blossoms.

The trail turns right away from the brook and then quickly left, resuming its ascent amid clusters of sheep laurel and wild oats. A long climb brings you to the top of a ridge at the edge of Hawthorne ravine. In the winter there is a nice view of Onota Lake to the south. Pine Mountain occupies the horizon to the northwest. The grade moderates as the path passes beneath a thick canopy of red oak and beech and crosses the now slender rivulet of Hawthorne Brook near the stream's headwaters on Pine Mountain. Hawthorne Trail then ends at its junction with Pine Mountain Trail.

Turning right along Pine Mountain Trail (north), the path climbs through a **mixed temperate forest** of windblown white pine, beech, and oak. The large fronds of pasture brake shade more wintergreen, and blueberries grow in the sunnier spots. The trail then arcs northwest, gaining the ridge crest where a cut-marble pillar marks the border of Pittsfield and Hancock.

A short walk along the level ridge brings you to the edge of a high buttress, a place where wild azalea forms tangled thickets beneath the oaks and the mountain dramatically drops away into the valley. The path turns right along a wooded ledge that offers a limited wintertime view of Tower Mountain to the northwest. At the edge of the ridge is a **stand of red spruce** that grows on a thrust of rock at the summit of Pine Mountain. As you turn into the grove a limited but beautiful view reveals itself. The forest recedes from the summit like a wave sliding back from the shore. Below, nestled in the surrounding woods, is Tilden Swamp with the pastoral hills and farms of Wyomanock, New York, beyond. The dogwood blossoms of bunchberry gather around the base of the spruce trees and small colonies of polypody fern huddle atop the rocks. Red spruce prefer the chill, windy places in the Berkshires and this overlook is no exception. On a hot day this grove is a wonderfully cool oasis.

The trail gingerly descends the hillside past outcrops of rock to a wide, level woodland that crosses the shoulder of the mountain to a junction where Pine Mountain trail divides. The left branch leads to Tower Mountain, the right to **Tilden Swamp.** Turn right (east) and follow the path to the outlet of the pond, where Parker Brook Trail enters right.

From the junction continue across the outlet and explore the pond's eastern shore. Beaver have managed to cut a twenty-yard swath around the perimeter of the pond, so the walking is easy and there are many lovely open areas in which to lie about and watch the world go by or picnic in the sun. The bronze-green foliage of leatherleaf intermingles with sheep laurel to form dense waterside thickets. Shy wood ducks share the pond with gregarious Canada geese, and sometimes coyotes come down from the mountain to stalk the shore for frogs or careless waterbirds. Snapping turtles like to lie in the mud of the shallows and belted kingfishers often perch in the taller trees near the shore.

When you're ready, return to Parker Brook Trail and follow the narrow footway southeast along the stream. The brook quickly carves a narrow ravine from the hillside and begins to tumble over **a series of low, rocky cascades.**

The trail follows alongside the brook, weaving in and out of the hemlock and yellow birch that grow in the cool, moist ravine and the oak and beech that prefer the drier upland hillsides. Trillium and spring beauty blossom along the path in May and the flowing water is a wonderfully cheerful companion any time of year.

After a pleasant walk a ski trail enters right and immediately leaves left where it crosses the brook on a bridge. Some **beautiful waterfalls** worth exploring are just a few yards downstream from here. From the intersection near the bridge the path heads southwest away from the brook, gradually swinging south until it comes to an east-west junction where you turn left (east). The path quickly merges with the main trail that leads back to the parking area.

Snapping Turtles

While growing up I would visit the pond behind the house almost every day. Bullfrogs croaked from hollows in the shore as water snakes basked on the rocks. Dragonflies streaked through the afternoon air, succeeded at dusk by the artful aerobatics of little brown bats. Yet of all the animals that lived in and around the water one held more mystery than any other: the snapping turtle. Old-timers said the one in the pond was the biggest turtle anybody had ever seen. Not many believed the stories, though, for this turtle was more phantom than fact. Many said it was there, but hardly any had ever seen it.

Turtles have been on earth for hundreds of millions of years. And of all the turtles in the Berkshires, that

A snapping turtle prepares to lay eggs in summer at Tilden Swamp.

prehistoric heritage is best represented by the snapping turtle. The snapper is the largest turtle in the Northeast, some specimens reaching more than fifty pounds. Its thick, muscular legs and neck are protected by a rough plated shell called a carapace, and the long tail is lined with rows of bony plates. A snapping turtle's mouth, however, is generally regarded as its most impressive feature.

People usually encounter snappers when the turtles cross a road in early summer on their way to lay eggs. At this time and place (pregnant and on land), a snapping turtle has very little patience. If you encountered it in the muddy shallows of a pond it would quickly swim away. On land, however, it is slow and awkward, with no easy escape route; so it fights, using its mouth to defend itself.

A snapping turtle will usually face its attacker head-on, opening its mouth to reveal a large, sharp-edged maw. When it strikes it does so with amazing speed, clamping its powerful jaws on whatever is threatening it. The muscular mandibles are strong enough to snap small branches but, like most creatures, the snapping turtle would just as soon leave well enough alone. If you don't disturb it, it will treat you in kind.

One hot summer day I came to the pond just as the sun was setting. As I walked along the warm boulders that rimmed the shore I looked out over the water for any sign of the turtle, but the surface of the pond was still. I had grown used to disappointment when it came to seeing the old turtle, but as I climbed atop the largest stone I suddenly stopped dead in my tracks. There on the rock below me was the snapper, enjoying the residual warmth of the rock. Our meeting lasted but a moment for the startled monster immediately plunged into the dark water. But that moment has endured in my mind ever since. In the coming years I continued to roam the shores of the pond, but I never saw the turtle again. Since then I've met many snapping turtles, but none like that one. It was a magnificent animal. And by the way, the old-timers were right; the thing was positively huge.

Getting There

From the intersection of Routes 20 and 7 in Pittsfield, take Route 20 west (West Housatonic Street) for 2.6 miles. Turn right on Hungerford and follow it to the West Street intersection. Turn left on West Street and drive 1.2 miles to Churchill Street. Take a right on Churchill and drive 1.7 miles to a second intersection with Cascade Street. Turn left on Cascade and follow it to the park entrance.

Balance Rock
Lanesboro

- **Balance Rock Trail**
- **0.5 mile (1.0 mile round-trip)**
- **118 ft. elevation gain**
- **0.5 hour**
- **easy**

In the forested hills just west of Pontoosuc Lake is a 330,000-pound boulder that is one of the enduring mysteries of the Berkshires. Somehow this roughly triangular behemoth rests atop another stone on a contact point of just a few square inches. Like an inverted pyramid it stands in apparent defiance of gravity. This walk explores the legendary Balance Rock as well as the unique ecosystem of the boulder field around it.

Balance Rock is in Balance Rock State Park and borders the much larger Pittsfield State Forest. The trail to the rock follows a paved road not open to automobiles and is very easy to follow.

Until recently Balance Rock State Park was closed due to vandalism of the site and lack of operating funds. However, through the efforts of Pittsfield Councilman Peter Arlos and employees of the Massachusetts Department of Environmental Management (DEM), the park was cleaned and recently reopened to the public.

Look Forward To
- Balance Rock
- wildflowers in a boulder field
- a spruce grove

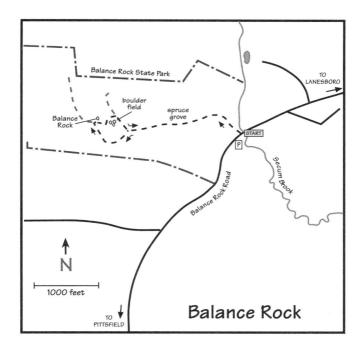

Balance Rock State Park

boulder field

spruce grove

Balance Rock

START

P

TO LANESBORO

Secum Brook

Balance Rock Road

N

1000 feet

TO PITTSFIELD

Balance Rock

The Trail

From the parking area cross Balance Rock Road to the entrance of the park. Secum Brook flows just to the right (northeast). The moist soil of the stream bank is crowded with red osier dogwood and the large green leaves of false hellebore. About Mother's Day the delicate fragrance of apple blossoms floats on the spring breeze.

The road leads along a level grassy lawn where young aspen shade the path and gray birch, cherry, and ash grow in the deeper woods. The trail makes a lazy westward turn, passing a thick grove of **Norway spruce** on the right. In its native range of northern Europe Norway spruce forms vast, exclusive forests. Its extreme hardiness allows it to drape even upper northern hemisphere mountains with a characteristic mantle of somber green. In America Norway spruce is planted for windbreaks and Christmas trees or to quickly stabilize disturbed watersheds. The tree escaped cultivation long ago and is naturalized throughout the north temperate region of eastern North America. The six-inch cones of Norway spruce are the largest of all the spruces and are a favorite food of **red squirrels,** who adroitly dismember the cones much as we eat corn on the cob.

The road then winds up the hillside past isolated clumps of delicate Solomon's seal to **Balance Rock.** The rock is a marble boulder of about 165 tons. Eons ago it calved from its parent bedrock somewhere to the northwest and was transported here in the ice of the last glacial age (see below). But Balance Rock seems to transcend empirical measure and bring harmony to contradiction. It is simultaneously delicate and massive, transient and eternal, possible and impossible. The more you gaze at it the more it seems that it shouldn't exist. And the more you explore it the more fascinating it becomes.

Downslope of Balance Rock is an impressive **boulder field** of huge marble monsters that have transformed this spot over the millennia into a unique ecosystem. As rain and ice erode the stone, calcium and other minerals characteristic of marble are leached from the rock and enrich the soil. A rich array of plants now occupies this area. **Wild ginger** grows from soil-filled crevices atop the rocks. If you gently scratch its stem you

The amazing Balance Rock of Lanesboro.

can smell the spicy fragrance that gives this plant its name. Nearby is miterwort, whose tiny flowers look like minuscule bells fringed with snowflakes. Clumps of yellow trout lily blossom atop buried ledges of stone and dainty bouquets of sharp-lobed hepatica dance in the May breeze. On the eastern face of one large boulder a colony of rare **walking fern** clings to the rock.

On the downhill side of the boulder field is a gravel path that leads back to the road. From the road it is a short walk back to the parking area.

Glaciers and Giants

If you asked a geologist to tell you the tale of Balance Rock he would tell you a story of glaciers. For at least the last ten million years there have been glaciers on earth.

Periodically conditions became favorable for these rivers of ice to grow into continental ice sheets that spread across the middle latitudes. As the ice surged down the valleys it dislodged boulders and soil from the hillsides, which then tumbled onto the glacier. The ice carried this rocky cargo on its journey south.

One of those anonymous boulders was Balance Rock. After falling onto the glacier the rock slowly became imprisoned in the ice as it drifted south. For millennia it lay in the frigid embrace of the Laurentide ice sheet until the climatic pendulum turned from omnipresent winter to spring. About 14,000–12,000 years ago the environment of the world quickly warmed and the landscape of ice began to melt. As it did the boulder slowly settled through the ice, eventually contacting the stone on which it now lies. As the last of the glacier ablated it left Balance Rock gingerly poised on its pedestal of stone—a thought-provoking monument to the Ice Age.

There is another story, of course, about the origin of the rock. One day hundreds of years ago some Indian boys were playing in the woods when they noticed another youngster through the trees. Hoping to get a reaction from him, the Indians teased the stranger, prodding him with insults. What the boys did not know was that the youth they were teasing was a powerful shaman descended from the ancient ones who brought civilization to the world. In horror they watched as the small boy grew into a fierce giant. He picked up a great boulder in his massive hand and placed it on top of another, then with words of power commanded the great stone never to move. The giant then taught the frightened boys the ways of peaceful people and told them to teach the rest of their nation as well. He then returned to his previous size and vanished into the woods, leaving Balance Rock as proof that the words he spoke were true.

Each summer the Indians would return to Balance Rock and gather at its base. An elder would climb the stone and repeat the teachings of the lawgiver.

Is Balance Rock a marvelous vestige of the Ice Age? If it is, its unerring balance has outlasted thousands of years of erosion, storms, and earthquakes, a record as incredible as its precariously fragile stance. Or is the rock something else entirely? Something powerful and peaceful that is beyond the logic of science. Perhaps we'll never know.

Getting There

From the traffic light at the entrance to the Berkshire Mall on Route 7 in Lanesboro drive north 0.2 mile to the junction with Bull Hill Road. Take a left onto Bull Hill Road and drive for 0.9 mile. Take a right onto Balance Rock Road. The parking area is on the left opposite the park at 0.8 mile.

Wahconah Falls
Dalton and Windsor

- **Wahconah Falls Trail**
- **0.3 mile (0.6 mile round-trip)**
- **144 ft. elevation gain**
- **0.5–1.0 hour**
- **easy**

Of all the walks in the central Berkshires the stroll to Wahconah Falls holds the most reward for the least effort. A short walk brings you to a series of cataracts that plunge through successive gateways of metamorphic rock and culminate in the percussive chorus of lower falls. In addition there are groves of pine and hemlock that shelter soapstone boulders and the remains of an old mill. All this and an ancient legend as well.

A wide unmarked woods road leads to the base of the falls. From there an unblazed but well-worn footpath leads uphill along the brook to the old mill. Although there is no formal trail system along the falls, the path is easy to follow.

Look Forward To

- impressive waterfalls
- pine and hemlock groves
- an old mill and soapstone boulders

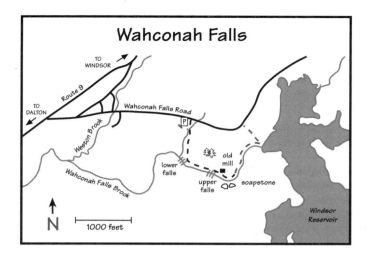

Wahconah Falls

The Trail

The trail begins at the southeast corner of the paved parking area where steps descend to a wooden bridge. At the base of the steps a short side trail leaves right to a hilltop picnic site, while the main path crosses the bridge and joins a wide, gravel woods road. Continue southwest along the road through stands of hemlock, yellow birch, and beech. False Solomon's seal and red trillium grow amid scruffy clumps of giant horsetail in the wetland to the right. The woods road then ends at a grassy picnic site a few feet north of **lower falls.**

This roaring cascade is what comes to mind when most people speak of Wahconah Falls. The rocks around the deep pool are cooled by waves of mist and offer an excellent view of the brook pouring through the aperture carved in the steep rock. This is also the place where the legend of Wahconah Falls takes place (see below).

From lower falls a footpath leads up the east side of the hill through century-old hemlock and small bushes of Canada yew. (You can tell the two plants apart by looking at their needles. Hemlock needles have two bluish white bands on their undersides while those of yew are solid green.) The trail quickly comes to a terrace atop the ledge of lower falls with a fine view downstream.

From the terrace it is a short walk through shady woods to the crest of **upper falls.** Chickadees and blue jays live here all year long, and Canada geese use the narrow valley as a flyway on their way to Windsor Reservoir just upstream. In spring hermit thrushes and black-and-white warblers return to the woods beside the stream.

Upper falls is a complicated jumble of boulders that squeezes the river through small openings in the rocks. The whitewater torrent that results is mesmerizing. A few yards due north of upper falls is an ancient grove of **cathedral pines** that occupies a low knoll. Some of these trees are more than a hundred years old and three feet in diameter. Decades ago the dense bed of needles beneath the pines was so thick that in summer the local kids would strap on their skis and slide down the hill atop them.

A few yards east of upper falls are the remains of the **Booth mill.** Built in the early 1800s, the stonework of the foundation is still in remarkably good condition. Just upstream of the mill is a boulder with a bore hole drilled through it. This rock is an excellent example of

Remains of Booth mill near Wahconah Falls.

soapstone. Soapstone, or steatite, is an impure form of the metamorphic rock known as talc. It is so soft that you can scratch it with your fingernail. In the 1880s the soapstone was mined briefly from a quarry that operated across the brook. Small amounts of asbestos and emery also have been found here.

To return, follow the path along the stream to lower falls, then walk up the woods road to the parking area.

The Legend of Wahconah Falls

Hundreds of years ago the Pequot Indians lived along the Mystic River in southeast Connecticut. In 1637 their nation was nearly destroyed in a war with the English. In an attempt to escape the bloodshed, a band of refugees headed west along the coast of Long Island Sound. The English caught them at the mouth of the Housatonic River, killing many. The survivors then followed the river north to the Berkshires, where they settled on the banks of a small stream by a waterfall we now call Wahconah Falls.

The summer of 1676 was hot and dry. One August day an Indian maiden named Wahconah, daughter of the Pequot sachem Miahcomo, was by the waterfall when an unfamiliar warrior appeared from the woods. She asked who he was and he told her that he was Nessacus of the Wampanoag. As she listened he told her of the bloody war in the east and that hundreds of Indians were fleeing west to escape the English.

Nessacus stayed in the village and fell in love with Wahconah. Miahcomo, however, was ignorant of these events, for he was visiting the Mohawk nearby. In a few days he returned with the warrior Yonnogah. Both warriors wished to marry Wahconah, so Miahcomo asked the shaman Tashnu what the wishes of the Great Spirit were. Tashnu told the sachem that the two warriors should stand on opposite banks of the pool below the falls. A canoe would be floated in the water so its bow touched the rock in the center of the stream. The flowing water would turn the canoe toward the warrior who the Great Spirit wished to marry Wahconah.

At this same time two hundred Narraganset, Nipmuck, and Quaboag were fleeing toward the Berkshires from eastern Massachusetts, just ahead of Major John Talcott's Connecticut militia. On August 11 the Indians crossed the Connecticut River on rafts at Chicopee. The next morning they passed the town of Westfield, just a few hours ahead of Talcott.

There were no English settlements beyond Westfield, and after reaching the banks of the Housatonic River in present-day Great Barrington the Indians rested, sure that Talcott had given up the pursuit. He had not, but he was bogged down in the thick forest near what is now Sandisfield. With his supplies running low Talcott selected his 60 strongest men, gave them all the remaining provisions, and sent his remaining 240 soldiers back to Springfield with the horses.

In the early evening of August 15, 1676, Talcott's soldiers crept up to the banks of the Housatonic opposite the Indian camp and attacked. Thirty-five Indians were instantly killed, including the sachem of the Quaboag. The rest, almost all women and children, scattered into the forest, eventually finding their way to the safety of New York.

At the base of the falls the canoe was set in the pool and released. Tashnu had told Yonnogah not to worry about the outcome, for the old shaman had rigged the test in the Mohawk's favor. For a moment the canoe balanced itself against the stone, then swung decisively toward Nessacus. In the ensuing celebration both Tashnu and Yonnogah vanished into the forest, never to be seen again.

The next day word reached the Pequots of the massacre to the south and that Tashnu was going to betray his people to Talcott. Wahconah and Nessacus were married, then with their people left the falls forever. The band headed west to New York, where they knew Talcott could not follow. For many years thereafter, they lived in peace. Talcott never did return to the Berkshires.

In 1677 the governments of Massachusetts and Connecticut made a formal request to Governor Andros of New York to return all the Indians that had fled across the border. He refused.

Getting There

From the junction of Routes 8 and 9 in Dalton, bear left onto Route 9. Follow Route 9 for 2.3 miles to North Road. Turn right onto North Road and drive for 0.1 mile to where Wahconah Falls Road bears right. Follow Wahconah Falls Road 0.3 mile to the parking area on the right.

Judges Hill
Windsor

- **Ant Hill Trail, Judges Hill Trail, Circuit Trail**
- **4.3 miles round-trip**
- **298 ft. elevation gain**
- **3.5–4.5 hours**
- **easy with moderate sections**

Judges Hill is the highest point in Windsor, a town where almost everything is more than two thousand feet in elevation. Along the way to its forested crest are acres of boreal woods, abandoned farms, wetlands, and wildflowers. In addition the summit holds the rough-hewn remains of Judges Fort, where people have picnicked for more than a century, and a tree that survived the touch of a lightning bolt.

The trails to Judges Hill are in Notchview Reservation, a 3,000-acre preserve of forests and fields atop the Berkshire Plateau. Visitors come year-round to enjoy the twenty-five kilometers of hiking and cross-country ski trails as well as visit the General Bates homestead and the Budd Visitor Center. Notchview is owned and maintained by the Trustees of Reservations, a conservation group that maintains many properties throughout the state.

All trails are marked with light yellow circular blazes and junctions are well signed. A $2 fee is charged to visitors.

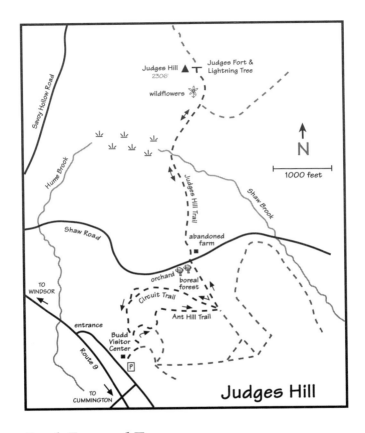

Look Forward To

- a walk through a boreal forest
- abandoned farms and wildflowers
- Judges Fort and a lightning tree

The Trail

From the Budd Visitor Center head through a grassy fence-lined passage to the woods. Bear left onto Circuit Trail beneath the red spruce, yellow birch, maple, and balsam fir of a **northern transitional forest.** These occur where temperate broad-leaved trees, such as maple and beech, coexist with the spruce and fir of the higher latitudes. These woodlands create a diverse habitat where a wide array of plants and animals live. After a short walk turn right onto Ant Hill Trail. The path heads uphill through thick stands of young spruce and fir where white-throated sparrows often flit among the branches. These birds are a hallmark of cool northern forests and their song (*Old Tom PEAbody, PEAbody*) is as silver as Chopin.

Continuing uphill the trail swings left through an undulating landscape of wet sags and drier hummocks. Circuit Trail then enters left a few yards before the junction with Judges Trail.

Turn left (north) onto the wide, level track of Judges Trail. Shining club moss and Canada mayflower grow in the moist soil to the left, while a beautiful stand of red spruce is to the right. A short walk brings you to an old orchard where fragrant apple blossoms sprinkle the trees in mid-May. In fall deer often come to browse the fruit that litters the ground.

After crossing Shaw Road the path heads downhill past the ruins of an abandoned farmhouse. The once-dominant red spruce quickly yields to a **mixed hardwood forest.** Goldenrod and dandelions mix with red trillium, wild oats, and stonecrop at the base of ash and red maple. The path gently descends through wet areas to the bank of Shaw Brook, which it crosses on a wooden bridge. From the brook the trail heads uphill through a woodland of beech and cherry with patches of hobble-bush beneath. Black bear sometimes stroll through here, but that wasn't always the case.

When the first European settlers came to Windsor in the 1700s the forests were full of gray wolves and black bear, animals the colonists viewed as threats to their safety. To encourage their extirpation a bounty was offered of 30 pounds sterling for each adult wolf or bear carcass and 15 pounds sterling for each pup or cub. In those times that was a fortune, and in the decades that followed both the black bear and the gray wolf disappeared from the forests.

Today the black bear is back and is often seen searching for beechnuts in autumn or nibbling blueberries from bogs in summer. The gray wolf, however, has never returned.

After a pleasant walk past beds of spring beauty and trillium the Windsor Trail leaves right. As the slope steepens look for ruffed grouse and pileated woodpeckers. If you find a grouse you'll know it, for they launch themselves skyward with thundering wing beats—quite a rush for the uninitiated. Close to the summit the floor of the woods becomes a mass of trout lily. In May these beds put on an amazing display, with hundreds of dainty yellow flowers everywhere.

The path makes a wide turn and gains the summit of Judges Hill just south of the stone ruins of **Judges Fort.** More than a century ago a social group called the Windsor Club built this patio-with-a-view atop the hill. They cooked lunches in the fireplace and served them on the stoneware table in the center of the fort. Some of the members of the club were judges in Berkshire County, their profession giving the hilltop and the fort its name.

Near the stone chimney is an **ash tree** that was **struck by lightning** around 1986 (see below). It is the tree with the narrow scar running from the ground up into the canopy.

Judges Hill is a wonderful place to picnic. Red-backed salamanders live beneath the rocks and sheaths of fallen bark, and wood thrushes and ovenbirds fill the summer days with song.

From here the return trip follows Judges Hill Trail back down the hillside to the junction with Circuit Trail.

Lightning struck this ash tree on Judges Hill, leaving a scar.

Turn right onto Circuit Trail and immediately right again into a pristine **boreal forest** of spruce and fir. The path carves a passage through the thick evergreens; in summer the air is filled with the fragrance of balsam. As hardwoods begin to mix in, the trail briefly forks, rejoining shortly before crossing a stream on a wooden bridge. Ant Hill Trail then enters left a few yards before the Circuit Trail turns right onto the grassy path above the parking area.

Lightning

The storm formed over the Gulf of Mexico in the second week of March 1993. The upper winds steered it north-east and as it crossed the Florida peninsula its strength grew explosively, the swirling clouds aglow with lightning. As it lashed the Outer Banks of North Carolina, lightning sensors recorded an astounding 5,000 flashes per hour. The storm then headed for New England.

Lightning is the visible discharge of atmospheric electrical energy. It results when droplets of water become charged as thermal turbulence circulates them through a storm cloud. The base of the cloud builds up a huge negative electric charge. At the same time the ground beneath it establishes a store of positive energy. So far this energy has been static, stored in the giant bell jar created by the earth and clouds. When the cloud can hold no more energy a conductive pathway of charged particles, called a leader, spreads out from the cloud. When this invisible passage descends to about a hundred yards above the earth, a companion leader rises from the ground to meet it.

When the two leaders make contact the lightning flash, or return stroke, manifests and moves up from the ground into the cloud at a speed of about 31,000 miles per second. Immediately several more flashes streak along the leader, ending only when the charge in the base of the cloud is exhausted.

Each lightning bolt may be more than a mile long, its strength measured in thousands of volts. As it rips through the sky it instantly heats the atmosphere around it to more than 30,000° F. The superheated air expands explosively, creating the shock waves that then roll over the hills as thunder.

A tree struck by lightning will bear a scar that extends from the ground up the trunk to the point where the bolt leaped toward the clouds. A weak strike carves a long sinewy wound along the trunk. These trees often survive, as the ash on Judges Hill attests. Strong strikes can literally explode the tree, blasting charged splinters of wood into the air that glow with an eerie red light as they rain down onto the ground.

For hours the 1993 storm pounded New England with heavy precipitation and howling winds. By the time it moved off into the North Atlantic, two feet of snow blanketed the Berkshires and nearly 60,000 lightning flashes had been recorded. In the unpredictable world of nature a blizzard had generated more lightning than any other recorded storm of any kind in history.

Getting There

From the junction of Routes 9 and 8A in Windsor center take Route 9 east 1.0 mile. The entrance to the reservation is on the left. Follow the entrance road a short way to the parking area and visitor center on the left.

Windsor Jambs
Windsor

- **Jambs Trail**
- **2.1 miles round-trip**
- **265 ft. elevation gain**
- **2.0 hours**
- **easy with moderate sections**

At the western edge of the town of Windsor, the lofty
Berkshire Plateau ends in a steep escarpment that
abruptly plunges into the Pioneer Valley to the east. Following the declivity of the rock, the streams transform
themselves from tranquil brooks into raucous cascades.
Of these waterfalls perhaps the most spectacular rushes
through the ravine called Windsor Jambs (see below for
the origin of this interesting name).

Jambs Trail is entirely within Windsor State Forest, a
woodland preserve owned by the state of Massachusetts
and managed by the Department of Environmental
Management. Parking in the monitored lot costs $2. The
trail is blazed with blue triangles throughout its length,
with turns noted with arrows.

Look Forward To

- magnificent waterfalls
- boreal spruce forest
- red-squirrel pyramids

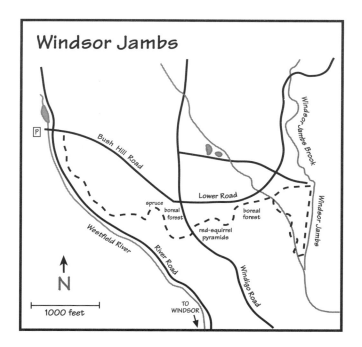

Windsor Jambs

Bush Hill Road

Lower Road

Windsor Jambs Brook

Windsor Jambs

spruce boreal forest

boreal forest

red-squirrel pyramids

Westfield River

River Road

Windigo Road

N

1000 feet

TO WINDSOR

The Trail

From the parking area on the west bank of the Westfield River, walk across the bridge and turn right into the campground. Proceed south to the comfort station, where the first blue blaze is on a large hemlock at the edge of the woods. From the trailhead the path wanders southeast over dry hummocks and sodden recesses. The higher ground is laced with tree roots, trillium, and wood fern while the wetter spots are host to jewelweed, bluebead lily, and wood sorrel. Trillium and bluebead lily blossom in May, while the shamrocklike wood sorrel displays its blush-pink flowers in late June. Jewelweed gets its name from the silver sheen the underside of the leaf reflects when held underwater.

After a brief walk beneath the tall red maple, hemlock, and yellow birch the trail crosses an intermittent stream on an old wooden bridge, then swings left (east). As the grade quickly steepens the hemlock and hardwoods yield to a dense **boreal forest** of Norway spruce. The path then crosses a stone wall and turns left (north) onto a mossy lane lined on both sides by an impenetrable partition of dark and stately conifers.

As beautiful as this forest is, it is not a natural one. In the lean years of the Great Depression, the Civilian Conservation Corps planted acres of Norway spruce plantations all across the Berkshires. The plantations grew into thick, exclusive forests that inadvertently robbed the area of its native biodiversity. If you're a red squirrel, living in this place is like winning the lottery, but not much else is here.

The trail turns right and soon crosses Windigo Road, a dirt track named for a creature you don't ever want to meet (see below). From the road the path dives again into the spruce forest. At the base of some of the trees you will notice large piles of dismembered spruce cones. These three-foot-tall pyramids are the creations of red squirrels. Red squirrels, or chickarees, are creatures of routine. When a squirrel finds a cone it brings it back to its tree, climbs up to its perch and begins to eat its cone. As it eats the seeds, it drops the cone scales. Over the years these little compost heaps can become impressively large.

An old corduroy bridge crosses a wet area where a **transitional forest** of red maple, balsam fir, and yellow birch grow above patches of bunchberry and partridgeberry. White-throated sparrows occasionally sing from the windfalls as juncos search the ground for tidbits. The trail then wanders back into the **spruce forest,** where a prairie of deep green moss reaches through the woods like a leprechaun's lawn.

At the edge of a small ravine the path descends steeply to the brook, which it crosses on stones. On the opposite bank the Jambs Trail forks; the Upper Jambs continues straight ahead (east) while the Lower Jambs turns right (south). Follow Upper Jambs as it climbs a rock-studded slope whose crest marks the height of land. Continue straight ahead to the fence where the **Windsor Jambs** begin.

The fence follows the edge of the gorge, offering countless opportunities to gaze down at the **boiling waterfalls** below. If you look at the rock that makes up the walls of the chasm you will see that the veins of the gray, fissile schist are almost upright. This alignment allows huge sheets to cleave cleanly from the wall, leaving a sharply vertical profile. To folks long ago the narrow ravine resembled a door jamb, hence the name Windsor Jambs.

Though the stone creates the frame of this masterpiece, it is the surging water that paints the picture. It races through the canyon like an animal in the frenzy of escape. And after a summer deluge or when spring drenches the mountains in meltwater, the frenzy becomes a foaming madness.

Maples overspread waterfalls at Windsor Jambs.

At the southern end of the fence the Lower Jambs Trail enters right and follows a tame rivulet north. As you walk upstream beneath the boughs of hemlock and birch, your feet pass the whorled leaves of Indian cucumber and the glossy leaves of bluebead lily. Hobblebush and mountain maple shade the wood sorrel as it dips its roots in the stream. If you are fortunate you will even find the pink moccasin of the lady-slipper blooming in early June. The path leads you back to the junction with Upper Jambs Trail. Here turn left (west) and return the way you came.

Mysteries of the Forest

Sooner or later it happens to everybody. On a lonely forest road the eye shine of an animal reflects eerily in the headlights. Then whatever it is turns away and melts into the darkness. Or on a walk in the woods the snap of a twig lets you catch a glimpse of a fleeting shadow moving through the emerald leaves. The taller the eyes, or the bigger the shadow, the more unnerving the experience. For whatever you saw, it saw you, too.

Imagination is a wonderful thing. It can turn a raccoon into a bear or a thirty-pound coyote into a sixty-pound wolf. Almost every sighting of scary animals in the woods is just a common creature seen from an uncommon perspective. Almost. Those few unexplainable events are investigated by people called cryptozoologists.

Cryptozoology, or the study of hidden animals, had its informal beginnings with Thomas Jefferson, who was convinced he had seen a new species of songbird in Virginia. The bird turned out to be a common towhee. From that inauspicious start cryptozoologists have tried to find everything from ivory-billed woodpeckers to Bigfoot to Champ, the creature of Lake Champlain. If all this seems removed from the Berkshires, it isn't. For we have the Thing and Windigo.

The Thing was first sighted in the late 1940s in the thick forests between Pittsfield and Peru. Those who saw it said it looked like a large, black mountain lion. For a while the Pittsfield black panther created quite a stir, but in the end no animal matching the description of the Thing was ever captured.

Black mountain lions are possible and in the early 1990s Vermont officially recognized that mountain lions were again part of the fauna of the Green Mountain State. That doesn't prove that the Thing exists, of course. It just makes it a bit harder to prove that it doesn't.

Perhaps the most frightening creature ever to walk the woods of the Berkshires was Windigo. The Algonquin Indians believed that certain places in the forest were inhabited by a large, hairy creature that walked upright like humans. But Windigo wasn't human. It lived in the moist woodlands of the Berkshire Plateau, and the sight of its huge footprints would frighten the bravest warrior.

Today the legend of Windigo lingers on in names like Windigo Road in Windsor. Whatever the circumstances behind the creation of stories like the Thing and Windigo, their future seems as phantasmic as they are. But the stories still appear. Even today, in the remote parts of northern Maine, Windigo is said to leave those frightening footprints beneath the balsam, its eyes reflecting red in the headlights of the trucks on lonely logging roads.

Getting There

From the junction of Routes 9 and 8A in Windsor, take Route 9 east 5.2 miles. Take a left and drive 0.2 mile to River Road. Take a left onto River Road and proceed 3.2 miles to the large paved parking area on the left opposite a campground.

Mt. Greylock Visitor Center
Lanesboro

- **Brook and Berry Trail, Cliff Loop Trail**
- **2.3-mile loop**
- **413 ft. elevation gain**
- **2.0–3.0 hours**
- **easy with some steep sections**

About thirty years ago the Mt. Greylock Visitor Center was built on the southern shoulder of Saddleball Ridge. It is perched on a narrow shelf of level land that is privy to an awe-inspiring view reaching the length of the Berkshires. From this beautiful overlook the Brook and Berry Trail and its companion, the Cliff Loop Trail, provide a varied walk through hardwood forests, open fields, and successional woodlands full of blueberries and azaleas. In addition the visitor center offers exhibits, nature programs, and a comfortable place to rest and enjoy the view.

The blue-blazed hiking trails are in the Mt. Greylock State Reservation, a preserve owned by the state of Massachusetts and maintained by the Department of Environmental Management (DEM). The state-owned visitor center is administered by DEM and managed by the Appalachian Mountain Club (AMC). AMC maintains its Berkshire offices at the center and in summer a naturalist is on staff to assist visitors.

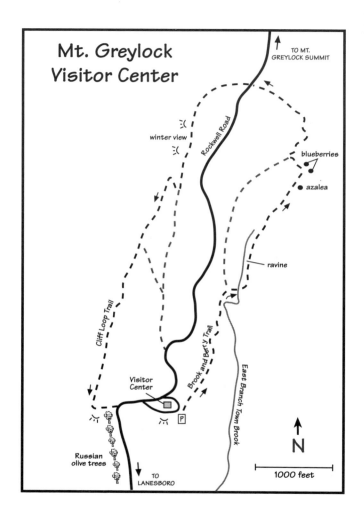

Mt. Greylock
Visitor Center

TO MT. GREYLOCK SUMMIT

Rockwell Road

winter view

blueberries

azalea

ravine

Cliff Loop Trail

Brook and Berry Trail

East Branch Town Brook

Visitor Center

Russian olive trees

TO LANESBORO

N

1000 feet

Look Forward To

- fantastic views
- blueberries and bluebirds
- birds, bugs, and flowers

The Trail

This walk begins and ends with **a magnificent view.** The visitor center and parking area are cradled between the bluffs of Savage Hill to the east and Constitution Hill and Potter Mountain to the west. The result is a dynamic southern vista that extends nearly to the Connecticut border. The silver sheen of Pontoosuc Lake sparkles in the foreground as the dual peaks of South and Lenox Mountains loom behind. Tom Ball Mountain in Great Barrington is just to the right (southwest) of Lenox Mountain. On clear days two sections of the southern Taconic Range are visible. Mt. Bushnell in South Egremont is just southwest of Tom Ball Mountain, and Mt. Everett, in faraway Sheffield, lies just southeast of South Mountain.

From the kiosk at the eastern end of the parking area the Brook and Berry Trail heads north along a stone boundary wall into a **mixed hardwood forest** of red oak, cherry, paper birch, and maple. A red-blazed snowmobile trail soon leaves left. The path ascends at a modest grade past trees whose trunks are pocked with the drillings of yellow-bellied sapsuckers. These large woodpeckers bore neat rows of holes into the inner bark of trees, lapping up the sap as it seeps from the wound.

After passing a large, weathered boulder and a ski trail that leaves left, the path bears right (northeast) and descends to the bank of Town Brook. This little rivulet has carved a small but picturesque ravine from the hillside. Graceful hemlock shade the stream as it flows effortlessly over the mossy rocks. From the brook the trail weaves past windfalls to the ridge, where it follows the edge of the ravine. Ancient oaks and ash blend into the dark green canopy of hemlock to create a mixed hemlock, hardwood forest. Beneath the tall trees striped maple grow that in turn shade carpets of princess pine and patches of Indian cucumber and starflower.

As the path continues northeast it enters an area of **overgrown fields,** abandoned to nature generations ago. A northern hardwood forest of beech, oak, and cherry rises above an open woodland dotted with blueberry and azalea. Gray catbirds perform their never-ending repertoire from the bushes with song sparrows and chickadees singing backup from the trees.

Soon a ski trail leaves left and the path crosses a section of ledgy ground where the thin soil supports rafts of spirea and raspberry accented with hawthorn, cherry, and oak. Deer are frequent visitors here, browsing on the new leaves of trees and bushes in summer and on acorns in fall. As the path swings to the west it enters a **dense thicket of maple** before crossing Rockwell Road at the trail's height of land about a mile north of the visitor center.

From the road Cliff Loop Trail descends through mixed hardwoods of ash, hop hornbeam, gray birch, and maple to the edge of a ridge where the buttress of the southern massif plunges into the valley. Turning south, the path wanders along the **breezy ridge crest** where in winter the leafless trees allow lovely views to the west.

The Mount Greylock Visitor Center is managed by the AMC.
(photo by Marny Ashburne)

At a double blaze a ski trail continues south while Cliff Loop Trail turns right (west), descending the steep slope along a narrow walkway of rock. At the base of the hill the path resumes its southerly course, crossing a stone wall and coming to another junction. From the intersection a shortcut leads left (southeast) to Rockwell Road while Cliff Loop turns right (southwest). Continue downhill on Cliff Loop Trail to a **wide, grassy field** with a windrow to the right and a south-facing view straight ahead.

There is an oceanlike beauty to a field of grass in summer. Waves of timothy and plantain roll toward windrow shores like swells about to break upon the beach. Meadowlarks and kestrels fly in place of terns and ospreys, and coyote leap through the grass like dolphins playing in the surf.

You could easily spend hours here poking for beetles and leafhoppers in the grass or admiring the flowers of hawkweed, meadowsweet, and daisy. As you meander east along the edge of the field there is a windrow of Russian olive trees to the south. In June these trees are covered with tiny yellow blossoms that radiate a wonderful fragrance well worth the short detour.

From the olive trees it is a short walk back to the visitor center, where snacks and cold drinks await inside.

The Ageless Daylily

Throughout the spring their long leaves grow until they form thick beds along the roadside. Then, about the time of the summer solstice, the first flowers appear high above the leaves. Each flower is a splash of sunset orange that in places has cooled to dusky cinnabar. It blossoms before the dawn is complete, and has withered before it comes again. No other flower combines intricate beauty with such fleeting transience, but no other flower is like the daylily.

The tawny daylily is not a native wildflower but is indigenous to eastern Asia, where it has been grown in the gardens of China and Japan for centuries. When trade routes between Europe and Asia were established, the daylily hitched along, entering Western gardens and literature in 1576. Some two centuries later the Swedish botanist Linnaeus officially recognized the tawny daylily as a unique species, giving it the name *Hemerocallis fulva*. When the Europeans began to colonize New England, the daylily again came along. It rapidly jumped the garden gate and has been a feature of the landscape ever since.

There is a mystery about the daylily, however. When Linnaeus described the tawny daylily he mentioned that it produced seed, but if you examine a patch of tawny daylily in late summer you will notice that not one of the flowers has set seed. What happened?

Sometime in the late 1500s a variety of tawny daylily was created that had an extra set of chromosomes. The triploid nature of the plant inhibited it from setting seed but gave it vigorous growth that allowed it to spread by sending up new shoots from older ones. This new variety was called Europa and quickly became more popular than the original species. The true tawny daylily faded from memory and the Europa variety has been mistakenly identified as the species for centuries.

Today in the Berkshires alone there are millions of Europa daylilies growing wild all over the county. That in itself is remarkable, but what is truly amazing is that all of those plants are genetically identical to the original one created more than four hundred years ago. The tawny daylilies of the Berkshires are living bits of history that have remained unchanged since the time of King Henry VIII.

Getting There

From Pittsfield take Route 7 north to the north end of Lanesboro. Just north of St. Luke's Church take a right onto North Main Street and follow signs to the visitor center.

Northern Region

The Northern Berkshire Hills

The northern Berkshire Hills is a region where the mountains crowd the valleys for room, and the towns squeeze into the narrow valleys. The Taconic Mountains form the western border of the region, their rocky spine separating Massachusetts from New York. Two walks take you along this windy ridge line.

The Hoosac Range rises in the eastern section of the region, where bear and moose are becoming commonplace. Two walks escort you through these wild woods.

In between the Taconics and the Hoosacs is the Mt. Greylock massif. The queen of the Berkshires is host to five walks, each a journey to a unique spot on this unforgettable mountain.

Between the highlands are charming valleys with fields and forests replete with animals and wildflowers. Four walks wander these lowlands, fields, and marshes, where the walking is often much easier than in the nearby hills.

Last, one walk explores that part of the Berkshires that is actually a bit of the Green Mountains nosing its way over the border. It takes you to a wonderful spot where the rest of the Berkshires lie spread before you in a long southern view.

Rounds' Rock

Cheshire and New Ashford

- **Rounds' Rock Trail**
- **1.1-mile loop**
- **157 ft. elevation gain**
- **0.75–1.0 hour**
- **easy**

On the south side of Mt. Greylock is a small plateau called Rounds' Rock, where unparalleled natural beauty mixes with a wonderfully mysterious past. A short, easy trail winds through fields of juicy blueberries and over ledges that offer spectacular views. In addition there are wildflowers, ferns, and the rusting remains of an airplane that crashed into the rock more than a half-century ago.

Rounds' Rock Trail is entirely in the Mt. Greylock State Reservation, a preserve of more than 10,000 acres owned by the state of Massachusetts and managed by the Department of Environmental Management. The trail is marked with blue blazes throughout its length.

Look Forward To

- spectacular views
- blueberries and more blueberries
- wildflowers and ferns

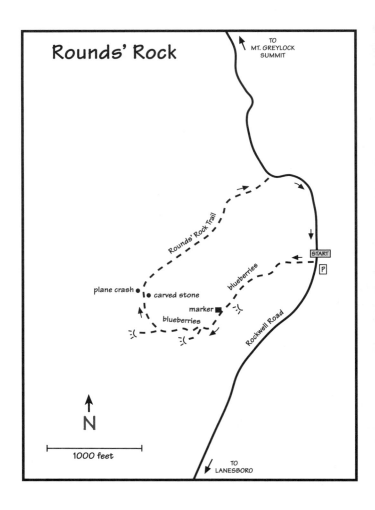

Rounds' Rock

TO
MT. GREYLOCK
SUMMIT

Rounds' Rock Trail

START
P

blueberries

plane crash ● ● carved stone

marker ■

blueberries

Rockwell Road

N

1000 feet

TO
LANESBORO

The Trail

From the parking area walk north along Rockwell Road to an exposed bedrock outcrop on the left. The trail begins near the rock and immediately climbs into a thick grove of gray-barked beech with patches of bluebead lily and princess pine growing beneath. A short way up the path the beech trees yield to a **transitional forest** of yellow birch, cherry, maple, and red spruce. These woods are particularly beautiful in autumn when the evergreen spruce provides a dark backdrop for the jumble of gold, crimson, and russet of the hardwoods.

After passing beneath a stand of red spruce where slate gray juncos and chickadees fly above clusters of goldthread and bunchberry, the trail leaves the large trees behind and enters an open area of scrub cherry and meadowsweet. Thorny canes of raspberry reach for you as you pass, while prickly vines of dewberry wind through the grass at your feet. Soon the briars are replaced by a thick **sea of blueberries** that grow between islands of cherry and mountain ash. The deep-blue fruit ripens in late July through August, and it is always pleasant to stop for a few minutes and enjoy one of nature's finest trailside nibbles.

From the blueberry field the path reenters the woods and descends to a level spot where a side trail leaves left to a limited view south. In summer the songs of hermit thrushes, warblers, and veeries float through the air. Deer often use the trail, sharing the woods with coyote, fox, and bobcats.

A little farther on a **gray stone pillar** stands just off the path. Erected in 1912, it marks the boundary of Cheshire (which you are leaving) and New Ashford

Lush acres of blueberries line the Rounds' Rock Trail in late summer.

(which you are entering). From the marker it is a short walk through oak, spruce, and mountain ash to a low stone cairn at the edge of Rounds' Rock's famous **blueberry barrens.**

Two hundred years ago this area was owned by Jabez Rounds, who cleared and cultivated much of the acreage around the rocky plateau that now bears his name. In 1915 the old farm was added to the Mt. Greylock Reservation. What were once fields and pastures are now forest and blueberry barrens.

The trail climbs through the berry bushes and crests a low hill where a side trail leads left to an **overlook** with a view that should not be missed. From the ledge the broad southern shoulder of Mt. Greylock forms a wooded shelf draped in the myriad textures of a hardwood forest. Far beyond the carpet of trees is Bear Mountain in northern Connecticut and the southern Taconics. To the right the majestic Catskills of New York fill the western horizon. On quiet days a group of ravens often come and perch on nearby ledges.

The main trail then wanders through more rocky blueberry patches and past lichen-covered maples to another side trail that leads to the **last overlook.** This ledge offers another fine view of the Catskills, visible in the notch just left of Jiminy Peak. Straight ahead lie the waters of Pontoosuc and Onota Lakes, with the southern Taconics far beyond.

A short walk brings you to the end of the blueberry fields and the beginning of a deep forest of yellow birch, maple, and cherry. Near the edge of the woods is a **gray slab of bedrock** with the date 12/7/48 chiseled into it. The carving is part of a story that began four months before, in the summer of 1948.

In the early evening of August 12, 1948, twenty-two-year-old John Newcomb rolled his plane down the runway of Bendix Field in New Jersey. Inside his twin-engine Cessna were bundles of the next day's edition of the *New York Daily Mirror.* It was John's job to fly the newspapers north so they could be sold in Albany the following morning. But the newspapers were never sold, for somewhere between northern New Jersey and upstate New York, Newcomb's airplane disappeared.

On December 7, 1948, three men were hunting on Rounds' Rock when they noticed the tops of some nearby trees had been snapped off. They followed the line of damage into the woods and quickly came upon the remains of a plane. The clock on the instrument panel had stopped at 7:19 and inside the broken aircraft were copies of the *New York Daily Mirror* dated August 13, 1948. Near the shattered wreckage lay the body of John Newcomb. As a memorial someone, perhaps one of the hunters, chiseled the date of that fateful day into the bedrock.

From the carved rock the path descends through the arching hardwoods to a level spot where a **rock cairn** topped by a worn wooden cross marks the place John Newcomb died a half-century ago. His plane, now a fragile assembly of broken wings and rusted bits of fuselage, is a few feet away. Wood and stone took his life that August night decades ago, and it is through wood and stone that he is remembered today.

From the crash site the path crests a small rise and then heads downhill into a moist glade of tall interrupted fern beneath ash and cherry. These regal-looking plants can grow nearly four feet tall and give the glen a distinctly Jurassic appearance. Interrupted fern got its name because halfway up each frond the series of green leaflets is interrupted by a few small spore-covered ones.

After a short walk the trail ends at Rockwell Road. Turn right (south) and follow the road back to the parking area. In summer look for the beautiful lavender flowers of the **large purple fringed orchid** that hide in the roadside grass. Each blossom looks like a miniature corsage and smells delightful.

Berkshire Blueberries

The hills of the Berkshires are home to two very different species of blueberry; the highbush and the lowbush. The highbush blueberry is the larger of the two, growing to well over six feet. It prefers moist, acid soils and is quite at home in wet fields or at the edge of a bog. Highbush blueberries don't usually grow in exclusive patches but are interspersed with such other plants as Labrador tea, leatherleaf, and sheep laurel.

In spring the branches are decorated with ivory-colored flowers that hang like tiny lanterns from the tips of the twigs. The dark-blue fruits ripen from July through August and harbor a sweet, tangy taste enjoyed by people and wildlife alike. In autumn the leaves turn from green to bright sunset red.

The first organized breeding program of highbush blueberries was started by the U.S. Department of Agriculture in 1906. Since then a host of varieties have been created and sold through garden centers.

The lowbush blueberry is a short plant, growing only one to two feet tall, and prefers the thin, rocky soils of abandoned pastures and hilltops. Once established in an area the lowbush blueberry spreads by sending out underground shoots called rhizomes that produce more plants. This method of reproduction quickly results in a thick carpet of plants that effectively chokes out most competitors. In parts of New England entire mountain-tops are virtually covered with blueberries.

Traditionally New England's lowbush blueberry fields have been called either blueberry barrens or blueberry pastures. *Barrens* because the land favored by blueberries is so poor that nothing else but blueberries can grow there. *Pastures* because blueberries easily colonized the compacted soils left after grazing land was abandoned.

The lowbush blueberry historically has been harvested as a wild crop, the fields being lightly burned every three years to thin the plants and increase berry production. During hard times the pastures and barrens were an important source of summertime food for rural people. It was the custom for the owner of the fields to let anyone pick as many berries as they wanted. In exchange the daily harvest was divided into thirds; one-third was given to the landowner and two-thirds to the pickers.

Blueberries are easily recognized because each berry is decorated with a crown of small spurs. These calyx lobes form a five-pointed star pattern at the base of each berry. As you browse the bushes remember to leave an ample supply of fruit for the birds and beasts; they have to eat, too.

Getting There

From the intersection of Routes 7 and 43 in South Williamstown, travel south on Route 7 for 9.6 miles to North Main Street in Lanesboro. Take a left onto North Main Street and follow the signs to the Mt. Greylock Visitor Center. From the visitor center drive 3.0 miles north on Rockwell Road to a small pull-off on the right.

From Lanesboro center travel north on Route 7 to North Main Street, just past the Old Stone Church. Turn right onto North Main Street and follow the signs to Mt. Greylock Visitor Center. From the visitor center drive 3.0 miles north on Rockwell Road to the pull-off on right.

Saddle Ball Mountain
New Ashford

- **Jones' Nose Trail, Appalachian Trail**
- **2.8 miles round-trip**
- **881 ft. elevation gain**
- **3.0–3.5 hours**
- **moderate with steep sections**

The backbone of Mt. Greylock is an undulating ridge called Saddle Ball Mountain. For two miles this narrow crest rolls southwest from the summit, its timbered crags filling the horizon like an evergreen serpent against the sky. It is a special place where 3,000-foot clouds still touch the ground and boreal groves of spruce and fir shelter gossamer gardens of wood sorrel and goldthread. In addition as you climb the mountain there are blueberries to nibble, flowers to smell, and views to enjoy.

The walk along the Jones' Nose Trail and a portion of the Appalachian Trail (AT) is entirely on the Mt. Greylock Reservation, a preserve owned by the state of Massachusetts and administered by the Department of Environmental Management. Jones' Nose Trail is marked with blue blazes and the AT is marked with white.

Look Forward To

- a walk through a boreal forest
- blueberries and wildflowers
- beautiful views

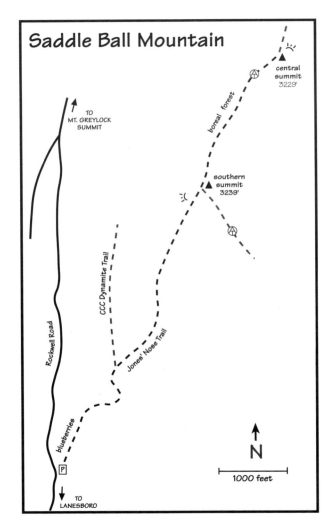

Saddle Ball Mountain

TO
MT. GREYLOCK
SUMMIT

central
summit
3229'

boreal forest

southern
summit
3239'

CCC Dynamite Trail

Jones' Nose Trail

Rockwell Road

blueberries

P

TO
LANESBORO

N

1000 feet

The Trail

From the parking lot off Rockwell Road head northeast into an **old field** overgrown with goldenrod, meadowsweet, and steeplebush. Both meadowsweet and steeplebush flower in August, but steeplebush sports a narrow cluster of pink blossoms while those of meadowsweet are white or very pale pink.

Nearby scattered stands of ash, aspen, and maple represent the vanguard of an ever-encroaching forest. The path then climbs to the top of a low rise where patches of **blueberries** mingle with yellow buttercups, rosy maiden pinks, and sweet goldenrod. From the knoll the trail passes through a small sag and continues through the open field toward the looming slope of Jones' Nose.

Jones was a farmer who tilled the land around Greylock many years ago. Apparently he was endowed with a proboscis whose profile matched the southern face of Saddle Ball Mountain, and over the years the ridge became known as Jones' Nose. Such is the price of immortality.

Soon you enter the woods and the grade steepens noticeably. In a few minutes it becomes clear that this is no ordinary nose. The climb is steep but in spring there are bluebead lilies, violets, and hobblebush in bloom. Summer brings pale touch-me-not and autumn's vibrant foliage colors of maple, birch, and ash. After traversing the slope the path crests a terrace where the CCC Dynamite Trail leaves left (north).

The treadway stays level for a brief while before tackling another steep section of the ridge. Outcrops of rock and boulders become more common, and soon the trail passes a wall of bedrock draped in a moist cloak of moss and polypody fern. Just beyond is a rocky clearing of wind-worn red spruce and yellow birch that is a nice rest spot.

From the clearing the path proceeds over rocks and exposed tree roots to a short side trail that leads to a **beautiful overlook.** The view extends from the Taconics in the south to the Catskills in the southwest to Jiminy Peak in the west. Raptors and ravens often glide overhead while bumblebees visit the goldenrod and aster flowers in summer.

From the overlook the trail continues uphill through rocky passages lined with balsam and birch to the AT junction at the 3,238-foot southern summit of Saddle Ball Mountain. Follow the AT left (north) into a **boreal forest** of balsam, spruce, and birch.

The boreal or northern forest is a broad belt of largely evergreen woodlands and bogs that wraps around the north temperate region of the world (see below). The climate is cool and moist, with short growing seasons and long winters. Many mornings the forest is cloaked in mist that wanders through the pathless wood like a ghost passing through a wall. In the afternoons the misty silence is replaced by a noisy wind that buffets the trees and mutes the songs of the hermit thrush and junco. The ground is spongy with sphagnum moss and decorated with assemblages of wood sorrel, goldthread, and bunchberry. Deer mice, voles, and red squirrels scamper along the forest floor and once in a while a bobcat passes by. It is often a harsh place to live, but that severity is also responsible for its simple beauty.

The path weaves through the woods, wandering along the western rim of the mountain. Starflower and club moss grow between the shallow roots of mountain

Red fruits of bunchberry in late summer atop Saddle Ball Mountain.

ash and red spruce, mountain maple and balsam fir. Soon you cross a small stream tinged brown with tannins the water has leached from the woods. The trail then climbs gently through rocky passages and muddy puddles to a **small crest with a view** that opens to the north and east.

This is the central summit of Saddle Ball, only ten feet lower than the one you passed nearly half a mile before. To the east are the Hoosac Mountains, while the war memorial tower and Bascom Lodge can be seen atop Mt. Greylock 2.2 miles to the northeast. If you can get a ride back down to the Jones' Nose parking area it is a pleasant walk from here to the summit of Mt. Greylock along the AT. Otherwise you can turn around and enjoy the easier return journey down the giant nose of farmer Jones.

Fir and Spruce

The days can be silent and deep. In winter the trees stand stiffly against the cold, backlit by a faraway sun. In summer the clouds sleep atop the mountains, draping the forest in organdy mist. Whenever you come, the boreal woods radiate an ambience of primeval magic, where the wildcats of Jack London stories coexist with the wizards and witches of fairy tales. Many types of trees make up the northern forest; two of the most dominant are the fir and the spruce.

The word *fir* is from a Scandinavian term that referred to the Scotch pine. Today it denotes a single-needle conifer with upright cones and needles that are attached directly to the stem. The only fir native to the Northeast is the balsam fir, a beautiful dark-green tree with a tight spire-shaped crown. Its aromatic needles give off a wonderfully pleasing scent when bruised.

Spruce trees are also single-needle conifers, but their cones hang down and the needles are attached to the stem on a woody pedicel. Both red and black spruce live in the Berkshires' boreal woods and they look remarkably alike. One way to tell them apart is that the cones of black spruce stay on the tree after the seeds have dispersed, while red spruce cones fall to the ground each year.

The word *spruce* comes from *pruce,* the term for a Prussian soldier. Prussians were known for their meticulous appearance and the neat, symmetrical habit of the spruce reminded people of the soldiers.

Both fir and spruce have evolved in similar ways to survive the harsh climate of the north woods. Their thick, resinous sap helps protect the trees from the cold of winter while a waxy cuticle covers the needles, protecting their precious reserve of moisture. The waxy covering allows the trees to keep their needles for many years, so as soon as the ground thaws the trees can begin photosynthesis instead of waiting for the new season's leaves to emerge.

The northern forest formed in the shadow of retreating glaciers and continues in the shade of the fir and spruce. Its beauty is subtle and simple: in the sound of the wind or the arrangement of wildflowers about the mossy rocks; in the song of the hermit thrush or the white-throated sparrow. It is easy to see the majesty of a distant mountain, but to appreciate the northern forest you must walk softly or the magic will pass you by.

Getting There

From the intersection of Routes 7 and 43 in South Williamstown travel south on Route 7 for 9.6 miles to North Main Street in Lanesboro. Turn left onto North Main Street and follow the signs to the Mt. Greylock Visitor Center. From the visitor center drive 3.75 miles up Rockwell Road to the parking area on the right.

From Lanesboro center drive north on Route 7 to North Main Street 0.1 mile north of St. Luke's Church. Turn right onto North Main Street and follow the signs to the Mt. Greylock Visitor Center. From the visitor center drive 3.75 miles up Rockwell Road to the parking area on the right.

Robinson's Point
Adams

- **Appalachian Trail, Robinson's Point Trail**
- **1.4 miles round-trip**
- **679 ft. elevation gain**
- **1.5–2.5 hours**
- **moderate**

Of all the places you can go in Massachusetts there is no place higher than the summit of Mt. Greylock. This walk takes you there, but with a twist. This time you start at the summit and hike to an isolated ledge high above the forested valley called the Hopper. Along the way there is the war memorial tower to explore as well as wildflowers and wild views. When you finish you can take your weary bones the short way to Bascom Lodge for a well-deserved rest and a relaxing snack.

This walk is entirely on the Mt. Greylock Reservation, which is owned by the state of Massachusetts and administered by the Department of Environmental Management. Bascom Lodge is owned by the state and operated by the Appalachian Mountain Club. The Appalachian Trail (AT) is a 2,000-mile-long National Scenic Trail administered by the Appalachian Trail Conference and maintained in Massachusetts by the Department of Environmental Management and the Appalachian Mountain Club. Both the AT and Robinson's Point Trail are plainly marked with white and blue blazes respectively.

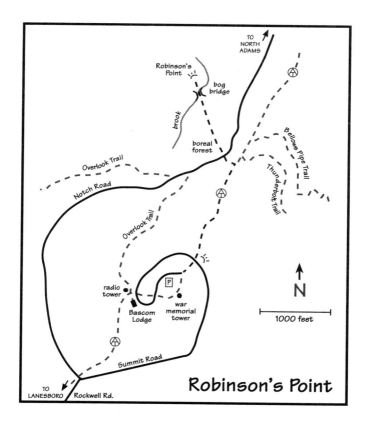

Look Forward To

- the war memorial tower and summit
- Bascom Lodge
- beautiful views and flowers

The Trail

From the summit parking lot walk east to the end of the parking area. Near the stone wall is a sign for the Appalachian Trail (right is south and left is north). Turn left and descend along a well-worn rocky path lined with balsam fir, meadowsweet, hobblebush, and steeplebush. If you are fortunate you will hear the sweet sound of the **white-throated sparrow,** a crystal clear *Old Tom PEAbody, PEAbody.*

White-throated sparrows are birds of the north country. Their plumage is dusky brown accented with muted streaks of black and gray. Their heads are crowned with black and white stripes, while a bright white bib covers their throats. You are most apt to see them in the winter when flocks fly down from Canada and visit backyard feeders. But it is in the summer mountains where their song transforms the day into something worth remembering.

The trail then crosses Summit Road and continues to descend. Straight ahead is the long profile of Ragged Mountain, with the Hoosac Range far beyond. The spreading branches of beech, mountain maple, and yellow birch create a leafy gallery along which mounds of meadow rue and turtlehead grow. The white flowers of turtlehead have a unique shape somewhere between that of foxglove and snapdragons. They blossom in August, while rue flowers bloom earlier in June and July.

Just after the path widens and passes an old campsite, the Robinson's Point Trail leaves left. Turn left (north) onto the blue-blazed path and enter a **rich woodland** of maple, beech, yellow birch, and balsam fir. In spring clumps of bluebead lily, wood sorrel, and

Turtlehead, one of the many wildflowers along the AT at Robinson's Point.

bunchberry bloom near the pock-marked trunks of trees visited by pileated woodpeckers.

At the intersection with Notch Road turn right and proceed down the road a few yards to where the Robinson's Point Trail again enters the woods left (northwest). The blue blazes lead you into a **thick boreal forest** of birch, balsam, and boulders. Rich mats of moss cling to the rocks and drip silver drops of water onto the leafy shamrocks of wood sorrel below.

Since beginning your walk you have been heading steadily downhill, but now the slope is briefly swallowed by the thick sphagnum moss of a **marshy bog.** The log bridge that crosses it is slowly becoming part of the bog, with tentacles of moss draping the decomposing wood. From the bog the trail crosses a small stream where the delicate sound of the water is often accompanied by chirping chickadees in the nearby trees. One last descent brings you to a rocky promontory high above a magnificent valley.

This is the place called **Robinson's Point.** In 1898 Mt. Greylock became the first state-owned wilderness park in Massachusetts. The park was administered by the Greylock Commission, whose membership included a man named Arthur Robinson. The overlook was named to honor his work.

Robinson's Point is a wonderfully comfortable spot that looks as if it had been carefully chiseled out of the cliff. The result is a rocky niche with steep, forested slopes behind and an **exquisite panorama** below. The huge bowl-like valley is called the Hopper because its shape resembles the hoppers used by farmers to store corn and grain. To the left is Stony Ledge, while to the right the long shoulder of Mt. Prospect looms two miles away. The farms of South Williamstown are visible through the mouth of the ravine while off in the distance lie the northern Taconics, with the summit of Berlin Mountain rising slightly higher than the adjoining ridge.

The view is striking all year long but is especially so on clear Indian-summer days. Then the frost has turned the mountains and fields into an ephemeral mosaic of cheerful color and the impending winter seems forever lost in the sapphire sky.

From Robinson's Point follow the path back to the Appalachian Trail, which leads to the top of Mt. Greylock where the war memorial tower and Bascom Lodge await (see below).

For more than 200 years people have tried to "improve" the summit of Greylock. Over that time there have been four towers on the mountain.

In 1830 a group from Williams College chopped down enough trees to construct a twelve-foot-tall building and briefly used it as an observatory. It was not maintained, however, and in less than ten years had rotted away. In 1841 another group from Williams tried again, this time constructing an observatory about thirty feet high. This tower lasted more than twenty years but vandals and neglect finally destroyed it. By 1866 the summit was devoid of trees and towers.

In 1885, with the montane forest a distant memory, a forty-foot iron tower was built by the Greylock Park Association, a group formed to conserve and protect the mountain. It cost ten cents to climb the tower and admire the view.

In 1931 the old iron tower was torn down and the present war memorial tower built. Originally a lighthouse designed to shine its light onto the Atlantic, the 100-foot granite structure was erected instead atop the Berkshire mountain, its beacon shining in memory of those from Massachusetts who died in war.

"The Dazzling Halls of Aurora"

On a summer morning in 1844 Henry David Thoreau was asleep in the wooden tower at the summit of Mt. Greylock. Emerson and Hawthorne had told him of the mountain, and now he had come to see it for himself. It was nearly dark when he crested the ridge and finally walked upon the highest land in the Berkshires. The summit was bare and cluttered with the ragged stumps that once had been a boreal forest of spruce and fir. He made a fire and fell asleep, never guessing what awaited him in the morning.

Overnight the clouds had settled over the valleys and mountains in such a way that just the tower poked above the mist and into the clear sky. When he awoke Thoreau found himself in a surreal world of sculpted vapor with no hint of earth beneath. "I found myself in the dazzling halls of Aurora," he wrote. "Drifting amid the saffron-colored clouds, and playing with the rosy fingers of the Dawn, in the very path of the Sun's chariot..." He watched in amazement as the early morning light danced on the sea of clouds, and he compared the world of mist and sky before him with the peaceful beauty of heaven. Later that day he descended Greylock, walking through the clouds that still embraced the mountain and thinking that someday, "I might hope to climb to heaven again."

Some things have no need for improvement.

Getting There

From the intersection of Routes 2 and 8 in North Adams follow Route 2 west 1.1 miles to Notch Road and turn left. At the reservoir make a hard left and continue to the gate at Mt. Greylock Reservation. Follow the road to the summit.

From Route 7 turn onto North Main Street just north of Lanesboro center (signs). Follow North Main Street/ Rockwell Road to the Mt. Greylock Visitor Center. From the visitor center follow Rockwell Road to the summit.

Money Brook and
Mt. Prospect
North Adams and Williamstown

- **Appalachian Trail; Money Brook Trail;
  Mt. Prospect Trail**
- **5.0-mile loop**
- **1,190 ft. elevation gain**
- **4.0–5.0 hours**
- **difficult**

This walk passes through some of the most beautiful country in the northern region, but it is also the toughest hike. There are waterfalls, deep spruce forests, rushing brooks, and a mountain that makes you work for every gorgeous view. This is a hike where most people will want to take their time, so pick a nice day, leave early, and relax at every overlook.

The trails are entirely on the Mt. Greylock Reservation, a preserve of more than 10,000 acres owned by the state of Massachusetts and administered by the Department of Environmental Management. The Appalachian Trail is marked with white blazes while the Money Brook and Mt. Prospect Trails use blue. All paths are well maintained.

Look Forward To

- waterfalls and brooks
- mountaintop views
- wildflowers and gliders

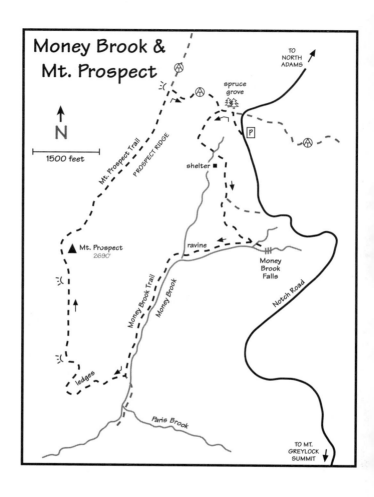

Money Brook &
Mt. Prospect

N

1500 feet

TO NORTH ADAMS

spruce grove

P

Mt. Prospect Trail

PROSPECT RIDGE

shelter

Mt. Prospect
2690'

ravine

Money Brook Trail

Money Brook

Money Brook Falls

Notch Road

ledges

Paris Brook

TO MT. GREYLOCK SUMMIT

The Trail

The trail begins on Notch Road opposite the parking area. The blue-blazed path immediately enters a **transitional forest** of tall red spruce, yellow birch, and maple. In spring the ground is peppered with the blossoms of goldthread, trillium, Canada mayflower, and bluebead lily. Beneath the understory of striped maple are patches of princess pine and Christmas fern whose dark green leaves lend a sense of coolness to the already shady woods.

At the junction with the Appalachian Trail turn left (west) into a majestic grove of **towering red spruce.** Log walkways lead you through corridors of evergreen undergrowth beneath the rugged canopy of 130-year-old trees. It is an enchanting place whose peacefulness is reinforced by the soft calls of chickadees and juncos.

The Money Brook Trail then leaves left (southwest), while the AT continues northwest. Turn left onto Money Brook Trail and begin a gradual descent, crossing a shallow stream on a log bridge and passing a red-blazed side trail that leads to an overnight shelter. The cool spruce yield abruptly to a **hardwood forest** of beech, birch, and maple. Clusters of shrubby hobblebush flower in early June, their fragrant white blossoms brightening springtime afternoons.

Soon after passing a side trail that leads to Notch Road the path winds down the steep hillside to a small stream. From here it is a short walk across the brook to the base of **Money Brook Falls.** Clusters of boulders lead the eye to a staired cliff high above. In spring the cascades are dressed in whitewater lace while in summer transparent rivulets of water pour over the dark rock,

*Money Brook
Falls.*

breaking into glimmering beads as they fall onto the stones below.

From the falls return to the small stream and turn left at the junction. The trail proceeds downhill following the course of Money Brook, which flows noisily about a hundred feet below. It is a gentle walk along the path, softened still further by bird songs drifting down from the trees. Sometimes barred owls call from the deeper ravines, their characteristic *who, who, who-who* echoing down the valley. It can sound a bit spooky on a gloomy day, almost as unnerving as the legend of the **ghosts that haunt the valley.**

After the Revolution the country was broke and its currency nearly worthless. To supplement their income a few folks tried their hand at counterfeiting. Small groups would set up shop in caves or other hideaways and hammer out coins. One band supposedly operated out of Money Brook ravine, hence the name of the stream. In some accounts the men were caught and hanged, in others they just clean got away. Whatever happened, the woods near the brook were once thought to be haunted by the ghosts of these counterfeiters. I've never seen them, but then, who knows?

The path comes to a hemlock grove at the lip of a wooded ravine, then descends to a small brook. After crossing the stream and climbing up the opposite side of the gorge the grade moderates and the walking becomes easy again. Black birch, beech, and yellow birch shade an understory of hop hornbeam and striped maple. Among the rocks below grow strands of partridgeberry and shrubby colonies of azalea and hobblebush.

After a long walk along the ridge, Money Brook Trail swings left (southeast) and Mt. Prospect Trail leaves straight ahead (west). Until now the hike has been an easy one, but in the next mile you will climb more than a thousand feet up the steepest trail anywhere on Mt. Greylock. This a good place to munch a light snack and have something to drink.

Turn onto Mt. Prospect Trail, which immediately tackles the mountain's southeast buttress. In spring Canada mayflower and starflower blossom and the talon-shaped fiddleheads of pasture brake appear. At the standing skeleton of a huge sugar maple the path turns northeast into a ragged boulder field accented with ledges of bedrock. A short scramble brings you to a rocky promontory where blueberries grow beneath stunted oak. The **view from the rocks** is gorgeous.

To the east is Mt. Fitch, while the radio tower atop Mt. Greylock is visible to the southeast. Between the two is the Hopper, the vast valley that forms Mt. Greylock's western flank. About midway up the Hopper you can see large groves of red spruce. These stands are rare **old-growth forest** nearly two centuries old. In 1987 the groves were designated a National Natural Landmark.

From the overlook the path climbs very steeply up the narrow ridge of Mt. Prospect's southern shoulder. Wild azalea, blueberries, lady-slipper, and trillium are some of the plants you pass here. As the summit edges closer another vista opens up to the left (west). From the clearing the neat farm fields of the Green River valley spread out like a country quilt, while the Taconic Range looms in the western horizon.

The rough trail continues up the mountain, passing through a brief level area before climbing the short way to the summit marked with a rock cairn beneath wind-pruned oaks. There is no view here but at least it's the top.

Mt. Prospect has shown you its worst at this point, and from here the walk is gentle as well as beautiful. The path meanders along the windy ridge, where a forest of red maple, beech, and yellow birch oversee natural gardens of wood sorrel, raspberry, goldthread, and bunchberry. At times the woods seem to have a fairy-tale enchantment about them while at other times they just feel wild, as windy places ought to be.

View from one of the many overlooks along the Mount Prospect Trail.

After a long walk the trail comes to the junction with the Appalachian Trail and what some have described as **the most breathtaking vista on all of Greylock.** From the west-facing ledge the pastoral valleys of the Green and Hoosic Rivers unfold below. In summer the sharp outlines of the rectangular fields are softened by rows of corn that sweep along unseen contours. To the west is the Taconic Range while to the northwest the Green Mountains of Vermont rise in the distance. In fall and spring this is a great place to watch migrating hawks glide by. Sometimes it is also a good vantage point to observe gliders. They usually sweep back and forth over the ridge just a hundred feet overhead. If you wave the pilots will wave back.

From the overlook take the Appalachian Trail south through the spruce forest. You will pass the turnoff to Money Brook Trail and shortly thereafter come to the connector trail (right) leading to the parking lot on Notch Road.

Silenced Voices

In the summer of 1972 a slender gray-colored bird returned to the thick balsam fir of Mt. Greylock's boreal woods. In the perpetual cool of the evergreens its soft, reedy song drifted through the trees as delicately as mist rising off the water. The ethereal tone of its melody was as prophetic as it was beautiful, for that single bird was the only one of its kind heard on the mountain all year. When it vanished on the autumn winds its song disappeared with it, and has never returned.

Bicknell's thrush was for years classed as a race of the gray-cheeked thrush. For generations the only place the birds bred in Massachusetts was Mt. Greylock, and even there they were not numerous. In the early 1960s about eleven pairs nested in the spruce and fir forest of the mountain. In 1967 the census was down to five pairs. By 1973 the birds were gone.

Bicknell's thrush winters in the lowland evergreen forests of the Dominican Republic and Haiti. In recent decades deforestation has nearly destroyed the forests of both countries. Many species of birds have traded the evergreen forest for plantations of coffee and cacao, but Bicknell's thrush has not. As the forest disappears, so do the birds.

When the few surviving thrushes migrate north they face more adversity in the form of radio and microwave towers. Many migrant songbirds are attracted to the lights and collide with the towers. In one night 20,000 birds died when they flew into a television tower in Wisconsin.

The birds' breeding grounds may have changed, too. The boreal forest of Greylock is much reduced from what it once was, but even where it is plentiful there might be too much human activity for the birds to successfully breed.

The loss of Bicknell's thrush is sadly unique because for years it has been an evolutionary work in progress. Categorized as a race of gray-cheeked thrush, its song was nonetheless a little different and the two birds did not look alike. In the summer of 1996 Bicknell's thrush was recognized officially as a separate species and given the scientific name *Catharus bicknelli.* It was also the twenty-third consecutive year that its song was absent from the balsam forests of Greylock.

Getting There

From the junction of Routes 2 and 8 in North Adams take Route 2 west 1.1 miles to Notch Road. Take a left onto Notch Road and drive about 3.0 miles to the gate at Mt. Greylock Reservation. From the gate continue up Notch Road 2.25 miles to a parking lot on left, or 0.1 mile beyond the point where the Appalachian Trail crosses Notch Road.

Ragged Mountain
Adams

- **Thunderbolt Ski Trail, Bellows Pipe Trail, Ragged Mountain Trail**
- **3.0 miles round-trip**
- **1,426 ft. elevation gain**
- **4.0–5.0 hours**
- **difficult**

Until a few years ago the windy crest of Ragged Mountain was a rarely visited place. No trail led to its summit, and if people noticed it at all, it was as the little mountain next to Mt. Greylock. The new hiking trail is still lightly used, but those who do climb the little mountain are dazzled by the view. It is a wonderful place to watch for ravens, listen to the wind, and read a little Poe.

The hike up Ragged Mountain passes through areas of Mt. Greylock Reservation, a 10,000-acre preserve owned by the state of Massachusetts and administered by the Department of Environmental Management. The Thunderbolt Ski Trail is marked with blue blazes. The Bellows Pipe and Ragged Mountain Trails are unblazed but easy to follow.

Look Forward To

- unique summit views
- the Bellows Pipe, Hawthorne, and Thoreau
- ravens, hawks, and blueberries

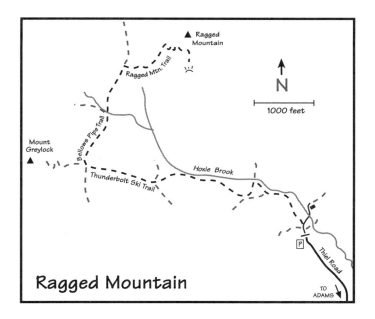

Ragged Mountain

The Trail

From the parking area on Thiel Road walk north along the road. The trailhead is just south of the spot where the Hoxie Brook passes beneath the road. There are no signs or blazes here, but the treadway quickly leads from the field into the woods and follows the south bank of the stream. A few yards along the brook you will see the first blue blaze on a tree.

The trail proceeds through a **northern hardwood forest** of beech and maple with clumps of dark green Christmas fern and sprigs of Indian cucumber scattered across the forest floor. A few hemlocks mix in with the hardwoods a few yards upstream, and in the spring the low-growing Canada mayflower blossoms, each plant a tiny bouquet of clustered white flowers with a fragrance like lily-of-the-valley.

The path then joins a wide woods road that climbs to a junction where an unmarked path leaves left (southwest) and the Thunderbolt Trail swings right. The succulent green leaves of pale jewelweed line the drainage areas while false Solomon's seal grows in the drier spots. At the brook the trail turns hard left (south), away from the water, and climbs moderately through an open woodland of birches to a high west-running ridge. **Many interesting flowers** grow along the ridge including bluebead lily, herb Robert, and helleborine. Herb Robert is a wild geranium with small, pink flowers and aromatic leaves while helleborine is a small orchid that displays a cluster of pale-plum blossoms in summer.

The trail continues west along the edge of the ravine, the noisy Hoxie Brook tumbling over the rocks far below. Soon an unmarked trail crosses near a granite post. From here to the Bellows Pipe junction the Thunderbolt climbs very steeply up the flank of Mt. Greylock.

The Thunderbolt is not an easy trail to hike and an even more difficult one to ski. Constructed by the Civilian Conservation Corps in the early 1930s, it drops more than 2,000 feet from start to finish. Its heart-stopping descent led to the trail being named the Thunderbolt, after the roller coaster at Revere Beach outside Boston.

In a small level area the Bellows Pipe Trail crosses running north-south. Turn right (north) onto Bellows Pipe, which is refreshingly level and easy. After crossing a small stream and passing through a switchback the

Helleborine, one of the wildflowers along the Thunderbolt Trail.

footway briefly follows a small drainage before traversing a high, breezy ridge. At an intermittent stream the trail branches; the left fork (north) leads uphill to the Appalachian Trail while the right fork (northeast) continues along the level ridge. Keep right and enjoy a pleasing stroll through the hardwoods.

The notch between the crests of Mt. Greylock and Ragged Mountain is called the **Bellows Pipe** in reference to the strong winds that sometimes blow through the valley. The contrasting beauty of hilltop and lowland, forest and sky has drawn thousands to this place, including **Nathaniel Hawthorne** and **Henry David Thoreau.** Where you walk, so have they.

Immediately beyond a stone wall the Ragged Mountain Trail leaves right (east). The path weaves through stands of Norway spruce and red pine, following the wall to a level area at the base of the mountain. The trail now ascends through woods of maple, yellow birch, and ash with an understory of hop hornbeam and striped maple. In spring goldthread and hepatica blossom on the hill, while thrushes sing on dew-drenched summer mornings.

Higher up the mountain the path snakes between **ledges of shiny mica schist** where starflower and trillium grow in the rocky hollows. A short walk brings you to the summit, a rugged bedrock shelf dotted with blueberry, oak, red spruce, and mountain ash. From the rocks you can see the Hoosic River valley as it wanders through Adams and Cheshire to the south. To the west the horizon is dominated by the massive east buttress of Mt. Greylock that rises nearly a thousand feet overhead. From this vantage point the war memorial tower crowning the summit is clearly visible, as is the large scar left on the mountain's flank by a recent landslide. To some this rocky wound is said to resemble the Virgin Mary, while others see the profile of Chief Greylock, a leader of the Waranoak Indians.

In summer you can relax on the sunny rocks, admire the view, and nibble on blueberries. The wind sometimes brings gliding hawks near the ledges, and ravens can often be heard chatting from nearby rocks. On the east side of Ragged Mountain is a place called **Raven Rocks** where the birds often nest (see below).

The return trip retraces your steps back to the parking area on Thiel Road.

"Quoth the Raven..."

In 1845 Edgar Allan Poe began to write a poem in which a mysterious bird was to be an omen of untimely death. Poe tried many birds, but eagles and crows did not convey the fear and dismay he desired. The raven, however, fit the role perfectly, and the image of the black bird perched above the chamber door became an intricate part of one of the most-recognized poems in American literature.

The raven's reputation as a harbinger of misfortune is centuries old. It foretold the death of the great orator Cicero, and Shakespeare used its hoarse croaking as a warning of danger in Macbeth. For generations its dark reputation was so ingrained that people persecuted the bird across much of its range. In many areas, including New England, the raven virtually disappeared. In recent years, however, the great black bird has returned to soar again over the ridges of the Berkshires and perch upon the rocks.

The common raven is a large bird, reaching twenty-seven inches in length and a wingspan of nearly three feet. Its plumage is jet black and, like its cousin the crow, the raven is very intelligent. Ravens were once observed stealing bait from ice fishermen by pulling up the fishing line and running back with it over the ice. When the bait popped out of the water they flew in and ate it.

Ravens nest in isolated crags of rock high up the sides of cliffs or mountains. There they build a stick nest and in late winter lay five to seven green eggs speckled with dots of brown. Three weeks later the young birds hatch. If left undisturbed a pair of ravens will return to the same nest for many years.

A raven's vocalizations range from raspy, primal croaks to a hauntingly human laugh. When you hear it as you sit atop some isolated ledge, it is easy for the sound's linguistic timbre to send a chill up your spine. But then that is why a raven sits upon the bust of Pallas above the chamber door. And why the bird's reply still lingers ever after.

"Quoth the raven..."

Getting There

From the traffic light on Route 8 in Cheshire continue north 1.9 miles to the intersection with Fred Mason Road. Turn left onto Fred Mason Road and drive 3.0 miles to Gould Road. Turn left onto Gould Road, bear right at the fork and continue to a parking area at the gate.

From the intersection of Routes 2 and 8 in North Adams follow Route 8 south about 3.5 miles to Friend Street. Turn right on Friend Street and continue about 1.5 miles to Gould Road. Take a right onto Gould Road, bear right at the fork, and continue to the parking lot near the gate.

Reflection Pond

Adams

- **Reflection Pond Trail**
- **1.0-mile loop**
- **30 ft. elevation gain**
- **0.5–1.0 hour**
- **easy**

A pond is a wonderful place to go and observe the nexus of water and land, and in the Berkshires there are scores of ponds and lakes to choose from. Reflection Pond, however, is different from any other you may visit, for its waters are literally crystal clear. But the pond is only one of the beautiful things waiting for you on this trail. There are marshes full of birds, flowers, and animals; beautiful views of nearby Mt. Greylock; and even a place to picnic and swim.

Reflection Pond Trail is on Greylock Glen, a protected area of land on the east slopes of Mt. Greylock. The trail is maintained by the Appalachian Mountain Club.

Look Forward To

- birds and wildflowers
- marshes and views
- Reflection Pond

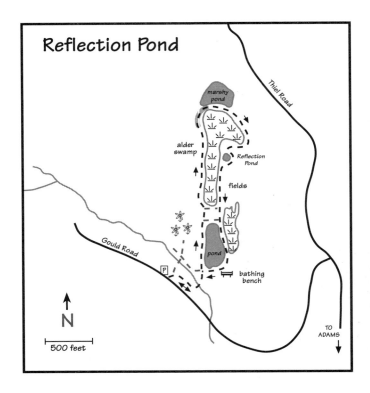

The Trail

From the trailhead on Gould Road head east into an **overgrown field** where isolated specimens of Scotch pine, poplar, and ash ride above a sea of Queen Anne's lace, goldenrod, and milkweed. Butterflies and bumblebees methodically visit the flowers while chimney swifts and swallows do acrobatics in the sky. High above, turkey vultures and ravens glide on the wind and every so often a ruby-throated hummingbird zips by.

The trail swings right and descends to the brook, which it crosses on a small bridge. At the intersection with a cart path that runs east to west, continue straight (north) along the west **shore of the pond.** The fields here are home to many fascinating plants including bird's-foot trefoil, common tansy, and yarrow. Bird's-foot trefoil is a bright yellow summer flower that in form resembles flowering pea. It is native to Europe but has naturalized throughout the Northeast. Yarrow sports a flat-topped cluster of small white flowers and very finely divided fernlike leaves. The foliage is pleasantly aromatic when bruised. Its Latin name, *Achillea*, comes from the tradition that Achilles used the herb to heal his wounded soldiers at the battle of Troy.

At the north end of the pond a bypass trail leads right (east) while the main trail follows a neatly mown lane straight (north). Thick bushes of willow and dogwood seem nearly swamped by waves of goldenrod interspersed with boneset and black-eyed Susan. A second bypass trail leaves right as you begin to walk along the shore of a **long marsh.**

The marsh was once, years ago, a beaver pond whose water drowned the ash, paper birch, and elm whose driftwood-gray skeletons still loom over the cattails. Flycatchers perch high in the branches of the dead trees, occasionally swooping through the air to catch an insect snack.

The trail continues along the edge of the marsh, where the chiffon pink flowers of joe-pye weed grow up to your eyebrows. Two short side trails (right) lead you into the marsh, ending in areas that afford views into the wet world of the **woodland swamp.** Dense thickets of alder and meadowsweet grow along the shore while sedges occupy the shallows. Dragonflies patrol the air like tiny fighter planes as grackles and flycatchers watch from the trees. In spring the air is alive with the calls of wood frogs and peepers; summer features the more sedate croaks of green frogs.

The neatly mown trail leads through an alder thicket and across a **bog bridge** constructed of plastic wood, an environmentally friendly alternative to pressure-treated wood. Waste plastic is recycled and shaped into timbers that are used to build footways across fragile habitats. No harmful chemicals leach into the marsh and the bridges last for decades, which means the swamp remains undisturbed.

The bog bridge ends along the shore of a **marshy pond** crowded with tangles of alder and willow, cattail and giant reed. The dense stands of reed and cattail filter the murky water, removing many pollutants from the swamp. You will often see great blue heron stalking fish on the far shore as well as groups of mallard and black ducks paddling through the maze of flooded windfalls. Bullfrogs lazily croak from protected niches and painted turtles sun themselves on half-submerged logs.

The trail passes between the marshes along a low earthen dike, then swings right (south) through overgrown fields bounded by forest and wet meadow. A short walk brings you to the edge of a spring-fed pool called **Reflection Pond.** The first thing you notice about this beautiful oasis is the water; it is absolutely crystal clear. Large pillows of skunkweed cover the bottom,

White birches and upended trees mark the marshes of Reflection Pond.

blossoming up from the depths like dark cumulus clouds in a summer sky. Skunkweed likes to grow in alkaline conditions, which gives a hint at the underlying geology of the pond.

Deep underground are mantels of limestone and glacial lake deposits. As the ground water percolates toward the surface it passes through these layers, which filter the water and add minerals that increase the water's alkalinity. The result is the magically vitreous Reflection Pond.

The trail continues through thickets of willow into a grove of paper birch and red maple. Canada mayflower and wintergreen huddle at the base of the trees while warblers and orioles flit among the leaves overhead. From time to time beaver wander through, and in summer the drone of red-eyed cicadas resounds from the treetops.

From the woods the path again enters open country and passes the two bypass trails (right). Scores of plants grow in waist-high waves around you. Dogwood, willow, and boneset mingle with cattails, reed, sedges, and blue vervain. Belted kingfishers patrol the nearby waterways for minnows, and swallows and flycatchers sweep through the sky overhead.

The overgrown field narrows into a slender corridor bounded by alder and willow that wanders between the marsh and swimming pond. The trail then crosses a bridge near the small **bathing beach** before swinging west across a closely cropped lawn. At the edge of the grass the path turns left (south) and heads back to the parking area.

Lake Bascom

Fourteen thousand years ago the massive continental ice sheet that covered New England had ground to a halt just off the coast. In a little over a millennium the warming climate had so thinned the glacier that the mountains reemerged, and the landscape became an ever-changing composite of advancing highland above the sinuous tongues of ice-filled valleys.

The dying valley glaciers did not surrender gracefully, but violently, calving massive blocks of ice into the perennial flood of their outwash rivers. Many times the combination of icebergs and alluvial till formed gigantic dams that held back miles of meltwater and created the immense ancient lakes of the late Pleistocene epoch.

Lake Hitchcock filled the Connecticut River valley from Hartford to northern Vermont, while Lake Albany flooded the Hudson valley from Staten Island to Troy. In the Berkshires an alluvial dam formed near Pownal, Vermont, and inundated the Hoosic valley with the frigid meltwater known as Lake Bascom.

For thousands of years Mt. Greylock was nearly surrounded by water, the giant massif becoming a picturesque peninsula rising thousands of feet above the lake. And what are now South Williamstown, Adams, Cheshire, North Adams, Pownal, and Williamstown were underwater.

Many of the great Pleistocene lakes drained away some eight thousand years ago and the dam near Pownal probably failed at about the same time. The marshes around Reflection Pond lie atop the gravel beaches and silty lagoons of that ancient lake, the thick deposits of sand and rock flour providing the matrix that makes the waters of the spring so crystal clear.

The warm summer breeze that gently bends the flowers in the fields tells no tale of vanished glaciers and massive lakes. The only signs that remain are hidden in the landscape; the soft shape of an ancient shoreline upon the mountain, and the whisper of the water that fills a crystal pond. The Berkshires have changed immensely over time, and knowledge of that history makes them more beautiful still.

Getting There

From the traffic light on Route 8 in Cheshire continue north 1.9 miles to Fred Mason Road. Turn left onto Fred Mason Road and drive 3.0 miles to Gould Road. Take a left onto Gould Road, bear left at the fork, and continue about 0.5 mile to a parking area on the right.

From the north take Route 8 south from the junction of Routes 8 and 9 in North Adams. Drive about 3.5 miles south on Route 8 to Friend Street. Take a right onto Friend Street and continue about 1.5 miles to Gould Road. Take a right onto Gould Road, bear left at the fork, and continue about 0.5 mile to a parking lot on the right.

Field Farm
Williamstown

- **North Trail, Oak Loop Trail, Caves Trail, Pond Trail**
- **2.4-mile loop**
- **100 ft. elevation gain**
- **2.0–2.5 hours**
- **easy**

The Trustees of Reservations (TOR) is a Massachusetts-based conservation organization with some outstanding properties throughout the Berkshires. Some of them, such as Monument Mountain and Tyringham Cobble, have abundant natural beauty. Others such as the Mission House and the Ashley House, are historic treasures. Field Farm, however, is in a class by itself, for it literally has some of everything.

On this 296-acre estate you will find miles of hiking trails that bring you to ponds, forests, pastures, and marshland. Wildflowers and wildlife are plentiful and there are even streams that disappear into limestone caves. The main house is architecturally beautiful and is also a charming bed-and-breakfast, with flower gardens and sculptures decorating the grounds.

Field Farm is owned and maintained by the TOR. The trails are marked with square yellow blazes throughout the property and all junctions are signed, although the cows do knock over a signpost now and again.

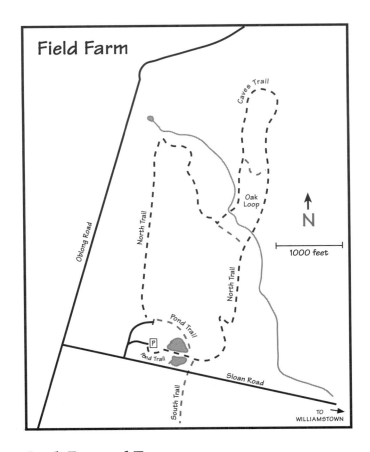

Look Forward To

- disappearing streams
- plentiful wildlife, flowers, and cows
- beautiful views

The Trail

From the trail's parking area near the maintenance garage walk along the driveway to the **Guest House.** The house was built by Lawrence and Eleanore Bloedel in 1948 in the American Modern style. Inside are artworks by Wolf Kahn, while the sculptures of Richard McDermott Miller are displayed on the lawn amid the roses, daylilies, and hummingbirds. Tours of the house are given from 8:00 A.M. to sunset. Just ring the doorbell and ask for the innkeeper.

To get to North Trail walk west across the lawn to the trail sign. The path proceeds north through a field where in summer the yellow flowers of St. Johnswort, goldenrod, and black-eyed Susan mingle with blue chicory and antique-white Queen Anne's lace. As you walk along a windrow of maple draped with hanging vines of fox grape and bittersweet, there is an **enchanting view** to the right (east) of Mt. Greylock.

Thousands of years ago as the last glaciers were melting, their outwash streams were dammed briefly by an immense jam of ice and alluvial till. The water backed up to form an immense body of water called Lake Bascom. The flat fields you are walking on were once a terrace of the lake whose waves lapped a shoreline far up the slopes of Greylock. At that time the mountain would have appeared as an island in an inland sea.

At the northeast end of the field you pass through a stile and enter a **cow pasture.** The footing can be slippery here, due to the moist ground and to the cows' contribution to the moist ground. Somewhere on your journey you will probably bump into the herd. Just walk on by and they will do the same.

The pasture is a maze of shrubby islands formed by multiflora rose and barberry, with the spreading branches of black birch, maple, hop hornbeam, and ash above. Goldfinches love to eat the seeds of thistle in the fall and common yellowthroats can be seen in the trees near the wetter places.

The trail leaves the pasture through another stile and enters a **tall maple sugar wood** with a few beech and paper birch mixed in. Christmas fern dot the ground in the dry spots while the moist areas are covered in jewelweed. Deer are very common here and their tracks often outnumber the boot prints of hikers.

The path then turns right (east) into a **northern hardwood forest** of birch, beech, and maple, with branches of witch hazel sweeping in graceful arcs overhead. Soon another stile ushers you into the cow pasture again. Catbirds and robins sing from the apple trees and honeysuckle bushes, while buttercups and wild peppermint grow in the dappled sunshine. Follow the blaze posts carefully here as the cows have made many paths that crisscross the main trail, creating an often-muddy maze.

In an open area covered with black-eyed Susan, boneset, and goldenrod the Oak Loop Trail leaves left (northeast). After passing through the pasture stile the path enters a **second-growth woodland** of paper birch, poplar, and ash, with shadblow and hornbeam forming the understory. A wooden bridge leads across a beautiful little stream where clumps of maidenhair fern overhang the water.

The trail briefly follows the brook, then leaves the water and weaves through a hardwood forest of beech, ash, and paper birch with a few towering specimens of red oak. At the foot of the trees grow glades of inter-rupted fern, maidenhair, and Christmas fern, creating a summer wonderland of leaves.

Just beyond a prominent boulder turn left (north) onto Caves Trail. The path follows an old logging road along the edge of a marsh. Beside the road-cut cotton-wood, beech and red oak grow above hobblebush and striped maple. In spring the small white blossoms of Canada mayflower mingle with wintergreen and thorny canes of raspberry.

The trail gently climbs a buried ledge of limestone until thrusts of rock begin to protrude from the ground to the left. Here a small stream flows from the marsh and disappears into one of the **McMaster caves,** a stony hol-low the brook has carved into the bedrock. This scene is repeated at two other places along the path where more streams vanish into the earth.

Just where the water goes remains a mystery, but it probably flows through the underground maze of stony passages for quite some distance. Sometimes in late win-ter the entrance to the caves becomes blocked with ice, causing the swamp basin to fill with water. The resulting vernal lake can remain for weeks, but as soon as the ice plugs melt the whole pond drains away in a matter of hours.

North of the caves the trail leaves the logging road and turns right (east). The path then swings south and climbs a rocky ridge into a beautiful **woodland savan-nah** where hop hornbeam share the ledges with dainty grasses. Some of the nearby boulders are home to colonies of walking fern, their delicate lancelike fronds clinging closely to the guardian rock.

From the ridge Caves Trail descends through a forest of maple, ash and oak and ends at the Oak Loop Trail junction. Follow Oak Loop Trail south (straight ahead) past areas where chipmunks, woodpeckers, deer, and **large brown land snails** wander through patches of maidenhair fern. The path then crosses a stream on another wooden bridge before reentering the pasture and ending at the North Trail.

Turn left (south) onto North Trail and walk through an open landscape dotted with mounds of prickly barberry and multiflora rose. Small groves of wild apple trees line a walkway where Queen Anne's lace, white clover, and yarrow blossom on sunny summer afternoons. A final stile leads you from the close-cropped

A snail hurries along the trail by Field Farm.

pasture into a **wide field** where corn is grown in the warmer months.

As you stroll down the windrow of apple and ash a limited view of Mt. Greylock begins to appear over the trees to the left. After the corn is cut in autumn many animals, including mice and Canada geese, come and search for morsels the harvester leaves behind. In turn, the fox and coyote come here to look for the mice.

After weaving through cornfields the path becomes a grassy ribbon of green that snakes through a **wooded marsh** of alder, aspen, pine, and ash. At the junction with South Trail turn right (north) and walk a few yards to another intersection. Here, turn left (northwest) onto Pond Trail and proceed across the earthen dam that forms the pond's southern shore. Red-winged blackbirds sing from the cattails while bass snatch bugs that land on the water. In spring the air is filled with the cheerful sounds of peepers and wood frogs, and migrating osprey often stop by in the fall. Deer, beaver, and even an occasional moose wander through, making this spot a wonderful place to stop and watch the world go by.

Along the shore arrow arum grows with forget-me-not, peppermint, and joe-pye weed, a tall plant with pink bouquets of flowers in August. This herb was named after joe-pye, an Indian healer who used the plant to help end an outbreak of typhus among the early colonists in Massachusetts.

From the pond the path passes to the left of a building called the Folly, for its unusual architectural design. It is open to the public by appointment. Pond Trail then continues through the woods, ending at the trailhead parking area next to the garage.

Of Deer and Cows

To many people nature ends where domestication begins, but that is not the case. Both wild and domestic animals influence the environment around them. And in some instances what appear as opposites may be linked by all-but-forgotten threads of history. Such is the case with the deer and the cow.

Thousands of years ago an animal existed in Europe called the auroch. The ancestor of most modern cattle, the auroch could weigh more than a ton and stood six feet high at the shoulder. Its hide was covered with hair of auburn and black, and its head was crowned with long, sweeping horns. Over the centuries this fierce animal was domesticated by the tribes of Europe and Asia.

In England, where there were no aurochs, the people tried to fulfill their needs with deer. Vast areas of the countryside were fenced or walled to create deer parks. These could be made only with royal permission, as the deer park was often the main source of meat and hides for nearby towns. When the Normans conquered the country, European cattle soon followed. In a few generations the deer parks were replaced with cow pastures.

Both deer and cows are herbivores, but deer browse while cows graze. *Browse* comes from the French word *broust*, which means "young shoot," and deer indeed eat the young shoots and leaves of trees and shrubs. *Graze* evolved from the Middle English word for grass and means to feed on growing grasses, which cows do.

Each manner of feeding alters the landscape differently. Browsing prunes bushes, forcing lush growth in some shrubs while favorite trees are kept trimmed as far up as the animals can reach. Grazing animals don't bother with leaves and bushes, but rather mow the grass. This produces the typical pasture landscape where islands of shrubs and trees are surrounded by a sea of closely cropped grass.

The two large animals you will see most frequently on Field Farm are white-tailed deer and Holstein cows. The deer have helped create the woodlands, their passing marked by sinuous trails through the forest. And the cows have made the pastureland, narrow savannahs of barberry and wild rose. Across both are the footprints of people, which represents, after all, what the cow and deer have most in common.

Getting There

From the junction of Routes 7 and 43 in South Williamstown take Route 43 west and then immediately turn right onto Sloan Road. Follow Sloan Road 1.1 miles to the farm entrance on the right. For hiking, follow the right fork of the driveway to the parking area near the garage. From here it is a short walk to the Guest House and the North Trail.

Berlin Mountain
Williamstown

- **Berlin Pass Trail, Taconic Crest Trail**
- **4.0 miles round-trip**
- **1,250 ft. elevation gain**
- **4.0–4.5 hours**
- **difficult**

The Appalachian Trail weaves across nearly ninety miles of the Berkshires. But it is not the only long trail that meanders the hills. Another is the Taconic Crest Trail which traverses the windy ridges along the border of Massachusetts and New York. The highest peak this footway crosses is Berlin Mountain, whose open summit offers views in any direction you choose.

This walk takes you to the top of Berlin Mountain, where the blueberries and the views are both delicious. Along the way you will visit Berlin Pass as well as walk through habitat where bobcat, deer, coyote, and bear live.

The Berlin Pass Trail is a wide woods road maintained by the Williams Outing Club (WOC). Despite the fact that the trail can go unattended for long periods of time, it is a popular route and is easy to follow. The Taconic Crest Trail is maintained by the Taconic Hiking Club (THC) and is blazed with white diamonds. *Caution:* both trails are regularly used by off-road vehicles.

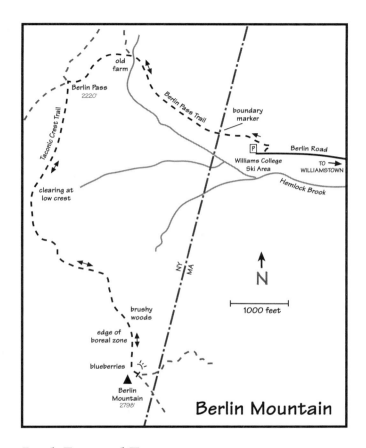

Look Forward To

- Berlin Mountain summit views
- blueberries
- windy ridges and wildlife

The Trail

From the northeast section of the parking area at the abandoned Williams College Ski Area follow a jeep road (north) into the woods. The trail immediately swings west, climbing easily through a mixed hardwood forest of ash, sugar maple, poplar, and red oak. Deer, turkey, and bobcat are frequent visitors here as well as higher up the mountain.

A short walk brings you to a gray stone pillar that stands just off the trail to the right marking the border of Massachusetts and New York. As the trail continues uphill the species of **trees begin to change**. In the rocky soil of the sloping hillside, beech and paper birch mix with oak, hop hornbeam, and maple. On the edges of the road-cut potentilla, Canada mayflower, and trailing arbutus grow. Trailing arbutus flowers in May, its delicate pink blossoms often hidden in the leathery green leaves.

The path steepens and passes areas where shards from the exposed bedrock pave the road with angular fragments of slate and phyllite. These are fine-textured **metamorphic rocks** that easily split into pearly sheets. Hundreds of millions of years ago this area was beneath a shallow sea. The quiet water allowed silty sediments to accumulate and consolidated over time into a rock called shale. When the Taconic Mountains formed during a collision between ancestral America and Africa more than four hundred million years ago, the shale was compressed and deformed into slate and phyllite.

The trail then crosses the north branch of Hemlock Brook, which pours down the steep gulf on the left. Just above the stream, where the woods are dominated with tall ash and groves of paper birch, are the foundation stones of an old farmhouse. The farm was here in the early 1800s when the road was part of the Albany-to-Boston network of post roads. There were about two dozen such roads through the Berkshires; they were used to deliver everything from newspapers to packages and letters. There was little money to pay for the postman's services then, so barter was used. Along this route even old linen rags were accepted as payment for services rendered.

An unmarked trail now leaves right as the Berlin Pass Trail continues west. The grade moderates and soon the path emerges into the brushy col called Berlin Pass. The Taconic Crest Trail runs north-south through the col, while a jeep road heads southwest toward Greene Hollow and Berlin, New York.

Low-growing maple, birch, and red spruce fill the col, and meadowsweet, goldenrod, wood fern, and raspberry crowd the sunny spots. You can find deer and coyote tracks at the edges of the frequent puddles and the scrub is a favorite habitat for bobcats. Warblers and thrushes sing in the spring and summer, while chickadees and brown creepers keep you company in the colder months.

At Berlin Pass turn left (south) onto the Taconic Crest Trail, a wide and often rutted road that leads through **beautiful woods** of yellow birch and beech. The path passes over a low rise and then climbs easily to another minor crest, where scattered blueberries grow among the steeplebush and meadowsweet. A few white pine mingle with the maple, and in June the bright pink flowers of wild azalea are sprinkled through the underbrush.

Nathaniel Smith walking through the overgrown scrub where bobcats like to prowl.

As you continue south the puddles become more numerous, sometimes completely blocking the road and serving as muddy nurseries for frogs. After a long, level stretch the trail climbs again through breezy stands of beech beneath the deeply furrowed path. The Taconic ridge is narrow here, only about a hundred yards wide, and blue sky often peeks through the branchy canopy to the left and right.

Soon the forest yields to a wide area of brushy woods, with wind-dwarfed maple and cherry interspersed with an ocean of thick meadowsweet, blackberry, and interrupted fern. As you climb out of the scrub you reach an altitude of about 2,700 feet, the border of the boreal zone. Red spruce groves begin to crowd the edges of the trail, and soon the path emerges onto the open summit of Berlin Mountain.

The clearing is full of steeplebush, chokeberry, and meadowsweet with large patches of lowbush blueberry. Come in early August and dessert is waiting to be picked. Windblown stands of beech and spruce surround the clearing, with many side trails winding through the woods. The four concrete footings spaced about the clearing once supported a fire tower that was removed.

The **turkey vultures** and hawks that ride the wind overhead and the cedar waxwings perched at the top of the spruce trees have the best view, but yours is not shabby. To the east the wide breadth of the Greylock massif rises above the valley while to the south is Jiminy Peak. To the southwest are the rolling hills of Southeast Hollow, with the Catskills beyond. To the northeast are the Green Mountains of Vermont.

If you are fortunate enough to have this spot all to yourself on a bright clear day, enjoy it. The act of walking instills a serenity that is magnified by the solitude of the summit. But on those days when the air is filled with oily exhaust and the grating sounds of ATVs and dirt bikes, it is best to walk someplace else.

From the top of Berlin Mountain the Williams Trail leaves east to Berlin Road, but recent logging and random maintenance has made it an unreliable route. The best way back is to follow the Taconic Crest Trail to Berlin Pass and descend to the parking area on Berlin Pass Trail.

Bobcats

Of all the animals I have observed in the woods the most beautiful is the bobcat. In grace and agility it rivals the white-tailed deer, and it can change direction on the dead run without ever seeming to lose balance. When hunting it can be as silent as a winter night, stalking through weeds and brush with no more noise than a snowflake makes as it falls from the sky. A bobcat is intense in a way I have seen in no other animal. It can seem cavalier and focused at the same time. And every so often it can send a chill down your spine.

Bobcats like to wander rocky forests and brushy woodlands. They eat a variety of things, from mice and birds to rabbits, snowshoe hare, squirrels, and the occasional porcupine. Most specimens grow to about thirty pounds but some have reached almost double that. They are most active at night, preferring to rest during the day in a thicket or crag of rock.

A bobcat's fawn-colored coat is richly spotted with cinnamon and black, with gray undertones in winter. When stalking, it places its hind foot in the track made by its front foot to minimize noise. Each print shows four toe marks and one heel pad. The print can be distinguished from that of a dog or coyote by the absence of claw marks and the shallow front scallop of the heel mark.

Don Reed, the naturalist at Bartholomew's Cobble, told me of a time when he stumbled on a sleeping bobcat. Being the kind of guy Don is, he sat down and watched. The bobcat slept for many minutes just thirty feet away. Eventually the cat woke up and stretched, stole a glance at Don, then walked away into the bush.

The only time a bobcat sent my fear to new levels was one dark night in late winter. The snow was deep and the night cold and still. Suddenly a hideous scream came from the nearby woods. The instant I heard it my blood instinctively ran cold. A moment later I recognized the sound as that of a bobcat who hadn't found a mate in a long time. There was no danger in the situation, just the horrific scream. It is like no other sound you will ever hear. And the bobcat is like no other animal you will ever see.

Getting There

From the junction of Routes 7 and 2 in South Williamstown turn onto Route 2 west. About 0.4 mile up the hill turn left onto Torrey Woods Road. In a little bit Oblong Road leaves left and Torrey Woods Road becomes gravel. Follow the gravel road (which somewhere along the way becomes Berlin Road, which some call Bee Hill Road) to its end in a large parking area adjacent to the abandoned Williams College Ski Area.

Snow Hole
Williamstown, Petersburg, and Pownal

- **Taconic Crest Trail, Snow Hole Trail**
- **5.8 miles round-trip**
- **450 ft. elevation gain**
- **3.0–4.0 hours**
- **moderate**

There is a certain thrill in seeing something that just should not be there. Such is the enchantment of the Snow Hole in summer. Months after the snow and ice have vanished from the surrounding mountains, it lingers here. In some years, during the hottest days of July, there is still ice at the bottom of the Snow Hole. And regardless how old you are, touching the frosty remnant of winter in the middle of summer is a magical moment you won't soon forget.

The walk to the Snow Hole is along a section of the Taconic Crest Trail, a twenty-nine-mile footpath that runs from Pownal, Vermont, to Pittsfield, Massachusetts. The trail is blazed with white markers and is maintained by the Taconic Hiking Club (THC). The Snow Hole Trail leads to the Snow Hole and is marked with blue blazes.

Look Forward To

- the Snow Hole
- beautiful views
- ice in July

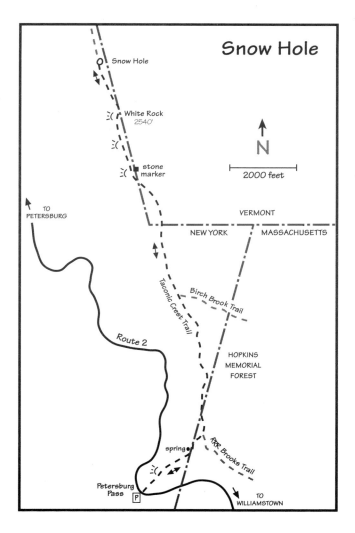

Snow Hole

Snow Hole

White Rock
2540'

stone
marker

TO
PETERSBURG

VERMONT

NEW YORK   MASSACHUSETTS

N

2000 feet

Taconic Crest Trail

Birch Brook Trail

Route 2

HOPKINS
MEMORIAL
FOREST

RRR Brooks Trail

spring

Petersburg
Pass

P

TO
WILLIAMSTOWN

The Trail

From the parking area off Route 2 at Petersburg Pass, cross the highway directly opposite the parking area. The Taconic Crest Trail rises from the roadbed and climbs through a short stretch of hardwood forest before emerging into a wind-swept clearing. In August rafts of blueberries and huckleberries cover the knee-high bushes and bumblebees drink nectar from the soft inflorescence of meadowsweet. Nearby is an unusually large bed of three-toothed cinquefoil, an alpine wildflower with small white flowers in July.

Continuing up the hill, a short side trail leaves left to a grassy vista west. Below are the farms of East Hollow with the village of Petersburg beyond.

For generations the people of Petersburg and Williamstown have traveled over the mountains to visit and conduct business. On the way they had to journey through Petersburg Pass, a notch known for its sometimes brutal weather. One day in late April 1857, four people and their dog walked from Williamstown to Petersburg to sell baskets to the local farmers. With the money they made they bought three bottles of whiskey and headed back home. On their way up the mountain it began to snow, and by the time they reached the pass the storm had become a blizzard. In the blinding snow they lost their way and wandered off the road. When they discovered they were lost they made themselves comfortable with sips of whiskey and decided to wait out the storm. In the morning there were six-foot drifts blocking the road, and only the dog was still alive. The bodies were brought to Petersburg, where they were buried in the cemetery near the village center below you.

The weather in the mountains can be harsh and unforgiving, but in each tragedy there is often a bit of mercy. The dog was adopted by one of the townspeople, and as far as can be determined, never again made the journey through Petersburg Pass.

From the overlook the trail climbs gently through a forest of low-growing maple, oak, beech, and birch, then descends into a hollow. A talus slope rises to the right and a **stone-lined spring** hides among the rocks and

The rocky phylite entrance to the Snow Hole.

wood fern. From the spring the trail makes an easy climb and at 0.5 mile reaches the junction of the red-blazed RRR Brooks Trail that enters right (southeast). Chickadees and nuthatches are residents here and in summer the sounds of warblers and thrushes can be heard.

From the trail junction the woods begin to break up into forested patches divided by clearings of goldenrod, huckleberry, and meadowsweet. Groves of beech underlain with carpets of grass make parts of the ridge a true walk in the park. Ruffed grouse like the beech groves, while fox and coyote prefer the cover of the brushy clearings.

After passing through a thicket of scratchy raspberry bushes the path enters the **Hopkins Memorial Forest,** a preserve owned by Williams College. For decades the Hopkins Forest has served as a place where students and faculty could study the intricate ecology of the Berkshires, and many internationally renowned experiments have been conducted here.

At 1.3 miles the Birch Brook Trail enters right (east) in a beautiful woodland of spreading trees and ferns that looks more like a fairyland than a forest. Continuing north the woods steadily thicken, slowly climbing through mixed northern hardwoods to the ridge crest and an overgrown clearing. Here an unmarked trail leaves right through waist-high goldenrod and ferns.

A short way north of the clearing the path enters the first of three open areas, with **spectacular views** to the west into Petersburg. Goldenrod, wild azalea, and huckleberry grace a field ringed by wind-dwarfed beech, maple, and spruce. An unmarked trail leads right (east) a short distance to a **stone monument** with the words

Vermont, New York, and Massachusetts carved into it. Over the years an observance has developed that involves circling the monument so people can say they've walked through all three states. The only problem is that the marker is not at the tristate border but some distance north of it.

As you continue along the trail an even **more beautiful view** presents itself, this one opening to the south as well as the west. As dazzling as these vistas are, the third overlook is the best of all. This promontory, called **White Rock,** stands 2,540 feet high and offers a wide panorama of eastern Rensselaer County, New York, while to the southeast is an excellent view of Mt. Greylock.

From White Rock the trail descends to the junction of the blue-blazed Snow Hole Trail. This path leads downhill through beech and wood sorrel to one of the area's least-known attractions, the **Snow Hole.**

The hole consists of a narrow fracture formed when some ancient force split the soft phyllite rock. The resulting crevasse is about thirty feet long by fifteen feet wide, narrowing to an opening perhaps two yards across. From the ledges at its crest, the hole drops thirty feet straight down into a rocky chasm so cold it will make you shiver on the hottest August afternoon.

At the north end of the hole are carvings passersby have cut into the rock, some of which date back to the 1880s. A slender path leads from these rocks into the Snow Hole. Many years you will find snow and ice tucked into the stony recesses well into July. Though you may not always find ice, you will always find cold. On a summer's day this rocky catacomb is as frigid as a refrigerator.

Follow the trail around the north end of the Snow Hole and back to the Taconic Crest Trail. Turn left (south) and retrace your steps to the parking lot in Petersburg Pass.

Forecasting the Weather

The weather is always a concern of hikers. Many times you walk miles from shelter and must rely on what you carry and what you know to make the time spent in the wilds safe and enjoyable. It is common sense to know the latest weather forecast before you set out. But the radio is only one way to know what kind of weather to anticipate.

Generations ago people relied on nature to tell them what kind of weather to expect. Once thought of as mere folklore, many of these traditions have been discovered to be based on accurate scientific information. Many plants and animals have been shown to be sensitive to changes in atmospheric pressure and humidity. Perhaps watching them will save you from being surprised by a sudden summer shower.

Many birds can help you determine if wet weather is coming. Blue jays call more frequently before a storm and Canada geese that honk loudly as they fly overhead may just be telling you of a shower headed your way. Swallows fly in great sweeping arches all the time, but swoop closer to the ground before foul weather hits.

Deerflies and black flies bite more before a storm, when they stay closer to the ground and are more active. Bees, conversely, will be less active before it rains. And some say that if you see bats flying about just after sunset then the next day will be fair.

Perhaps the most sensitive forecasters of the weather are plants. In spring the delicate flowers of hepatica will open on sunny days and close on cloudy ones or in the evening. But the most reliable prognosticator is hawkweed. These plants blossom in summer and have tufts of orange-red or yellow flowers atop succulent stems. They like fields and dry hillsides but can be found almost anywhere. Hawkweeds open their blossoms in the morning and close them in the evening. This schedule changes when a storm approaches, prompting the flower to fold well before sunset.

Sometimes it takes years to develop the skills necessary to see the message of the swallows or heed the warning of the jays. But while you learn there is pleasure in stopping to smell the flowers and ponder the signs of sun or shower reflected in the attitude of the petals.

Getting There

From the junction of Routes 2 and 7 in Williamstown turn onto Route 2 west and drive for 4.2 miles. A large parking area is on the left at the top of the ridge in Petersburg Pass.

Natural Bridge
North Adams

- **easily followed footpaths**
- **0.5 mile**
- **25 ft. elevation gain**
- **1.0 hour**
- **easy**

In all of North America there is but one place where a stream has carved an arch from white marble. Yet the unique wonders of Natural Bridge State Park do not end with its famous natural bridge. The stream and the bedrock have combined to create a fascinating landscape of narrow canyons and potholes. Human activity has added a marble dam and quarry where unusual wildflowers grow in the alkaline soil.

The walk around the natural bridge follows fenced footpaths near Hudson Brook. There are no paths in the quarry itself, but it is small and easy to explore.

Natural Bridge State Park is owned by the state of Massachusetts and administered by the Massachusetts Department of Environmental Management (DEM). There is a $2 parking fee in season.

Look Forward To

- the natural bridge
- canyons and potholes
- a marble quarry and wildflowers

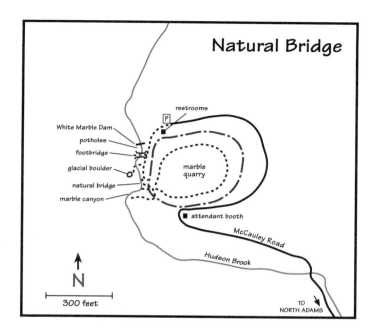

The Trail

From the parking lot the gravel footpath heads southeast across a manicured lawn whose edges are lined with the delicate yellow sprays of goldenrod and purple bouquets of New England aster in late summer. After passing the restrooms and a small wetland where cattails, sedges, and speckled alder grow, the gaping maw of the abandoned quarry appears to the left (east).

For nearly a century workers methodically cut apart the marble bedrock, hauling away blocks of stone and creating the horseshoe-shaped quarry before you. The white marble that underlies this area is millions of years old, and its creation is a story in itself (see below).

To the right (west) is Hudson Brook and the celebrated **white marble dam.** When the North Adams Marble Dust Company began operating here in the middle of the nineteenth century, the firm needed to build a dam for a power source. When workers constructed the barrier they logically built it of local marble. No one knew that they were building a wonderfully unique structure, but since its completion in 1850 this has been the only white marble dam on earth.

Just below the dam is a **metal footbridge** that spans the brook's narrow gorge. The steep sides of the chasm are home to daylilies and aster, hemlock, spruce, and white cedar, with bulbet fern hanging in lacy valances from clefts in the rock. The streambed itself is pocked with large, bowl-shaped potholes.

These potholes are still being formed, yet most of their genesis occurred thousands of years ago. As the mile-thick glaciers of the last Ice Age melted away they produced enormous volumes of water and sediment. The force of the water coupled with tons of swirling stone abraded the bedrock and produced the potholes. Today the stream is docile in comparison to times past, but the slow shaping of the gorge continues, albeit at a much more relaxed pace.

The trail then leads to a wooden stairway that descends into the chasm beneath the **natural bridge.** Before you is the white marble arch that Nathaniel Hawthorne visited in 1838. Below is the twisting labyrinth of passageways the brook has patiently carved through the pale stone. In some places the gorge is twenty feet

Potholes carved by Hudson Brook in the white marble near Natural Bridge.

deep and but six feet across, creating a landscape of claustrophobic beauty and surreal ambience.

From the natural bridge a walkway crosses the stream on the right and leads to a view of a large boulder. This great stone is called a **glacial erratic,** a geologic term for a boulder of one rock type that now rests on bedrock of another type. The erratic is made of granite, a light-colored, coarse-grained igneous rock, while the bedrock is marble, a metamorphic rock composed primarily of calcite.

Backtracking to the natural bridge, another path leads to a view of the arch from the opposite side. This perspective is equally spellbinding.

From here it is a short walk to the stairway that descends into the quarry. Once on the floor of the quarry follow the contour of the cliff south, then west to a dead-end walkway. This path leads into a spectacular **marble canyon** whose sculpted walls tower above you.

From here return to the quarry floor. In summer this area is a colorful collage of wildflowers. Thimbleweed's simple white flowers contrast with the golden hues of black-eyed Susan, goldenrod, and St. Johnswort. Indian paintbrush and yellow hawkweed grow next to mullein, aster, and boneset, while the sapphire flowers of viper's bugloss sparkle like pieces of blue sky that have fallen to earth. At the east end of the quarry is a place where horsetail and bulrush grow and green frogs and garter snakes like to hide in the undergrowth. In September the vibrant blue flowers of fringed gentian blossom in the grass providing a treat for wildflower lovers. Please note that gentian is a rare plant and must not be picked or disturbed.

From the quarry it is a short stroll along the walkways to the parking area.

Making Marble

The creation of the white marble of North Adams began about 500 million years ago. Then all of the northeastern United States was submerged beneath the warm waters of the Potsdam Sea. The first plants were evolving to live on the barren shoreline, and primitive coral and shellfish populated the ocean. The coral and shellfish created exoskeletons of calcium they gleaned from the sea. When these animals died, their shells became part of the ocean floor.

Over millions of years the calcium deposits became thick beds hundreds of feet deep, which eventually consolidated into limestone. About 450 million years ago the Potsdam Sea began to close as forces deep in the earth's mantle pushed what are now Africa and America together. As the continents collided the Taconic Mountains began to take form.

As the continental convergence continued, some of the limestone became the heart of a section of the new mountain range. The intense pressures deformed the rock, changing its mineral makeup without melting it and transforming the sedimentary limestone into metamorphic marble.

Born in the tectonic vice of a continental collision more than 400 million years ago, the white marble of North Adams remained buried for hundreds of millions of years. As the mountains slowly eroded, the veins of marble came to the surface, where they have been abraded and sculpted by ice and water.

With lifetimes of less than a century, it is easy for us to view stone as an unchanging constant. But it is not. As you touch a bit of white marble you are touching the remains of extinct creatures that lived here 500 million years ago, as well as feeling the core of a mountain 400 million years old. Now that's humbling.

Getting There

From the northern junction of Routes 2 and 8 in North Adams take Route 8 north 0.5 mile to McCauley Road. Take a left onto McCauley Road and immediately bear right. Continue 0.5 mile to the parking area at the top of hill.

Cheshire Cobbles
Cheshire

- **Appalachian Trail**
- **3.4 miles round-trip**
- **885 ft. elevation gain**
- **2.5–3.0 hours**
- **moderate**

The Appalachian Trail (AT) was created to give people a place to retreat to nature. Yet this 2,000-mile footpath does more than wander the wooded spine of the Appalachians. It also visits many small towns from the deep South to northern Maine. The resulting blend of nature and rural village is essential to the AT experience.

This walk takes you through the heart of Cheshire, one of the Berkshires' friendliest trail towns, and passes the monument to the famous Cheshire Cheese. From town the AT leads you up the flank of the Hoosac escarpment to a memorable view from the quartzite boulders of the scenic Cheshire Cobbles.

The Appalachian Trail is a National Scenic Trail administered by the Appalachian Trail Conference and maintained in Massachusetts by the Department of Environmental Management and the Appalachian Mountain Club. It is marked with white blazes throughout its length, with access trails blazed in blue.

Look Forward To

- the Cheshire Cheese monument
- giant boulders
- memorable views

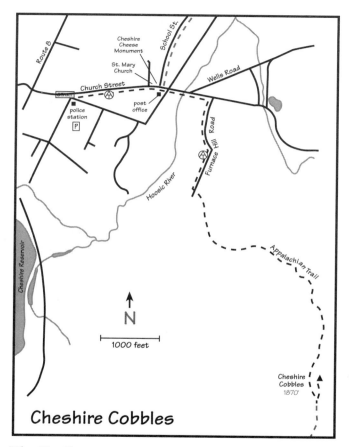

Cheshire Cobbles

The Trail

Note: Parking is not permitted on Furnace Hill Road. The Cheshire Police Department asks hikers to use the police lot in town and walk the short way to the wooded trailhead.

From the south parking lot outside the Cheshire Police Station walk east along Church Street, passing St. Mary of Assumption Church on the left. In the friendly spirit AT towns are noted for, the church operates a free hostel for the many through-hikers who pass by each summer.

Just past the church, at the junction of School Street and Church Street, is the monument to the **Cheshire Cheese.** The early years of United States politics were dominated by one party, the Federalists, whose policies favored wealthy landowners and merchants. While on vacation in Bennington, Vermont, Thomas Jefferson and James Madison conceived of a more democratic party that valued individual talents over aristocratic birthright. To celebrate Jefferson's election to the presidency in 1800 the people of Cheshire made a huge wheel of cheese. The 1,235-pound cheese was then shipped to Washington by wagon, sled, and boat, where it was placed in the East Room of the White House. In appreciation for the town's support Jefferson donated $200 to the church of his most enthusiastic backer, John Leland.

From the cheese monument continue east on Church Street past the post office on the right. The road crosses the **Hoosic River** on a metal bridge, then forks. Bear right, walking the short distance to Furnace Hill Road. Turn right onto Furnace Hill Road and proceed uphill through a quiet residential neighborhood. After walking for 0.3 mile the Appalachian Trail enters deep spruce woods on the left.

The path heads uphill to a sign that reads Cheshire Cobbles 1.0 mile. From the sign continue uphill through a **second-growth hardwood forest** of red maple, black birch, and red oak with a few hemlock sprinkled here and there. Shining club moss, princess pine, and partridgeberry decorate the ground with ever-green color, and starflower blossoms spark things up in May.

As the trail gains altitude the forest becomes more diverse with beech, yellow birch, and cherry adding to the mix. In summer the translucent white flowers of **Indian pipe** poke through the leaf mold. Indian pipe does not get nourishment from chlorophyll as green plants do, but rather through a symbiotic relationship with soil-borne fungi. This relationship is called mycor-rhiza, literally fungus-root (see below).

As you climb higher the woods become a beautiful assemblage of straight-trunked trees and acres of lacy

After the flower fades, a bright red berry decorates the trillium along the AT.

ferns. The snow-white bark of paper birch gleams beneath a summer canopy of green or autumn's multi-colored leafy collage. Deer browse beneath the trees where gray squirrels scramble from branch to branch. Chickadees and nuthatches call in winter while thrushes and warblers sing in the spring.

The trail then swings southeast along a **forested talus slope.** Yellow birch grow atop the boulders, clinging to the rock with tentacle-like roots. Between the stone and wood are colonies of deep-green polypody fern, their tiny fronds nodding in the breeze. A short walk brings you to the base of cobble cliff, where **boulders** the size of cars litter the ground. The path proceeds along the base of the rock face where mountain laurel grows in tangled thickets. Huge vertical fractures scar the stone above you, like dark lightning bolts chiseled in the rock.

The white blazes lead around the steep hillside to a junction where a short blue-blazed trail leaves left (north) for the cobbles. The soils around Cheshire Cobbles are very fragile, sandy loams that erode quickly once disturbed. With this in mind, please stay on the trail and don't bushwhack to the overlook.

The path wanders through mountain laurel and hemlock, which abruptly yield to bare rock at the edge of a sheer precipice. Follow the cliff edge to a rocky west-facing promontory where a **spectacular view** awaits.

Below, the narrow Hoosic valley cradles the town of Cheshire straight ahead and Cheshire Reservoir to the southwest. The western horizon is dominated by the terraced profile of Mt. Greylock. The overlook of Rounds' Rock is visible at the head of the southernmost terrace. Just north of Rounds' Rock is the clearing at the base of Jones' Nose, the steep ridge which leads to Saddle Ball

Mountain and finally to the summit of Mt. Greylock. To the right of Mt. Greylock is Ragged Mountain, with the Green Mountains of Vermont farther north (right).

In spring and fall the rocks are also a good place to watch migrating raptors glide up and down the valley. Broad-winged hawks and turkey vultures are some of the birds who regularly fly by.

As you relax on the rocks take a moment to look at the plants around you. Windy Berkshire cliffs are usually the realm of white pine, bear oak, or balsam fir. In contrast, the Cheshire Cobbles are home to hemlock, mountain laurel, wild azalea, and **mountain holly**. Mountain holly is a tall deciduous shrub that is easy to overlook until late summer, when the plant is covered with bright red fruit. On sunny days the fruit appears luminescent, with a sheen of hazy violet overlying the crimson skin.

To return to the parking area follow the blue blazes to the Appalachian Trail, which you can then follow back to town.

Mycorrhiza

One of the basic lessons everyone learns in science class is that a plant's roots absorb moisture and nutrients from the soil. What most people don't learn is that almost all roots need a lot of help to do the job.

At the very tip of a plant's growing root is an area where fuzzy growths called root hairs appear. These single-celled filaments weave around soil particles and absorb moisture and minerals. Even the smallest plants have an enormous number of root hairs. For example, a single clump of winter rye can contain as many as 14 billion root hairs.

Even this extraordinary number of root hairs cannot supply the needs of most plants. What completes the quota is the complex relationship between fungus and plant called mycorrhiza.

Mycorrhizal fungi exist in almost all soils as slender filaments. These threads invade the epidermal layer of young roots, sometimes producing swollen, nodulelike growths and at other times forming nearly invisible sheaths of fungus that completely encase the root. The fungus secures complex foods from the root and in exchange helps translocate minerals and water into the plant.

Mycorrhiza works best in boggy and organic forest loams, as fungi can glean nutrients from these soils when simple roots cannot. Recent studies have indicated that some mycorrhizal relationships can even allow plants to take nitrogen directly from the air, bypassing the soil completely.

The study of mycorrhizal relationships is still a fairly young discipline that promises many surprises in the decades to come. The overriding lesson so far is that just about everything in nature is a partnership, and nothing is as simple as it first appears.

Getting There

From the traffic light at the junction of Route 8 and Church Street in Cheshire, turn onto Church Street and proceed 0.1 mile to a fork in the road. Bear right and then turn left into the small parking lot between the town hall and the police department. Before you begin your walk, let the officers know about how long you'll be gone.

Spruce Hill and Hawk Lookout

Florida and North Adams

- **Busby Trail**
- **2.6 miles round-trip**
- **700 ft. elevation gain**
- **2.0 hours**
- **moderate with steep sections**

The Hoosac Range is composed of the eroded remnants of ancient mountains. Worn down to their hearts, the rounded summits nonetheless still stand above the landscape like senior elders watching over a geomorphic tribe. Chief among the peaks is Spruce Hill, a 2,566-foot crag that commands exceptional views from its rocky crest.

The overlook is but one feature that makes a journey up the mountain rewarding. There are dark spruce plantations and miles of deep hardwood forests that harbor bear, deer, and coyote. And if nature isn't enough there are tales of ghosts around old cellar holes and even reports of alien spaceships that hover nearby in the night. You would have to travel light-years to find a walk with more variety.

The hike to the summit of Spruce Hill is entirely within Savoy Mountain State Forest, a preserve of more than 10,000 acres owned by the state of Massachusetts and managed by the Department of Environmental Management (DEM). The Busby Trail is marked with blue blazes and is easy to follow.

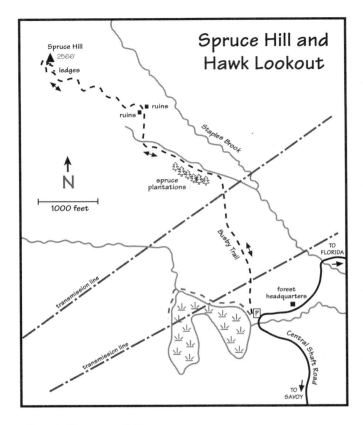

Spruce Hill
2566'
ledges

Spruce Hill and
Hawk Lookout

ruins
ruins

Staples Brook

N

1000 feet

spruce
plantations

Busby Trail

TO
FLORIDA

transmission line

forest
headquarters

P

transmission line

Central Shaft Road

TO
SAVOY

Look Forward To

- summit views from Hawk Lookout
- forests of spruce and hardwoods
- ghosts and spaceships

The Trail

From the parking area off Central Shaft Road walk west down the wide dirt lane called Old Florida Road. After about thirty yards the Busby Trail leaves right (north) and enters a **second-growth hardwood forest.** Yellow birch, red maple, and gray birch grow above an understory of shadblow, striped maple, and hobblebush. Shadblow sends out rafts of dainty white flowers in spring before the leaves appear, while hobblebush shows its flat-topped bouquets of creamy blossoms in May and June.

The trail soon passes beneath a power line and quickly reenters the woods, where it turns hard left (west). This short bypass wanders through a moist woodland where hemlock and red spruce mingle with the hardwoods. In summer cinnamon-colored veeries sing their flutelike song from the deep woods, while in fall gray squirrels leap through the trees searching for tasty beechnuts.

The trail soon rejoins the original woods road and passes by a picturesque grove of **century-old hemlock** that loom over clusters of mossy boulders. Brown creepers methodically climb the furrowed trunks looking for bugs while pileated woodpeckers find insects by hammering out huge holes in the trees.

After passing under another power line the trail climbs gently into a **plantation** of deep-green Norway spruce. Planted in the 1930s by the Civilian Conservation Corps (CCC), the seedlings have matured into a forest composed almost exclusively of spruce. Recently narrow strips, called clearcuts, have been carved through the dense growth in order to encourage biodiversity (see below).

The path then comes to a small stream on the right, which it follows through waves of spruce and hardwoods.

Trailing arbutus shows off its lightly scented flowers in May while white baneberry blossoms in wet spots nearby. In late summer baneberry is decorated with a bunch of polished white fruits, each distinctively marked with a small black dot. The appearance of the berries gives the plant its other name of doll's-eyes. As attractive as the fruits are, do not touch them, as baneberry is very poisonous.

As the brook narrows, the trail crosses it, passing a drainage where water-eroded ledges hang out over a mossy gully. Just north of the runoff is the stone foundation of a small barn on the left, followed by the **neatly cut cellar hole** of the main house on the right. Thick, serpentine roots of yellow birch coil around the topmost stones, and chipmunks peek out warily from crevices littered with nutshells.

According to records at the forest headquarters the house was built in 1831 by Kelly Sherman and his wife. Later that year the couple had their only child, a girl named Maria. In 1847, when Maria was sixteen years old, her mother went off to visit relatives, leaving her daughter and husband behind. When she returned a few weeks later, tragedy was waiting. Just what happened remains a mystery. Some say that Maria died naturally; some insist that her father murdered her. Whatever happened, the legend persists that the ghost of Maria Sherman haunts the area around the old foundation and that on moonlit nights she can be seen gliding over the stone steps that rise from the cellar hole.

From the ruins the trail winds up the steep hillside on switchbacks, passing a side trail left (southwest) near a stone wall. The Busby Trail continues northwest a short distance to a signed junction where the path splits into

Nature has nearly reclaimed the old foundation of the Sherman home at Spruce Hill.

the north trail and the south trail.

Take the north trail (right) through an imposing landscape of **ledges and boulders.** The path curls between the rocks and trees where goldthread and blue-bead lily form delicate springtime gardens. In June the bright pink blossoms of wild azalea look like brilliant sparks as they hang from the slender branches. Near the summit you pass through tangled groves of chokeberry and clearings of bedrock and blueberries until you final-ly climb out onto the mountain's **impressive overlook.**

Spruce Hill is the highest point on the Hoosac Range, with grand western views of the entire Greylock massif. North of Mt. Greylock are the Taconics of New York and the Green Mountains of Vermont. To the southwest are the peaks of the southern Berkshires, while due south is Borden Mountain and its fire tower. The towns of Adams and North Adams are spread out before you, filling the Hoosic River valley with a colorful mosaic of buildings and streets.

This rocky promontory is called **Hawk Lookout** for the large numbers of the birds that pass by during their spring and fall migrations. The most-numerous species is the broad-winged hawk, a brown-plumed raptor with distinctive black and white tail bands. Sometimes thousands of them can glide overhead in a single day.

Hawks aren't the only things people have seen flying near Spruce Hill, however. A few years ago UFOs were reported hovering over Savoy State Forest. But they don't seem to be regular visitors.

When it's time to go you can leave by following the edge of the cliff to the south trail, which leads back to the north trail junction. From there follow the Busby Trail back to the parking area.

Biodiversity

The Norway spruce plantations off the Busby Trail are peaceful places. Thick beds of fallen needles blanket the ground and soften the step. The sun and sky disappear behind a green tapestry that hangs from a thousand gray-barked branches. There is little noise here, just the whisper of passing breezes or the scolding chatter of red squirrels. And that is the problem: when a forest is perennially quiet, something is wrong.

The silence of the spruce plantation originates from

the exclusivity of the forest. Wherever you walk things look pretty much the same. As soon as you leave the spruce woods and venture into the surrounding northern hardwood forest, the scene changes dramatically. Instead of one species of tree there are now maple, birch, beech, and oak. Where the ground was littered with spruce cones there are husks of beech nuts, wings of maple seeds and acorns. Black bear eat beechnuts, deer consume acorns, and gray squirrels munch on maple seeds. In a nutshell the more diverse a forest is, the more diverse it becomes.

Throughout most of the twentieth century foresters have been planting fast-growing spruce and pine plantations to protect watersheds and logged areas from erosion. What they inadvertently created were beautiful patches of forest that support a very narrow spectrum of wildlife. To correct the mistakes of the past, thin ribbons of plantations have been clearcut. These areas will grow back with a blend of plant species that in turn will support even more kinds of birds, mammals, and insects.

There is beauty in the silence of the plantations, as there is beauty in many human creations. Yet the silence is also a messenger that tells us of our failure to reckon with the complex systems of nature. And therein hides the lesson. We can create the woods, but not the wood thrush. We can make the silence, but we cannot inspire the song.

Getting There

From the junction of Routes 8 and 2 in North Adams follow Route 2 east 5.3 miles to Central Shaft Road. Turn right onto Central Shaft Road and follow signs to Savoy State Forest. The parking area is a narrow pull-off 0.1 mile past the DEM forest headquarters.

Tyler Swamp
Savoy

- **Tyler Swamp Trail**
- **1.75-mile loop**
- **70 ft. elevation gain**
- **1.0–1.5 hours**
- **easy**

The area around Savoy and Florida is sometimes called the backwoods of the Berkshires because it is so wild. Vast forests and plentiful swamps and lakes provide suitable habitat for a rich array of wildlife. White-tailed deer and coyote are here, as well as black bear and moose. Beaver and muskrat swim in the shallow woodland ponds while mink and otter run the riverbanks. If you wish to observe animals, Savoy State Forest is one of the best places to visit. On this walk you will see a great blue heron rookery, bear trees, an area where does give birth to fawns in spring, and beautiful orchids.

The trail around Tyler Swamp is entirely within the Savoy State Forest, a preserve of more than 10,000 acres owned by the state of Massachusetts and managed by the Department of Environmental Management (DEM). Tyler Swamp Trail is a wide, easy-to-follow footway lightly marked with blue blazes.

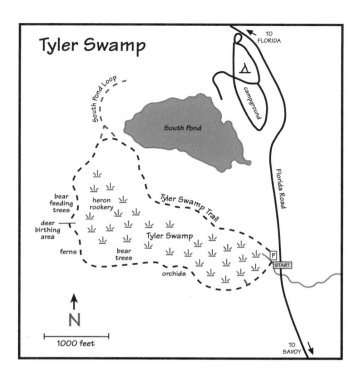

Look Forward To

- a heron rookery
- bear trees
- wild orchids

The Trail

At the trailhead Tyler Swamp Trail immediately splits into north and south loops. Bear left and take the south route into a **second-growth woodland** of red spruce, hemlock, and hardwoods. The path quickly crosses a stream and the open horizon of the swamp becomes visible through the trees to the right. A fifty-yard bushwhack north will bring you to the edge of the **grassy wetland** with nice views across the swamp. The thickets of leafy bushes are sweet gale, a wonderfully aromatic plant the foliage of which is used in sachets. The sinuous paths through the knee-high grass and sedge are made by black bears, who browse the marsh in the cool of the evening or early morning.

Once back on the path the footway widens, revealing the shallow side cuts of an old logging road. Many times of the year this area is muddy and wet, crossing many small drainages along the way. Hardwood saplings form a thick understory while mature trees of ash, beech, and yellow birch tower overhead. The common ephemeral flowers of goldthread, bluebead lily, and Canada mayflower grow here, as well as the more unusual **large round-leaved orchids.** This plant has two large, round, shiny green leaves that lie flat against the ground. In July it sends up a spike of showy white flowers that are truly gorgeous.

The old woods road then leads uphill past a forested talus slope to the left, good habitat for bobcat and porcupines. To the right grow a few **enormous old hemlock** that dwarf the hardwoods around them. Bear sometimes rest in the shelter of the grove, earning the place the epithet "the bear trees."

The path then swings to the north through an area where many species of fern grow including broad beech fern, identifiable by its pair of reflexed pinnules, or leaflets. A short downhill walk brings you to the west edge of the swamp, where a short unmarked side trail descends the few yards to the edge of the marsh. This section of the swamp is completely different from the view you saw earlier. A forest of driftwood-gray tree trunks crowds the shallows, nearly obliterating the tree-line at the far side of the swamp.

About forty yards into the swamp is a place where **great blue herons** raise their young each year. The nest is a large platform of sticks that is clearly visible only with binoculars. These birds do not like visitors, so please watch quietly from the edge of the swamp.

Autumn is the season when white-tailed deer mate. Seven months later in the warmth of spring the pregnant does come to the grassy area on the right to give birth. There they care for their spotted fawns until they can follow their mothers on summer-long browsing walks.

The heron rookery deep in the tangled dead forest of Tyler Swamp.

Many of the dead trees harbor colonies of ants. In late summer, when the nest populations are largest, **black bears** come to feast on the insects. They rip open the rotting trees with their claws, pulling away large pieces of wood. As the ants spill out the bears lick them up.

From the swamp the trail continues north to the junction of South Pond Loop Trail which leaves left (north). Tyler Swamp Trail then coincides with a section of South Pond Loop Trail, traveling east a short distance where South Pond Loop Trail leaves left and Tyler Swamp Trail continues right (southeast).

On its way back to the parking area the path passes through a picturesque woodland accented with rustic boulders. Barred owls sometimes call from the deeper woods and bear have left claw marks on some of the trees in their search for food. In summer the air is replete with the songs of hermit thrush and veeries, while in the fall small flocks of chickadees follow you about.

Soon the outline of Tyler Swamp appears through the trees to the right, and from here it is a short stroll to the parking area.

Bear Stories

If you are curious you will find folks around Savoy State Forest who are willing to talk about the bears they have known. There is no shortage of stories. And regardless of the epithets and expletives used during the telling of the tale, most people will end the conversation by expressing a bit of admiration for the beasts. They are smart, resourceful, and aggravatingly persistent, traits New Englanders hold dear to their hearts. As an example, I pass this tale on to you.

One evening a bear came out of the woods and strolled up to the big green dumpster behind the Savoy State Forest headquarters. The heavy metal doors were closed and at first there seemed to be no way to get to all the lovely garbage inside. But bears are smart animals, and after studying the situation for a while she hooked her claws under the hinged door and gave it a flip. Dinner was served.

For months the forest employees tried to baffle the bear and for months she met each challenge and ate very well, thank you. But one day the old dumpster was gone and another, more secure container stood between her and supper. None of her old tricks worked on this new contraption, and it seemed that the bear had met her match.

In the morning the forest employees once again found garbage strewn all around the container. After trying all her old tricks the 300-pound bear had climbed onto the top of the dumpster and stomped her forefeet until the entire top of the thing collapsed under the assault. She landed inside, partied a while, and then returned to the forest.

The contest between human and bear could have gone on for months, but eventually the humans' patience with the game was exhausted. The bear was trapped and relocated to deeper woods. Sometimes people just don't play fair.

Getting There

From the junction of Routes 2 and 8 in North Adams, follow Route 2 east 5.3 miles to Central Shaft Road. Turn right onto Central Shaft Road and follow the signs to Savoy State Forest. After entering the forest you will pass the state forest headquarters on the right. From the headquarters travel 1.7 miles to a small pull-off on the right.

Pine Cobble
Williamstown

- **Pine Cobble Trail**
- **3.2 miles round-trip**
- **1,200 ft. elevation gain**
- **3.0 hours**
- **moderate**

Pine Cobble is a rocky quartzite promontory on the southwest lip of East Mountain. The view from the ridge is one of the nicest in the northern region, encompassing Mt. Greylock, the Taconics, and parts of Vermont's Green Mountains. Along the way you will pass through forests filled with many species of plants that are common farther south but rare in northern Berkshires. And visit a tree that tells an unusual story.

Pine Cobble Trail is maintained by the Williams Outing Club (WOC) and is marked throughout its length with blue blazes. The path is well maintained and easy to follow.

Look Forward To
- unusual species of plants
- a wide selection of beautiful views
- the tree with a story

The Trail
Pine Cobble Trail begins opposite the parking area on Pine Cobble Road. The path leads southeast to a large

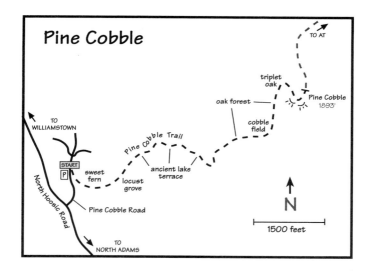

Pine Cobble

TO AT

triplet oak

oak forest

Pine Cobble
1893'

cobble field

Pine Cobble Trail

ancient lake terrace

TO
WILLIAMSTOWN

START
P

sweet fern

locust grove

North Hoosic Road

Pine Cobble Road

TO
NORTH ADAMS

N

1500 feet

sign that reads Pine Cobble Summit 1.6 miles. From the sign walk up the road-cut banking to a cluster of spruce at the edge of a second-growth hardwood forest. Hickory, red maple, ash, and white oak are the primary trees, with an understory of hornbeam, witch hazel, and wild azalea. The glossy leaves of wintergreen pepper the forest floor and a few specimens of **sweet fern** can be seen nearby. A delicious tea can be made by steeping a few leaves of wintergreen and sweet fern in a cup of hot water. It also gets rid of headaches.

The trail climbs easily, passing through a grove of **black locust.** These trees, with their deeply furrowed bark and contorted trunks and branches, are easy to identify. The twisted growth habit of locust gives the woods a haunted appearance, and the weird creaking of the trees as they sway in the wind only adds to the ghostly ambience.

From the locust grove the path climbs to a level area where large oaks dominate the smaller paper birch and maple. This **large terrace** marks the ancient shoreline of glacial Lake Bascom (see pg. 260). The waves deposited a sandy, well-drained soil that, combined with the mountain's southern exposure, has created a warm microclimate. This unusual habitat has allowed plants such as sassafras, normally too tender for northern Berkshire winters, to thrive here. You will also find maple-leafed viburnum whose purple-black fruit and scarlet leaves brighten the autumn woods. Wild azalea shows its spicy pink blossoms in June along with the far less conspicuous sheep laurel.

At the end of the level terrace the path begins a moderate climb through an **oak forest** that grows above thick patches of blueberry, huckleberry, sheep laurel, and stump sprouts of American chestnut. Squirrels and chipmunks often scold you as you pass by. In contrast the resident woodpeckers, chickadees, and nuthatches note your presence with gentle calls and friendly squeaks. In autumn wild turkey and deer come to forage on acorns, and the winter snow often reveals the footprints of coyote.

The path briefly levels out as it traverses a **narrow field of cobbles** that have been freed from the underlying bedrock by the seasonal freezing and thawing of water. The wind is a frequent companion the rest of the way, its omnipresent assault reflected in the dwarf oaks around you. Beneath the trees sassafras and azalea mingle with tall bracken fern, huckleberries, and spring-flowering lady-slippers.

A long, easy climb brings you to the triplet oak growing in the middle of the trail. At its center is a water-filled basin formed from the remains of the original stump. This tree's story began about a century ago when an acorn sprouted where the basin is now. The oak grew for more than fifty years until it was cut down. The next spring three suckers began growing from the old stump. As the new trees grew taller they also kept the edges of the old stump alive while the center rotted away. The triplet oaks are about forty years old now, yet they are actually part of the original tree that began its life near the turn of the century.

From the triplet oak the trail scrambles up a steep slope graced with mountain laurel, azalea, and trailing arbutus. At the ridge crest the terrain levels out and the

The triplet oak, where three trees grow from a single stump.

path leads through the windy woods to the exposed overlooks of **Pine Cobble.** There are many to choose from, each area blessed with a wonderful blend of quartzite boulders, wind-sculpted flag trees, and open horizons that reach to the mountains. From the various promontories you can see Mt. Greylock to the south and the undulating spine of the northern Taconics to the southwest and west. To the north are the forested slopes of the Green Mountains.

Weaving between the mountains are the valleys of the Hoosic and Green Rivers, each graced with Grandma Moses farms and Norman Rockwell towns. It is that symbiotic blend of humanity and nature that makes the views from Pine Cobble so magnificent. From up here the world really looks like a peaceful place.

Hindsight

When Henry David Thoreau walked through the Berkshires he carefully wrote of the beauty he saw here. He recorded his experiences the night he slept atop Mt. Greylock and vividly recounted the ethereal beauty of the next morning's sunrise.

Nathaniel Hawthorne lingered longer than Thoreau, spending pleasant months in a cottage that overlooked the tranquil vista of Stockbridge Bowl. There he wrote stories of the hills, including tales of a journey to the marble canyon beneath a natural bridge.

William Cullen Bryant was here, immortalizing Monument Mountain in the tragic verse of his poetry and giving life to the legends of Squaw Peak.

Herman Melville would abandon his farm chores and disappear into his room. There he would write and gaze out the window at Mt. Greylock in the distance. His novel *Moby Dick* was based in large part on unrelated true events he gathered together over many years. There really was a white whale called Mocha Dick that swam the Pacific, and a sperm whale really did ram a whaler and sink it in the southern ocean off Chile. But while those events were in his mind, the profile of the mountain was always in his eyes. With a mantle of snow upon its back, it is said that Mt. Greylock became the image of the white whale to Melville as he wrote.

There have been many more. Yet whether they wrote or painted, danced or sang or played, the Berkshires have been reflected in what they have done. And what they have done is blend humanity and nature. To show that both are a part of the beauty that makes the area priceless.

Getting There

From the junction of Routes 2 and 7 in Williamstown take Route 2 east 0.7 mile to Cole Avenue. Turn onto Cole Avenue and drive 0.7 mile to the junction with North Hoosic Road. Turn right onto North Hoosic Road and proceed 0.4 mile to Pine Cobble Road. Turn left on Pine Cobble Road and continue 0.15 mile to the parking area on the left.

Walks and Highlights

Region	Walk	Page Number	Difficulty Level	Distance (miles RT)	Waterfalls	Scenic Vista
Southern	Bartholomew's Cobble	2	moderate	3.0		✔
	Sheffield Plain	11	easy	3.6		✔
	Race Brook Falls	19	easy	1.0	✔	✔
	Sage's Ravine	27	moderate with steep sections	7.8	✔	✔
	Bash-Bish Falls	35	moderate with very steep sections	2.6	✔	✔
	Guilder Pond and Mt. Everett	43	moderate	2.4		✔
	Jug End	51	moderate with steep sections	2.2		✔
	Monument Mountain	58	moderate	2.5	✔	✔
	Benedict Pond	66	easy	1.5		
	Ice Gulch	73	easy	2.2		✔
	Bowker's Woods	81	easy	1.0		
	Laura's Tower and Ice Glen	87	moderate	3.3		✔
	McLennan	95	moderate	2.8	✔	
	Tyringham Cobble	102	moderate	1.9		✔
Central	Yokun Ridge	111	easy	1.1		✔
	Pleasant Valley	119	moderate	2.1		
	Kennedy Park	127	easy with moderate sections	3.4		✔

Bogs & Marshes	Ponds/ Lakes/ Rivers	History	Fields	Forest	Wild Life	Plants/ Wild Flowers	Geology
	✓		✓	✓	✓	✓	✓
✓		✓	✓	✓	✓	✓	
	✓		✓	✓	✓	✓	✓
✓	✓	✓		✓	✓	✓	
	✓			✓	✓	✓	
✓	✓			✓	✓	✓	
				✓	✓	✓	✓
		✓	✓	✓	✓	✓	✓
✓	✓			✓	✓	✓	
		✓		✓	✓	✓	
	✓	✓		✓		✓	✓
	✓	✓		✓	✓	✓	
✓	✓	✓		✓	✓	✓	
			✓	✓	✓	✓	✓
			✓	✓	✓	✓	
✓	✓		✓	✓	✓	✓	
	✓	✓		✓	✓	✓	✓

Region	Walk	Page Number	Difficulty Level	Distance	Waterfalls	Scenic Vista
Central	Finerty Pond	136	easy with moderate sections	3.2		
	Northern Transitional Forest	143	easy	2.0		
	Shaker Mountain and Holy Mount	150	moderate	3.5		
	Canoe Meadows	160	easy	1.2		
	Rice Sanctuary	168	easy with moderate sections	1.5		✔
	Tilden Swamp	174	moderate with steep sections	3.5	✔	✔
	Balance Rock	182	easy	1.0		
	Wahconah Falls	188	easy	.6	✔	
	Judges Hill	195	easy with moderate sections	4.3		
	Windsor Jambs	202	easy with moderate sections	2.1	✔	
	Mt. Greylock Visitor Center	209	easy with moderate sections	2.3		✔
Northern	Round's Rock	217	easy	1.1		✔
	Saddle Ball Mountain	225	moderate with steep sections	2.8		✔
	Robinson's Point	232	moderate	1.4		✔
	Money Brook and Mt. Prospect	239	difficult	5.0	✔	✔
	Ragged Mountain	248	difficult	3.0		✔
	Reflection Pond	255	easy	1.0		

Bogs & Marshes	Ponds/ Lakes/ Rivers	History	Fields	Forest	Wild Life	Plants/ Wild Flowers	Geology
✔	✔			✔	✔	✔	
✔	✔			✔	✔	✔	
	✔	✔	✔	✔	✔	✔	✔
✔	✔	✔	✔	✔	✔	✔	
✔	✔		✔	✔	✔	✔	
	✔			✔	✔	✔	
		✔		✔	✔	✔	✔
	✔	✔		✔	✔	✔	✔
	✔	✔	✔	✔	✔	✔	
✔	✔	✔		✔	✔	✔	✔
	✔		✔	✔	✔	✔	
		✔	✔	✔	✔	✔	
		✔	✔	✔	✔	✔	
✔	✔	✔		✔	✔	✔	✔
	✔	✔		✔	✔	✔	
	✔	✔	✔	✔	✔	✔	
✔	✔		✔	✔	✔	✔	✔

Region	Walk	Page Number	Difficulty Level	Distance	Waterfalls	Scenic Vista
Northern	Field Farm	263	easy	2.4		✔
	Berlin Mountain	272	difficult	4.0		✔
	Snow Hole	280	moderate	5.8		✔
	Natural Bridge	288	easy	.5	✔	
	Cheshire Cobbles	294	moderate	3.4		✔
	Spruce Hill	301	moderate with steep sections	2.6		✔
	Tyler Swamp	308	easy	1.75		
	Pine Cobble	314	moderate	3.2		✔

Bogs & Marshes	Ponds/ Lakes/ Rivers	History	Fields	Forest	Wild Life	Plants/ Wild Flowers	Geology
✔	✔	✔	✔	✔	✔	✔	✔
		✔		✔	✔	✔	✔
		✔	✔	✔	✔	✔	✔
	✔	✔	✔			✔	✔
		✔		✔	✔	✔	✔
	✔	✔		✔	✔	✔	
✔	✔		✔	✔	✔	✔	
			✔	✔	✔	✔	✔

About the Author

CHARLES W. G. SMITH has written about nature and the environment for more than a decade. His articles have appeared in many publications, including *Country Journal, Berkshire, Harrowsmith Country Life, New England Monthly,* and the *Social Issues* Resource Series. He grew up in rural southern New England and received his bachelor of science in environmental horticulture from the University

Nathaniel Smith

of Connecticut. Over the ensuing years he has taught natural science to emotionally disturbed youth, worked for the Appalachian Mountain Club at Mt. Greylock, and trained teachers on peaceful methods of crisis intervention. He is presently the horticultural editor of Storey Communications.

Smith lives with his son, Nathaniel, and fiancee, Christine Dupuis, in a log cabin on the banks of the Umpachene River in Mill River, Massachusetts. Together they maintain four miles of the Appalachian Trail in the southern Berkshires and periodically lead interpretive hikes along it. He has backpacked in New England for more than twenty-five years and plans to keep walking for at least twenty-five more.

About the AMC

SINCE 1876, the Appalachian Mountain Club has promoted the protection, enjoyment, and wise use of the mountains, rivers, and trails of the Northeast. The AMC believes that successful, long-term conservation depends on first-hand experience and enjoyment of the outdoors. A nonprofit organization, the AMC's membership of more than 72,000 enjoy hiking, canoeing, skiing, walking, rock climbing, bicycling, camping, kayaking, and backpacking, while—at the same time—help to safeguard the environment. All AMC programs and facilities are open to the public.

AMC Huts & Lodges

AMC offers unique overnight lodgings throughout the Northeast. Spend an overnight at one of eight huts, each a day's hike apart, in the White Mountains of New Hampshire, or drive to Bascom Lodge atop Mt. Greylock in western Massachusetts. Also accessible by car are Pinkham Notch Lodge or Crawford Hostel in New Hampshire, and Mohican Outdoor Center in the Delaware Water Gap of western New Jersey. For reservations, call 603-466-2727.

AMC Outdoor Adventures

Whether you're new to the outdoors or an old hand, the AMC offers workshops and guided trips that will teach you new skills, refine your expertise, or just get you outside in good company. Choose from more than 100 workshop and adventures offered. Whether you're going solo, with your family and kids, or with friends, there is something for everyone.

Each of our 11 chapters—from Maine to Washington, D.C.—offers hundreds of activities close to home. Chapter leaders arrange hiking and bicycling trips and teach the basics of cross-country skiing, whitewater and flatware canoeing, and other outdoor skills.

Volunteering

If you like to hike, discover the lasting satisfaction that comes with volunteering to maintain or build trails. No experience is necessary—we'll teach you what you need to know. The AMC leads volunteer trail building and maintenance crews throughout the Northeast. Our professional and volunteer crews take great pride in maintaining 1,400 miles of trails throughout the region.

Paddlers can help clean up a river, monitor water quality, or help negotiate access with private landowners. Volunteering is a great way to give something back to places that have given you so many memorable moments.

Conservation Leadership

Much of the northeast's outdoor recreation opportunities would not be possible without a commitment to protecting land and keeping trails, rivers, and mountains accessible. Since its founding, the AMC has been at the forefront of the conservation movement. AMC members fought for the creation of the White Mountain National Forest in 1911. More recently we have been active in protecting the Appalachian Trail corridor, improving access to and the health of rivers and land around hydroelectric dams, and improving water and air quality. Our conservation policies are backed by solid scientific research, conducted by our own professional researchers in conjunction with such organizations as the Harvard School of Public Health, Dartmouth College, U.S. Forest Service, and the National Park Service. We're working to keep our air clean and healthy, our waterfalls clear, our rivers running free, and recreational activities open.

AMC Books & Maps

The AMC publishes an extensive line of books, including nature guides, New England history, outdoor skills, conservation, and our famous trail guides and maps. AMC guidebooks are essential companions for all kinds of outdoor adventures throughout the eastern U.S. Our publications are available at most bookstores and outdoor retailers as well as our main office in Boston and Pinkham Notch Visitor Center in New Hampshire. To order by phone, call 800-262-4455. Also available through the AMC is *Appalachia*, the country's oldest mountaineering and conservation journal.

AMC Membership

We invite you to join the Appalachian Mountain Club and share the benefits of membership. Your membership includes a one-year subscription to *AMC Outdoors*, the Northeast's premier outdoor magazine—telling you where to go for outdoor recreation and keeping you informed on conservation issues. Members also enjoy discounts on AMC books, maps, workshops, and lodgings, as well as free affiliation to one of AMC's eleven chapters.

For more information on AMC, call 617-523-0636. To join, send a check for $40 for an adult, or $65 for a family to AMC Membership, 5 Joy Street, Boston, MA 02108; or call 617-523-0636 for payment by Visa or MasterCard.

Index

Alphabetical Listing of Areas